FORWARD *through* THE AGES

BICENTENNIAL
ATHENS FIRST UNITED METHODIST CHURCH

Forward
Through the Ages

BICENTENNIAL
ATHENS FIRST UNITED METHODIST CHURCH

Forward Through the Ages

A Bicentennial History of Athens First United Methodist Church

THOMAS H. JACKSON, JR.

Independently published by Thomas H. Jackson

Jr. First printing, March 2025

The contents of this publication, Forward Through the Ages - A Bicentennial History of Athens First United Methodist Church, were meticulously researched, compiled, and written by Thomas H. Jackson Jr. This work reflects extensive effort to provide an accurate and comprehensive account of the church's rich history. While every effort has been made to ensure accuracy, any errors or omissions are unintentional.

The publication is intended for historical and educational purposes, celebrating the enduring legacy of Athens First United Methodist Church. Reproduction or distribution of any portion of this publication without explicit permission is prohibited.

BICENTENNIAL
ATHENS FIRST UNITED METHODIST CHURCH

ꝮDEDICATION ꝲ

To all those on whose shoulders we stand at this 200th anniversary of the founding on its current site of Athens First United Methodist Church, particularly those saints who have guided the author's path since arrival as a student at the University of Georgia in 1971. Those very special servants of God and this church, many of whom are mentioned in the text, now have joined the great cloud of witnesses who eagerly anticipate seeing the great things this congregation will accomplish next.

Table of Contents

∽ ACKNOWLEDGMENTS ∽

This book was designed with professional expertise and loving care by Janet Beckley, a longtime colleague of the author, who forever is in her debt for the generous gift she has given our church through her offer to perform this significant task with no expectation of return other than to the glory of God.

Sincere appreciation goes to each of the current and former pastors, church leaders and members, and church staff who contributed feature essays, photographs, information and context. Likewise, the many who have offered encouragement and expressed interest in this project have kept us moving forward even when it seemed mired in the weeds.

Credit for the striking bicentennial logo is due to Eleanor Sams. It captures our historic steeple but has a feel for the future.

The author was a much younger man when I was privileged to know Dean Robert Wilson and Mr. John Bondurant, previous historians of the church. Both are gone now, but their writings on church history live on and were invaluable in this project. Perhaps they can feel our thanks from that great cloud where they now reside.

It is difficult to adequately express our indebtedness to Mr. David Pass of Rocky Face, Georgia, who while perusing an antiques mall at Dalton in the summer of 2024 spotted the lost minutes and other record books of our church covering 1838 through 1930. He had the wisdom to obtain and return them, and for that this church should be forever grateful.

And last but not least (Matthew 20:16, Luke 13:30), to my wife Sherry. Not only did she spend countless hours hauling bound copies of church bulletins from the church to home and back, reading every word of every page from 1955 to the present, but she accompanied me on trips to the Candler School of Theology Library, spending hours in the stacks poring through Conference Journals. Most of all, Sherry had the forbearance to allow me time to pursue this project to the exclusion of all else, or surely it must have seemed to her. We celebrate our 50th wedding anniversary this year because of that very kind of unwavering assistance, support and care she has offered over many decades.

FORWARD through THE AGES 18 23 20 23

BICENTENNIAL
ATHENS FIRST UNITED METHODIST CHURCH

Introduction

Forward Through the Ages

1. For-ward through the a - ges, in un - bro - ken line,
2. Wid - er grows the king - dom, reign of love and light;
3. Not a - lone we con - quer, not a - lone we fall;

move the faith - ful spir - its at the call di - vine;
for it we must la - bor, till our faith is sight.
in each loss or tri - umph lose or tri - umph all.

gifts in dif - fering mea - sure, hearts of one ac - cord,
Proph-ets have pro - claimed it, mar-tyrs tes - ti - fied,
Bound by God's far pur - pose in one liv - ing whole,

man - i - fold the ser - vice, one the sure re - ward.
po - ets sung its glo - ry, he - roes for it died.
move we on to - geth - er to the shin - ing goal.

Refrain

For-ward through the a - ges, in un - bro - ken line,

move the faith - ful spir - its at the call di - vine.

Have you ever looked up your family history?

It wasn't too many years ago that such an endeavor would often require countless hours of genealogical research and scavenger hunt-like historical investigation. But these days, for a relatively nominal fee, there are websites that will do all of the work for you. You simply enter your information, submit a saliva sample, and in seemingly no time at all, you can get an impressively thorough report that tells you who you are, where you're from, and how you got here.

Wouldn't it be great if a similar website existed to look up our church family history? Just think of how easy it would be to learn about our church genealogy if all we had to do was plug in our church's information, submit a sample worship bulletin or sermon manuscript, and, voila! A fully detailed church history that tells us all we need to know about our church family tree.

Sadly, at least according to my research, no such website or service exists. Which I'm sure has you wondering,"So, how am I holding a fully detailed and impressively thorough history of Athens First United Methodist Church?"

Well, about eighteen months before we were set to celebrate our church's bicentennial, one of our long-time church members, Tom Jackson, asked if he could have the honor of researching our church's 200-year history. I fretfully informed him about the dearth of websites that could do the work for us fearing it might discourage him from tackling this herculean project.

But he didn't even flinch. He simply smiled and said, "It'll be my pleasure." Eighteen months— and countless hours of genealogical research and scavenger hunt-like historical investigation—later, he has given our church a timeless and inestimable gift that is so much more than just a church history book.

It's the story of our church's family tree that tells us who we are, where we're from, and how we got here. More than that, it traces the history of how God has been at work in our church, in our community, and throughout the city of Athens for the last two centuries.

Maya Angelou once said, "You can't know where you're going unless you know where you've been."

It's for that reason that I'm immensely grateful to Tom and Sherry Jackson for the blood, sweat, tears, and love that they've invested in this project. I'm grateful to God for 200 years of faithful mission and ministry in the Classic City. And I'm grateful to you for being a part of our church family history as well as our future.

Two Centuries of Worship, Service, and Growth

Our church really has two founding dates to celebrate. The first is founding of the Methodist Society in Athens in 1801 by Rev. Hope Hull, a professor at the fledgling Franklin College, which more formally was the University of Georgia. After meeting in homes and then in two rustic meeting houses along South Lumpkin Street near Pinecrest Drive, the Society finally gained a permanent home. That was our second founding date, when in 1825 the Society obtained the land lot on North Lumpkin Street between Market (now Washington) Street and Hancock Avenue.

Our celebration in this year of 2025 is the 200th anniversary of the first church built on the land that our congregation still occupies. But this church historian would suggest a 250th anniversary celebration be held in 2051 marking the semi-quincentennial of the Methodist Society founding. And in 2075, marking the 250th anniversary of location on the current site would be in order. It's not my plan to be around to join in either of those celebrations, other than (hopefully) being among the great cloud of witnesses.

This book started out to be a pamphlet, but grew into a larger project as I delved into the very rich history of that little congregation that started out in a log cabin and has grown into today's Athens First United Methodist Church, with more than four thousand members, an annual budget of more than three million dollars, and a physical plant now covering an entire city block-and-a-half of downtown Athens, and fronting two blocks of Lumpkin Street from Washington to Dougherty Streets. This work benefitted from the serendipitous recovery of a full century of the oldest church records missing since the 1940s, allowing us to develop a deeper, more complete and richer history than our predecessors were able to do.

Athens First United Methodist Church is rooted in this plot of land granted to the Methodist Society of Athens by the Trustees of the University of Georgia at the behest of Methodist Society member Thomas Hancock. Examining this history has developed into one of the great privileges of my life. It is not our intention that this be a comprehensive history, in that it would be a daunting task to highlight every member who made significant contributions, or to ferret out details such as membership and budget year-by-year. If there are errors to correct or details the reader can supply, please send them to us. The publishing method allows updates should there be future printings, so this can be an ongoing project.

Our hope is that this book will convey to the reader a picture of this congregation growing and maturing over two centuries, through the entirety of its existence standing as one of the leading churches of Georgia Methodism. As Athens First steps into its third century in this location, we look back year-by-year at how the congregation began and has developed. We lift up some who have gone before us in this endeavor, on whose shoulders we stand, who preceded us in their dedication to Athens First Methodist over the past two centuries. We learn from their lessons and build on the foundation they established. Through this we will learn the story of how this church has moved forward through the ages, counting now 224 years as Methodists in Athens and a full two centuries on this site. In this our third century, let us be dedicated ever more deeply to our mission of making disciples of Jesus Christ for the transformation not only of Athens, but of the world.

Prelude

1783 - 1824

9**1783** 9

As Europeans moved ever-inward from the Georgia-Carolina coast, encroaching upon lands which for time immemorial had been the home and the hunting grounds of the Cherokee Indian nation, Governor Lyman Hall of Georgia signed a treaty May 31, 1783 in which the Indian nation ceded to the state a large area of what is now North Georgia, including the area that is now Athens.

9**1784** 9

The land ceded from the Cherokees was formed into Franklin County by act of the General Assembly on February 25, 1784. At its formation, Franklin County extended from the Savannah River to today's Gwinnett County and south to the Apalachee River, having a population of barely one thousand.

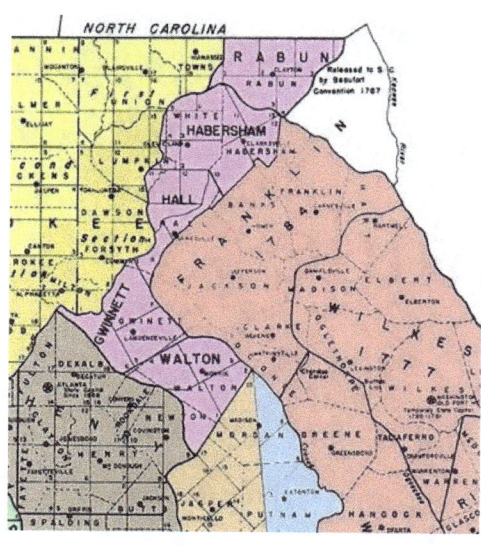

Detail from State of Georgia Map "Original and 1895 counties and land lot districts"

9**1785** 9

On January 27, 1785, almost three years before the U.S. Constitution was ratified, the Georgia General Assembly chartered the

University of Georgia, the first public university to be established by one of the United States. That UGA charter that calls Georgia's youth "the rising hope of our land" also is a fundamental founding document for the Athens Methodist Church. Without it we likely would not be here. That same year, Governor Samuel Elbert granted 1,120 acres of land in the new Franklin County to William Few, who two years later in 1787 would sign the U.S. Constitution on behalf of Georgia. Few had served on the commission that in 1783 gained the cession from the Cherokee Nation of this land and much of what is now North Georgia. His acreage encompassed what would become the UGA North Campus and downtown Athens, including the current site of Athens First United Methodist Church.

That same year, the South Carolina Methodist Conference was formed, encompassing South Carolina and Georgia. In 1819, the Conference would be expanded to include all of Florida, newly-acquired that year from Spain.

෧1786 ෧

The first official census of Methodist membership showed 78 Methodists in Georgia.

෧1787 ෧

On September 17, 1787, William Few, who at the time owned the land on which Athens First United Methodist Church now stands, signed the U.S. Constitution on behalf of the state of Georgia, along with Abraham Baldwin, who at the time was serving as President of the University of Georgia Board of Trustees, which had not yet chosen a site for the newly chartered institution.

WILLIAM FEW
Nov. 1748 – Oct. 1828

෧1789 ෧

William Few became Georgia's first United States senator, arriving at the Senate's first session at Federal Hall in New York City on March 4. Georgia's second senator, James Gunn, did not arrive to be sworn in until April 20.

Courtesy of Hargrett Rare Book and Manuscript Library, University of Georgia Libraries.

෧1796 ෧

On February 11, 1796, the southwest portion of Franklin County, including the area now Athens, became Jackson County, with the county seat at Jefferson.

෧1799 ෧

Having served as Georgia's first U.S. Senator and becoming disenchanted with the institution of slavery, William Few moved permanently to New York, where he became a bank president and an alderman. As such, he served a rotating term as mayor of New York City. Few sold 693 of his Jackson

County acres to Daniel Easley, who operated a mill on adjacent property at the Cedar Shoals of the North Oconee River. This would become the site of the historic Athens Cotton Mill, later known as the O'Malley's Building, and in recent years home to the UGA School of Social Work, on the North Oconee River at Williams and Oconee Streets in today's downtown Athens. The land Few sold to Easley also included what has become today's North Campus, downtown Athens, and the site of our church.

The first Baptist church to be founded in the immediate area was in the Mars Hill community northwest of Watkinsville. By the time of the founding of the Athens Presbyterian and Methodist churches some two decades later, Athens-area Baptists attended what had become a relatively large and active Mars Hill Baptist Church, as well as the Trail Creek Baptist Church located on the east side of the Oconee River about two miles below Athens.

Ꭽ1801Ꭴ

Although chartered 16 years earlier, a site for the university had not yet been chosen. The *Senatus Academicus*, a governing body consisting of the university Trustees and Board of Visitors, met in the State Capitol at Louisville to appoint a site selection committee, with instructions that a site be chosen somewhere in what was then Jackson County. In June 1801 the committee, comprising John Milledge, Abraham Baldwin, George Walton, John Twiggs and Hugh Lawson, met at Billups' Tavern on the road from Athens to Lexington. The group toured several sites – some property already in the University land grant and other sites privately held. It accepted a proposal from Daniel Easley to purchase some of the former Few land as the university site. Trustee Milledge, soon to become Georgia Governor (1802-1806), personally purchased 633 acres, all but 60 acres of the Few land from Easley, donating it to the Trustees. It included the current sites of UGA North Campus, downtown Athens, and Athens First United Methodist Church. Among the deciding factors was a "copious spring of excellent water" located on the hillside above the river, on what today is Spring Street in downtown Athens. Classes began under the trees of what is now North Campus before any buildings were yet constructed.

Rev. Hope Hull, Pastor, The Methodist Society, 1801-1818

Ordained at (or shortly after) the Baltimore Conference of Christmas 1784, the first annual conference in America, Hope Hull was a colleague

4

of the first American Methodist Bishop Francis Asbury. In 1801, Rev. Hull arrived in Athens to join the faculty of the fledgling Franklin College (the University of Georgia). Born in 1763 in Worcester County on Maryland's eastern shore, Hull served in the American Revolution. A carpenter by trade, Hull came to be known as the founder of Methodism in Georgia, having been Asbury's traveling companion for several years. He was admitted on trial in 1785, granted full connection in 1787, was named deacon in 1788 and ordained elder in 1789. Bringing Methodism with him to Franklin College, Hull followed John Wesley's teaching, conducting meetings in local homes. He previously had served in Maryland, the Carolinas, Amelia Island, in 1788 moved to Washington, Ga., 1790 Savannah, 1791 Burke County, Ga., 1792 Hartford, Connecticut, and in 1793 back to Savannah. As with many early Methodist leaders, Hull's controversial preaching of Methodist doctrine had brought violent reactions in Savannah and elsewhere over the previous decade. "In 1793 he was back again laying siege to Savannah and riding that circuit," reports Augustus Longstreet Hull's *Annals of Athens*. Hope Hull married Anne Wingfield in 1796 and settled again in Washington, Ga., as teacher in a preparatory school which he helped build (literally, as a carpenter) before his relocation to Athens. Dr. Lovick Pierce described Hull's preaching: "His words rushed upon his audience like an avalanche, and multitudes seemed to be carried before him like the yielding captives of a stormed castle." Augustus L. Hull called his grandfather a "naturally eloquent preacher with no affectations." Hope Hull is said to have "convinced many of his hearers that he had pried into their personal sins and was now spreading them before the entire congregation." An indication of the wide admiration Hull drew is the Alabama town of McGehee's Switch in Montgomery County, which changed its name to Hope Hull, Alabama. He would become one of the most active members of the University Trustees, serving 1802-11 and again from 1816 until his death in 1818. One of his sons, Henry Hull, served as a UGA trustee 1825-29, and Henry Hull, Jr. was trustee 1857-67. The Hull line of church leaders continued with William Hope Hull and Augustus L. Hull, although they do not appear in the roll of trustees.

Also in 1801, the southern portion of Jackson County became Clarke County, with the county seat at Watkinsville.

Ə**1803** Ə

After meeting in homes for two years under Hope Hull's leadership, the Methodist Society congregation moved into a 22x24-foot log cabin along a creek near today's Lumpkin Street, between present-day Milledge Avenue

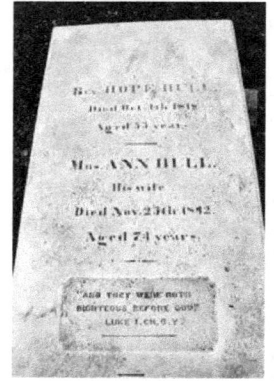

Rev. Hope Hull's grave
in Oconee Hill
Cemetery, Athens

and Pinecrest Drive, south of what is currently the UGA football complex and Barrow School. *Sketches of Athens* 1810-1825 by Henry Hull, edited by A. L. Hull, describes the property as "the land of Josiah Freeman, near a spring 500 yards east of Mr. Barwick's house." It is believed to be the first Methodist Meeting House built west of the Oconee River. It was covered with pine boards with the bark on, a door on one side, and no chimney (thereby, no heat in the winter). Inside, directly across from the door was a pulpit made of the same pine boards. According to Hull's *Sketches*, "In this miserable cabin two of the most eloquent men of the time used to preach sometimes to a

dozen, never more than a hundred hearers." The South Carolina Methodist Conference organized the Apalachee Circuit in 1804, part of the Oconee District, which covered all of Georgia from Greene County north and west.

Two conceptual sketches of the rudimentary, unheated cabin that was the first Hull's Meeting House. This and following sketches of the early wooden church buildings are from John P. Bondurant's 1988 history of Athens First Methodist Church (left) and from promotional materials prepared during the 1963 renovations (above).

6

The first appointee was Hope Hull, his duties including weekday meetings in Hull's Meeting House and a Sunday service in the college chapel, predecessor of the current UGA Chapel built in 1832. Joining the Circuit in 1804-05 were Benjamin Watts and Eppes Tucker, and in 1806, Lovick Pierce and Joseph Tarpley. In 1807, new additions to the Circuit were James Russell and Judge Hilliard. The small Methodist Society in Athens had preaching on weekdays by one of the Circuit preachers, occasionally Hope Hull. After his death in 1818, Athens was left out of the list of appointments until a Methodist Church was constructed in 1825.

◉1806 ◉

The city of Athens was incorporated, extending in a one-mile radius from the high point on the campus, site of the current UGA Chapel. The University Trustees divided their land along Front Street (now Broad Street), selling lots to the north of Front to provide a community to support the University to the south. The first lots sold were in the area bounded by Front, Hull and Foundry Streets and Hancock Avenue. All north of Hancock remained dense forest at the time.

Bishop Frances Asbury visited Athens in December and preached at Hope Hull's meeting house.

A BRIEF HISTORY OF THE METHODIST CHURCH AT WATKINSVILLE

The first Methodist church in the immediate vicinity was founded at Watkinsville shortly after 1800, forerunner of today's Watkinsville First United Methodist Church. The village known as Big Spring was renamed Watkinsville in 1802 at the time it was selected as site for the courthouse of newly created Clarke County. The Methodist Meeting House was located adjacent to the oldest part of today's Watkinsville City Cemetery on Simonton Bridge Road, the cemetery beginning as the church burial ground. Watkinsville was part of the Apalachee Circuit, in the Oconee District of the South Carolina Conference, a circuit which included 22 churches and two missions stretching from Greene to Hall Counties. The first appointed pastor of the section including Watkinsville was Rev. Isaac Cook, whose area covered all of Clarke, Greene and Oglethorpe Counties and part of

Warren County. That first meeting house was struck by lightning and burned in early 1830 and was replaced by a new meeting house built on the rear of the Clarke County Courthouse property off Main Street, the northwest corner of the property fronting on Water Street. By 1850, there was a parsonage on Water Street adjacent to the church. A massive fire swept downtown Watkinsville in 1855, destroying the courthouse and several businesses, but leaving the church and parsonage unscathed. In 1856, the circuit was further divided, placing 12 churches in a new Jefferson Circuit, leaving Watkinsville with ten: Antioch, Asbury's Chapel, Farmington, Lebanon, Prospect, Ray's Chapel, Salem, Tigner's and Veal's Chapels. In 1861, Watkinsville Methodists built a new church on Main Street, a white clapboard structure which today is covered in brick and serves as the Watkinsville Christian Church. Future Bishop Atticus Haygood served Watkinsville as pastor during that period. The former building on Water Street was given to the Black Methodist congregation of Watkinsville and served as a church and school for local Blacks until 1922. Another great fire swept downtown Watkinsville during a January 1887 snowstorm, destroying what by then was the Oconee County Courthouse, two stores, a home, the Masonic Lodge and a printing office. Once again, the church was spared. In 1893, two brothers and five children of the late Louisa Booth Ashford determined to build the Methodists a new church as a memorial to her. A. W. Ashford deeded to the Watkinsville church a lot on the southwest corner of Main Street and Harden Hill Road, diagonally across from the 1861 building which stood at the northeast corner of the same crossroad. The Ashford family built and gave to the congregation the Gothic church structure of white clapboard that stands today on that site, in exchange for the older building and land. At the same time, they built the home next door, known today as Ashford Manor. The former church stood vacant until 1897, when it was purchased by two local businessmen, members of the Christian Church board of trustees, purportedly to forestall it being turned into a tavern or dance hall. County records show that it was sold directly from A. W. Ashford to the Christian Church trustees for $500. Watkinsville Methodist Church voted in 1979 to seek property to relocate because of a shortage of building space and parking at the existing location. A subsequent vote the same year split almost evenly – a three-vote margin – to proceed to build a new sanctuary on New High Shoals Road, where the first services were held in September 1982. Sentiment was strong among almost half of the congregation that opposed the move, leading the church to split between those who wanted to stay in the old building and those supporting the new. Attempts to create a new United Methodist congregation in the old building were not approved by the North Georgia Conference, so the group desiring to stay determined to become an independent Methodist church, purchased the old building from the departing group for $122,500, and began holding services in their former church building on May 29, 1983, with the name Ashford Memorial Methodist Church. The United Methodist congregation continues today as Watkinsville First United Methodist Church. (Reul, Myrtle R. "*Beacon on the Hill.*" Athens, Ga.: ABC Printing, 2003).

ɘ**1810** ɘ

The Athens Methodist congregation moved to a larger version of Hull's Meeting House which Dr. Henry Hull in 1875 reported to have been located "where is now the Fair ground,"which today is the UGA Track. At this writing in 2025, a new complex for UGA Track and Field is being constructed off South Milledge Avenue outside the Athens Loop. The location of the former track (and Hull's Meeting House) will be assumed by the football practice complex. Henry Hull reported his father's home at that time was "a few hundred yards east of it." This site served 15 years, until the first Methodist church was built on the present site at Lumpkin Street and Hancock Avenue.

A larger version of Hull's Meeting House built in 1810 on present-day South Lumpkin Street where the UGA Track is in 2024.

ഐ1816 ഐ

From the first classes in 1801 until 1819, the University and community languished from inadequate enrollment and income. To help remedy the situation, in 1816 the state authorized the University trustees to sell part of the original land grant (not the Few/Easley property). The original grant, signed by Governor Samuel Elbert on October 13, 1785, was in the name of William Few, apparently on behalf of the university trustees, and included 1,120 acres in Franklin County (now Clarke) bounded "NorthEasterwardly by the North fork of the Oconee River, part South and west by Unknown lands and on all other sides by vacant land."

ഐ1818 ഐ

Asbury Hull, head of the Methodist Society, 1818-1825
Hope Hull died in Athens at age 55, with his last words as quoted in Hull's *Sketches*, "God has laid me under marching orders. I am ready to obey." He was buried in Oconee Hill Cemetery. The South Carolina Conference did not appoint a successor to Hull, leaving local Methodists to find supply preachers from among the college faculty. The congregation struggled, but carried on under the leadership of his son, Asbury Hull. Born in 1797 while his parents were at Washington, Ga., the younger Hull graduated from Franklin College in 1814. For 47 years (1819-1866) he would serve as UGA's secretary and treasurer, and for many years a UGA trustee. He would become the founding president of Southern Mutual Insurance Company, which over the years produced many church trustees and leaders. As a state legislator, Asbury Hull would serve as both House Speaker and Senate President, voting at the state secession session in 1861. He died in Athens in 1866 and was buried in Oconee Hill Cemetery.

ഐ1819 ഐ

U.S. President James Monroe visited Athens, taking lodging and holding a reception for the entire community in a third-floor ballroom of the town's hotel, a building known today at the Franklin House at the corner of Broad and Thomas. His 1819 tour of Southern states included other Georgia stops in Savannah, Washington and Lexington.

With the authorized sale of University land-grant acreage accomplished, and the hiring that year of Dr. Moses Waddel as University president, the

University had the needed infusion of cash and leadership to hire faculty, buy equipment, construct buildings and move forward.

ꙅ**1821** ꙅ

President Waddel, like many of the early college administrators a Presbyterian clergyman, organized the Athens Presbyterian Church. That congregation constructed its first building in 1828 at the main entrance to campus where the Holmes-Hunter Academic Building now stands. There was little compunction at the time about the intermingling of church and state interests.

ꙅ**1824** ꙅ

Thomas Hancock, a member of the Methodist Society, who lived at the southeast corner of Lumpkin Street at Hancock Avenue, was in the process of acquiring from the UGA Trustees the lot on the southwest corner, across Lumpkin Street from his home, where our church now stands. He apparently had not yet made sufficient payments to secure the deed. Hancock relinquished his right to the lot with the desire that the land go instead to the Methodist Society. The UGA Trustees granted the land to the Methodists, provided a house of worship was erected within two years. It may be that Hancock found himself financially unable to complete the transaction to purchase the lot, so arranging for the Methodists to have it was an excellent outcome for both Hancock and the congregation. Hull's Sketches reports the Hancock family was "reduced from affluence by commercial losses." In their home on Hancock at Lumpkin "they opened a house of public entertainment, where all were welcome, both those who paid and those who did not; and most welcome of all were those who could not." This apparently grew into Hancock's Tavern, which for some years was located on the northwest corner of the same intersection, site of today's Saye Building.

FORWARD *through* THE AGES

BICENTENNIAL
ATHENS FIRST UNITED METHODIST CHURCH

The First Half-Century

1825 - 1874

Conceptual sketch of the first Athens Methodist Church built in 1825 at the present site on Lumpkin Street at Hancock Avenue (From the 1988 Bondurant history of the church)

୨1825 ୧

Thomas W. Stanley, Pastor, 1825

The Methodists built a 40x40-foot meeting house on their new land at Lumpkin and Hancock and named the Rev. Thomas W. Stanley as pastor. Methodism had been in Athens since 1801, but this marked the beginning of the Athens Methodist Church on its present site.

Rev. Stanley came to Athens in 1823 to head the Athens Female Academy, located in a home along Front (now Broad) Street between College Avenue and Lumpkin Street. Admitted on trial to the Conference in 1812, Stanley became a deacon in 1814 and an elder in full connection in 1816. Before coming to Athens, his appointments were: 1812 Pee Dee, S.C.; 1813 Little River (Ogeechee District); 1814 Sparta; 1815 Wilmington; 1816 Charleston; 1817 Columbia; 1818 Located (meaning he took a position outside the church appointment process). A Thomas W. Stanley was reported in Savannah during the period of his location, likely in a position similar to the one for which he came to Athens in 1823.

Construction of the Methodist sanctuary and at least five houses in the community was surprisingly rapid, all accomplished by a family of carpenters from Vermont. The head of the household, according to Hull's *Sketches*, was "a live Yankee named Peck" joined by "his three or four sons and several kinsmen, all active carpenters." The church was built with a gallery on three sides for the seating of African-American members, and a raised pulpit under which a man six feet tall could stand. Judge Augustin S. Clayton led fundraising and superintended the construction. A graduate in the University's first class in 1804, Clayton returned to Athens in 1808 with his wife and young son, established a law practice, and became a leading citizen. He became secretary of the University Trustees, confidant and mediator for each University president of his time, and the only lawyer in Athens for 15 years. He became judge of the Superior Court and was elected to the legislature and to Congress. The founding congregation also included the families of Hope Hull's two sons, Henry and Asbury, and Revolutionary War General David Merriwether and his family, among others. Henry Hull would live well into the latter part of the 19th century, being a member of the Athens Methodist Church for more than fifty years. Hull served as secretary of the Quarterly Conference, the governing body of the local church, from 1834 – 1866. Merriwether, who died in 1822, served in the Georgia House of Representatives from 1796-1802 and as House Speaker all but his first year there. He served three terms in the U.S. House of Representatives 1806-12. He was personal friend of President Thomas Jefferson and was a cousin to the explorer Meriwether Lewis. Meriwether County, Georgia, is named in David Merriwether's honor. A son, James Meriwether, also an Athens attorney, served in Congress and was a UGA trustee 1816-1831. *(Notes: The Merriwether name evolved over time to using only one "r." The duties of the church assembly originally known as a Quarterly Conference later were assumed generally by a Board of Stewards, which became the Official Board, then the Administrative Board, and today it is called the Church Council.)*

ᵹ**1826**ᵹ

Lovick Pierce, Pastor, 1826-1827

The first pastor appointed to the new Athens Methodist Church by the South Carolina Conference was Lovick Pierce, who remained involved with the congregation the rest of his life and whose descendants have been church leaders through generations. He was well established in the Conference, having been admitted on trial in 1805, as deacon in 1807, and as elder in 1809. After appointments at Pee Dee, Apalachee Circuit (which included the Methodist Society at Athens), Augusta and Columbia, he was Presiding Elder (a position now called District Superintendent) of the Oconee District 1809-11 (which also included Athens), the youngest ever to hold such a position to that date in Methodism. Born March 24, 1785, in Halifax County, North Carolina, Pierce had been a Methodist chaplain in the U.S. Army in the War of 1812. He earned an M.D. degree from the University of Pennsylvania and a Doctor of Divinity from Randolph-Macon College, where he later was as a trustee. He was a founder of Wesleyan College at Macon and served on its first board of trustees. He also was a trustee at Emory College. He was a delegate to General Conference in 1812. Appointed to the Athens-Greensboro Circuit in 1826, Pierce maintained a home in Athens, preaching two Sundays a month in Greensboro and two in Athens. The next year, Pierce again was appointed to Athens, but the circuit was changed to Athens-Madison. Dr. Pierce's report to the Conference regarding his second year at Athens: Membership, Whites 107, Colored 70. Total collection from both Athens and Madison for the year: $9.41. *(Note: The terminology "Colored" is used in that era to refer to persons known today as Black, or African-American. The word may be jarring to the modern eye, but it is of that day and appears widely in church reports of that time.)* On the Sundays when Pierce did not preach, the Athens church utilized local supply preachers,

Lovick Pierce in Smith's *History of Methodism in Georgia and Florida* and the 1892 North Georgia Conference Journal

among them a gifted preacher from the faculty, Stephen Olin. Pierce would serve three separate times as pastor at the Athens Methodist Church: 1826-27, 1831-32, and 1834. His subsequent appointments included: 1828 Eatonton-Madison; 1829 Eatonton-Clinton; 1830 Milledgeville-Clinton; 1831-32 Athens-Madison; 1833 Presiding Elder, Augusta District; 1834 Athens; 1835 Presiding Elder, Savannah District; 1836-37 Columbus (the future St. Luke); 1838-39 Georgia Female College; 1840-41 Columbus; 1842 Montgomery, Alabama; 1843 Mobile, Alabama; 1844-48 American Bible Society; 1849 Presiding Elder, Columbus District; 1850 Columbus; 1851 American Bible Society; 1852 Trinity and Andrew Chapel, Augusta; and further appointments in conference positions including city missionary, Sunday School agent, and conference missionary, during which times he was based in his Athens home. In 1866 he helped organize Pierce's Chapel AME Church, today the First AME Church of Athens, not to be confused with the Pierce Chapel at Wesleyan, named for his son, Bishop G.F. Pierce. Lovick Pierce retired from active appointment at the end of 1878 and died at Bishop Pierce's home in Sparta on November 9, 1879.

In Pierce's first year as Athens' pastor, his 16-year-old son, George Foster Pierce, was converted in a revival that began among students at Franklin College and spread to the Athens Methodist Church. The younger Pierce would become president of Wesleyan College, then Emory College, and finally a Bishop of the Methodist Church. He was elected a clergy delegate to General Conference in 1840, 1844, 1846, 1850, 1854 and 1858. A great-great-grandson was Dr. Robert C. Wilson, a longtime member of Athens First who in 1924 would become founding dean of the UGA College of Pharmacy. Dean Wilson was baptized as an infant by Dr. Lovick Pierce and would die in Athens in 1981 at age 102.

୭**1828**୭

Ignatius A. Few, Pastor, 1828

The third pastor appointed to Athens Methodist Church, Ignatius A. Few, had a famous father, Ignatius Few, and three famous uncles, William, Benjamin and James Few, each known to all Georgians. William Few signed the U.S. Constitution for Georgia, was first individual owner of the land on which UGA, downtown Athens and Athens First UMC now stand, and became U.S. Senator from Georgia and mayor of New York City. Our pastor's father, also named Ignatius, was a noted Revolutionary War captain.

Ignatius Alphonso Few
Portrait from Oxford (Ga.)
Historical Society

His mother was Mary Candler of the Georgia family famously associated with Emory University and the Coca-Cola Company. His uncle James Few, known as "the first martyr of the American battle for independence," was hanged by the British in 1771 following the Battle of Alamance in North Carolina. Benjamin Few, eldest of the brothers, was a Colonel in the Revolution, leading troops in battles at Savannah, Augusta, and the Carolinas, who later became a large landowner and member of the General Assembly. *(Benjamin Few is five-great-grandfather of your author).*

Pastor Ignatius A. Few was born in Columbia County, Ga. (then Richmond County) in 1789, studied at Princeton and lived much of his early life in New York City with his uncle William Few after the bitter separation of young Ignatius's parents over an allegation his mother attempted to poison his father. An "avowed infidel" in his youth, young Ignatius inherited his father's Augusta plantation at an early age but was an unsuccessful farmer. Rather, he found success as an Augusta lawyer, only to have that career cut short by a bout of apparent tuberculosis. In 1826, a religious conversion under noted circuit rider Joseph Travis led him to membership on trial in the South Carolina Conference in 1828, the same year he was appointed to the Athens-Lexington Circuit. He was ordained deacon in 1830 and elder in 1832. He was a founding member of the Georgia Conference in 1830. Subsequent appointments were: 1829-30 Macon; 1831 Savannah; 1832 Columbus; 1833 Presiding Elder, Columbus District; and 1834 Macon. He was elected a clergy delegate to General Conference in 1832 and 1840. In 1835 he was appointed to start a manual labor school at Covington, which would become Emory College the next year, with Few as the founding president. He named the community around Emory for the English seat of learning at Oxford. He returned to the Savannah church for a final year in 1840 before retiring to Athens, where he died in 1845. Few was buried in the historic cemetery at Oxford, Ga.

In a single act, the Georgia General Assembly granted separate charters incorporating the trustees of the Methodist and Presbyterian churches at Athens. Passed by the General Assembly and signed by Governor John

Forsyth on December 20, 1828, it named as original "Trustees of the Methodist Church at Athens" James Meriwether, William Lumpkin, Cicero Holt, Asbury Hull, and Right Rogers. The act vests the property of the church in the trustees, and provides that they may "appoint such officers as they may deem necessary for conducting the business of said corporation," phraseology which some over the years have asserted to mean the trustees could appoint the church pastor if they desired, though it has not been tested.

Original trustee James Meriwether was a son of Revolutionary War General David Meriwether, a founding member of the Methodist Society and our church. A native of Washington in Wilkes County, Georgia, he graduated from Franklin College (the University of Georgia) in 1807. He briefly practiced law before entering farming. After fighting in the 1813 war

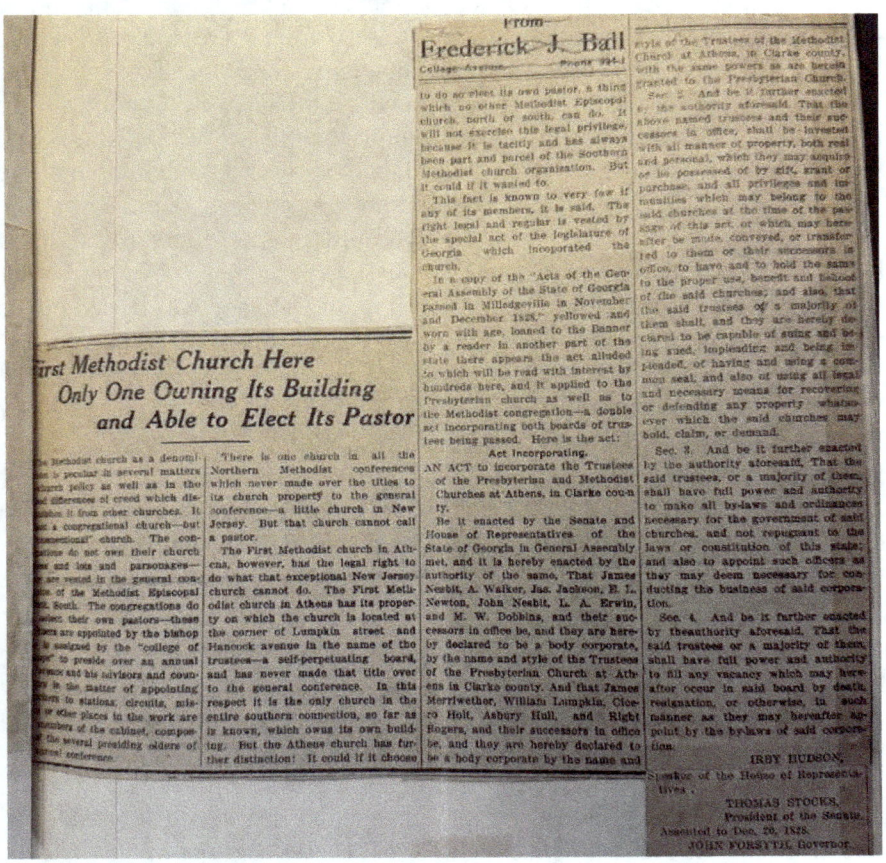

A 1918 article from the Athens Banner regarding the authority granted by the Georgia General Assembly in the 1828 charter of the Trustees of the Methodist Church at Athens.

against the Creek Indians, he became U.S. Commissioner to the Cherokee Indians and a trustee of the University of Georgia 1816-1831. Meriwether served as a judge of the Superior Court, represented Clarke County in the General Assembly 1821-1823 and was elected to the U.S. Congress from the district including Athens for one term 1825-1827. He is listed in *The Appendices of Antebellum Athens* as one of the major slaveholders in Clarke County during the decade of the 1820s. He died in 1854 in Memphis, Tennessee while on a trip to the West and was buried in the Meriwether family cemetery, which today is protected by a stone wall in the back yard of a home on Cherokee Ridge behind Georgia Square Mall.

Original trustee William Lumpkin was a Virginia native and brother to Georgia Governor Wilson Lumpkin, who served 1831-1835, and Joseph Henry Lumpkin, first Chief Justice of the Georgia Supreme Court. The youngest of William's nine children was Martha Lumpkin, for whom Marthasville was named, the community that grew to become Terminus, later Atlanta. William was 57 years of age when he left Clarke County in 1837 to join a son in Mississippi, moving with more than 60 slaves, 32 horses and mules, 50 head of cattle, his wife, four daughters, four grandchildren, three other White men, a coach and four horses, two large wagons pulled by five mules each, two other wagons and a sully. In Marshall County, Mississippi, he established Lumpkin Mill and a plantation he named "Athenia," after Athens. He died in Holly Springs, Mississippi in 1840 and was buried on his plantation there.

Original trustee Cicero Holt was Solicitor General of the Western Judicial Circuit. He practiced law in Clarke County and was elected to the General Assembly in 1828. He was an honorary member of the UGA Demosthenian Society, whose members wore black crepe on their arms for thirty days following his death in October 1830, when he had been a church trustee for only two years.

Original trustee Asbury Hull was a son of founding pastor Rev. Hope Hull, who along with his brother Henry was a longtime leader in our church. Asbury had six sons, one of whom, also Henry Hull, likewise would have long service as an Athens Methodist Church trustee. Asbury Hull served in the General Assembly, holding at various times the positions of Speaker of the House and President of the Senate, his last session being the secession meeting of 1861. He was cashier of the State Bank at Athens, President of Southern Mutual Insurance Company, and secretary of the

University of Georgia Board of Trustees. His wife was the widow of the American artist George Cooke, who painted the monumental *Interior of St. Peter's* that has hung in the UGA Chapel since 1867.

Original trustee Right Rogers (whose name at times was spelled "Wright") was a shoemaker and repairman in Athens, who founded a local organization known as the "Mechanics Mutual Aid Society" dedicated to discussions of matters "other than religion and politics," helping one another in their mechanical professions, giving aid to widows, visiting the sick, helping settle disputes, and raising money with intentions of starting a school. The group maintained a public reading room which carried newspapers from across the United States. He had moved to Walton County, Georgia, by 1848.

9**1829** 9

John Owen Andrew, Pastor, 1829-1830

Born of Puritan parents in 1758 at Midway, Ga., John Owen Andrew was orphaned at age 15 and raised by uncles. After fighting in the Revolution at Midway Church, Brier Creek, Savannah and in South Carolina, he served in the legislature before moving to Elbert County. There he was a schoolmaster and became the first native-born Georgian to be ordained a Methodist minister, being accepted on trial in 1789 and as a deacon in full connection deacon in 1791. His first two wives died in childbirth, leaving a daughter each, and the third bore him eleven children. While serving the joint appointment at Athens and at Mount Zion Methodist near Bishop, Rev. Andrew died March 10, 1830. He was buried in the Andrew-Akridge Cemetery at Mt. Zion Church, one mile south of Bishop on today's U.S. 441, where his gravesite is marked by a state historical marker. Neither the church nor the community remain, but the cemetery is well-maintained.

Rev. John Owen Andrew's gravesite
along U.S. 441 in Oconee County

21

Bishop James Osgood Andrew
From *New Georgia Encyclopedia*

John Owen Andrew's son, James Osgood Andrew, was elected a Methodist bishop in 1832. The younger Andrew's purchase of a mulatto girl as slave and his third wife's owning two other slaves when he married her led to the 1845 split between the northern and southern branches of the Methodist Church. Bishop James Osgood Andrew died in 1871 in Mobile, Ala. and was buried in the historic cemetery at Oxford, Ga.

ᗝ1830 ᗣ

The Georgia Conference of the Methodist Church was formed, separating from the South Carolina Conference. It stretched from Blairsville, Georgia, to Key West, Florida, including most of Georgia and the Florida Territory, which had been ceded from the Spanish in 1822 and would not become a state until 1845.

Lovick Pierce, Pastor, 1830-1832

Upon the death of Rev. John Owen Andrew, former pastor Lovick Pierce, already living in Athens while serving a church at Milledgeville, resumed the duties. He was elected a clergy delegate to General Conference in 1832, 1836, 1840, 1844, 1845 (interim session, Louisville), 1846, 1850, 1854, 1858, and 1866. There was no General Conference in 1862 because of the Civil War.

Athens residents who were members of the Baptist church at Trail Creek formed the Athens Baptist Church, meeting at first in the Presbyterian Church building on the University campus. They built a "plain cheap house" nearby on the campus at the corner of Broad and Lumpkin which would serve until 1860.

ᗝ1832 ᗣ

An invitation to a "cotillion party" at Jackson's Hotel, among whose managers is "that staid and sober old Methodist S. J. Mays," set tongues in town wagging, according to Hull's *Annals*. Dancing was widely frowned upon before the Civil War. "Who that ever knew Mr. Mays would suppose that he ever aided and abetted this worldly amusement…?"

Athens Station clergy past and future representing the Georgia Conference as delegates at the 1832 General Conference of the Methodist Episcopal Church were James O. Andrew, Ignatius A. Few, Benjamin B. Pope, William J. Parks, and Lovick Pierce.

9**1833** 9

Benjamin B. Pope, Pastor, 1833

Born in 1804, Benjamin Pope was son of an early Georgia preacher, Henry Pope. Both were pastors at Pope Chapel Methodist Church in Wilkes County, Benjamin serving there in 1827-28 beginning at age 22. He was admitted on trial in 1828, became a deacon in full connection in 1830, and was ordained elder in 1832. His appointments were: 1828-29 Apalachee; 1830 Savannah; 1831-32 Macon; 1833 Athens-Madison; 1834 Columbus; 1835 without appointment at his own request, apparently because of illness. Demonstrating the esteem the young man had attained, Pope was elected a Georgia delegate to General Conference in 1832 at age 28. He was appointed to Athens the next January, becoming the youngest pastor to serve Athens Methodist Church to that date. Pope died in December 1835, just two years after leaving the Athens pulpit, and was buried in the Barrow-Pope Cemetery in Lexington, Ga. "Benjamin Pope had run a short career, but one of the most brilliant. An unusual combination of excellence entered into his character. He was gentle and brave, gifted, cultivated, and humble, an heir of

The gravestone of young Benjamin Pope at Lexington, Ga. He died at age 31, two years after leaving the Athens Methodist pulpit.

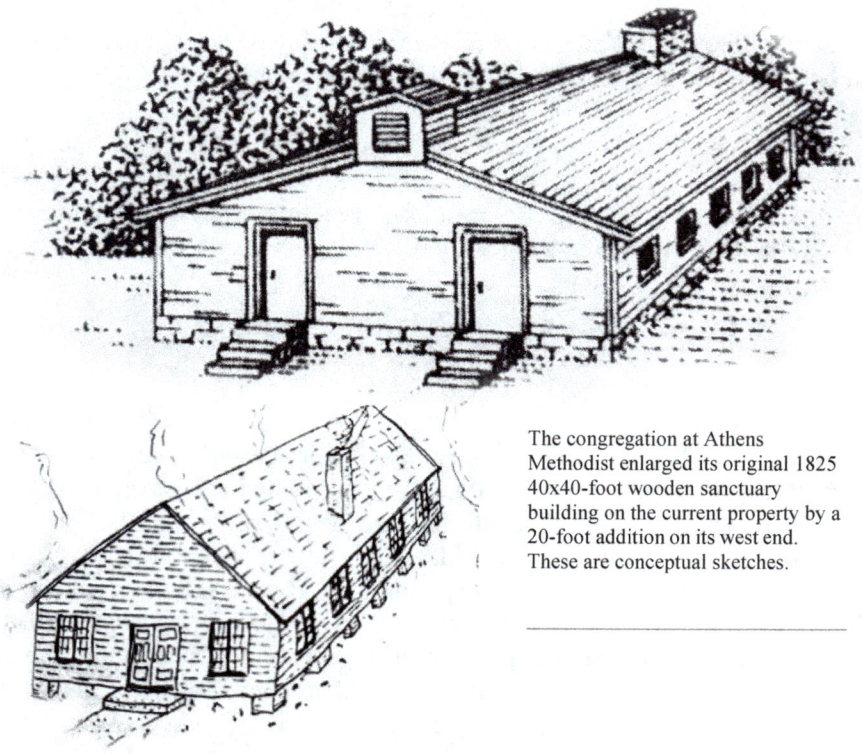

The congregation at Athens Methodist enlarged its original 1825 40x40-foot wooden sanctuary building on the current property by a 20-foot addition on its west end. These are conceptual sketches.

wealth, yet willingly surrendering all its comforts that he might preach the Word." (Smith, *History of Methodism in Georgia and Florida*).

ꝯ1834ꝯ

Lovick Pierce, Pastor, 1834

During this appointment, Lovick Pierce served a two-point circuit that included the churches at Athens and Madison.

ꝯ1835ꝯ

William R. H. Moseley, Pastor, 1835

Pastor William Moseley was admitted on trial in 1829, to full connection in 1831, and was ordained elder in 1833. His appointments included: 1829 Abbeville; 1830 Yellow River; 1831 Broad River; 1832 Pensacola Mission; 1833 Montgomery. He requested and was granted to have no appointment in 1834. After his one year in Athens in 1835, he served Waynesboro in 1836 before being "located," that is, accepting an appointment beyond the local pulpit.

ᵒ**1836** ᵒ

Jeremiah Norman, Jr., Pastor, 1836-1837

Pastor Jeremiah Norman, Jr. was a native of far eastern North Carolina, born October 1, 1771, son of the noted Methodist pastor Jeremiah Norman. The younger Norman was admitted on trial in 1825, became a deacon in full connection in 1827, and was ordained elder in 1829. His appointments included: 1825 Cedar Creek, Milledgeville; 1826 Houston; 1827 Monroe; 1828 Chattahoochee, Tallahassee; 1829 Sparta; 1830 supply; 1831-33 LaGrange; 1834 Quincy, Fla.; 1835 Sparta; 1836-37 Athens; 1838 Eatonton-Monticello, 1839 Supply. Called "a most excellent preacher" in Smith's *History*, "his looks, however, did not indicate it…. His beauty had not increased, though his intellect had improved by the time he came to Athens." At his death on October 30, 1843, he was a "lonely man" who "lived unmarried and seems to have had none near of kin to him in this land." He was buried in the Norman family cemetery in Bladen County, North Carolina. His father had been a pioneer minister of the Methodist Episcopal Church in Virginia, the Carolinas and Georgia. Called to the Methodist ministry in 1792, the elder Norman had met Bishop Francis Asbury. Norman, Sr. was assigned in 1798 to Augusta as a pioneer missionary. By the end of the year, he had established the Augusta Methodist Circuit of the South Carolina Conference. He served further appointments throughout the Carolinas and Georgia. Norman, Sr.'s detailed journal is housed in the Southern Historical Collection at the University of North Carolina, Chapel Hill. It describes "the rigors and discouragements encountered by the Methodist itinerants" with vignettes of people and places he encountered.

Rev. Lovick Pierce was a delegate to the 1836 General Conference of the Methodist Episcopal Church.

ᵒ**1837**ᵒ

The Georgia Annual Conference met in Athens in 1837 for the first time of record, convening December 13, 1837, with Bishop Thomas A. Morris presiding. From western Virginia, Bishop Morris had been a preacher since age 20. He had been elected bishop at the General Conference in Cincinnati the previous year, and this was his first tour through the South. He came to Georgia only once more, choosing to go with the Northern church in the split of 1845. Over the next 177 years, as of this writing the Athens Methodist Church has hosted Annual Conference 33 times, with the first eight of those meetings in our sanctuary, and beginning in 1999, 25 of the last 26 years in the Classic Center. At this writing, the Conference has contracted to continue meeting in Athens at the Classic Center through June 2026.

෨**1838**෧

Whitefoord Smith, Pastor, 1838-1839

Rev. Whitefoord Smith, Jr.
From Wofford College archives

Born November 7, 1812, in Charleston, Whitefoord Smith, Jr. was son of Whitefoord Smith, Sr. and Margaret Shand. He graduated from South Carolina College and married Martha Ann Mouzon. He was admitted on trial in 1833, became full connection deacon in 1835 and was ordained elder in 1836 at Annual Conference in Columbus. His appointments were: 1833 Sandy River, Columbia; 1835 Camden; and 1836 Augusta. He came to Athens Methodist Church in 1838 at the tender age of 26 in only the fifth year of his ministry. The youngest senior minister in the 200-year history of our church, Smith reported finding 101 members on roll upon his arrival, "and among them were some most excellent people." During his time at Athens, Smith accomplished a "gracious revival.... He was very popular as a preacher, and the spiritual interests of the church began to revive." In his first year alone, 57 White and 25 Colored members were added. Among the converts was Superior Court Judge Augustin S. Clayton, a former member of Congress and noted skeptic, and Alban Chase, who held a long and widely known political hostility for the judge. At the altar call, as the two approached from opposite sides, they extended a warm handclasp, bringing the entire congregation to tears at the sight. Sixty members joined the church during that revival. Records begun by Pastor Smith in his own handwriting and continuing through 1843 show 316 names on roll at some point during that six-year period. Notes show most "received by certificate" and some "removed by certificate," some died, and thankfully, only a few "dropped" or "expelled." After Athens, Smith returned to the Carolinas with these appointments: 1840 Charleston; 1841- 42 Columbia; 1843-44 Wilmington; 1845 Presiding Elder, Wilmington District; 1846-47 Trinity, Charleston; 1848-49 Cumberland; 1851 Washington Street, Columbia; 1852-53 Cumberland; 1854 supply; 1855 Greenville; 1856 Washington Street; 1857-59 professor, Wofford College; 1860 President, Columbia Female College; 1861-62 professor, Wofford College; 1866 Spartanburg. He continued to teach at Wofford College until shortly before his death in the 1890s. He became a noted evangelist and orator, speaking to the South Carolina Conference and delivering commencement addresses at Wofford and Emory colleges. He served for a time as director of the Methodist Publishing House. His papers are held by Duke University and include sermons and diaries dating from 1839 when he was at our church. He wrote on the Confederate press, the religious instruction of slaves, the temperance movement following the Civil War, his pastoral duties, and letters exchanged with an uncle in Scotland discussing the War of 1812, the Napoleonic campaigns in Spain and current events in England. Whitefoord Smith, Jr. died January 27, 1893, and was buried in Magnolia Cemetery in Spartanburg, South Carolina.

Church records from 1838 entitled "Records of White Members of the Methodist Episcopal Church in Athens," in the handwriting of pastor Whitefoord Smith, list 316 names as members. Listed as "class leaders" are Asbury Hull, Whitefoord Smith, John Reynolds, Right Rogers, William M. Morton, D.D. Tichener, Joseph B. Jones and Alsa Moore, Jr. Stewards are listed as Asbury Hull, Henry Hull, Thomas Hancock, Burwell Pope, Daniel Grant, William L. Mitchell, William Brown, Blanton Hill, and Albon Chase.

⊝1840 ⊜

James Ezekiel "J.E." Evans, Pastor, 1840

Whitefoord Smith and James Evans swapped appointments, with Smith going to Charleston whence Evans came to Athens. Born February 4, 1810, in Wilkes County, he was son of Llewellen and Mary Evans. Pastor Evans' ministry was described as "always successful in winning souls." His memoriam describes him as a "noble man, possessing a magnificent frame...

his bearing dignified and his manners courteous...." Further, "his learning was not so much the culture of the university as the wisdom of the prophets, learned in the school of Christ and taught by the Spirit." Evans oversaw a continuing great revival in Athens, with 63 White and 47 Colored members joining the church during one quarter of his single year here. Sunday School enrollment reached 100 for the first time. Likewise, he was noted for leading construction of new church buildings, which he accomplished at Trinity, Savannah; Trinity and Cumberland, Charleston; and Mulberry Street, Macon. New parsonages were built on his watches at St. John, Augusta and in Rome. He served as trustee at both Emory College and LaGrange College. Converted in 1824 at age 14, Evans was a local preacher beginning in 1829. He married Parmella J. Mays in 1831. He was admitted on trial in 1833, became a deacon in full connection in 1835, and was ordained elder in 1836. His appointments were: 1833 Houston; 1834 Hawkinsville; 1835 Forsyth; 1836-37 Savannah; 1838-39 Charleston (where he survived a terrible epidemic of Yellow Fever); 1840 Athens; 1841-42 Savannah; 1843- 44 Presiding Elder, Augusta District; 1845-46 Columbus; 1847-48 Augusta; 1849-50 Wesley Chapel, Atlanta; 1851 Macon; 1852-53 Presiding Elder, Columbus District; 1854-55 Augusta; 1856 Book Agent at the Publishing House in Nashville, Tennessee, but left the position after five months for a vacant pulpit at Macon; 1856-57 Macon and Vineville; 1858 LaGrange; 1859-61 Presiding Elder, Macon District; 1862-63 Macon and Vineville; 1864 Presiding Elder, Columbus District; 1865 St. John, Augusta; 1866- 69 St. Luke, Columbus; 1870 Trinity and Isle of Hope, Savannah; 1871-72 Trinity, Savannah; 1873-74 St. James, Augusta; 1875-76 Presiding Elder, Atlanta District; 1877-78 Trinity, Atlanta; 1879 Presiding Elder, Griffin District; 1880-81 Rome; 1882 Griffin; 1883 Commissioner of Education for the Colored, Paine Institute; 1884-86 Presiding Elder, Augusta District. He was a trustee of Emory College for 44 years and of Wesleyan College for 45 years. He headed a committee in 1868 which developed a plan to complete separation of the Black and White churches and continued as chair of that committee through 1874 as the plan was implemented. In 1878, he chaired a committee to revise the Discipline of the M.E. Church, South. Much concerned about Wesley's theology of personal sanctification, he finally professed he had achieved this "blessed state" in 1882, declaring even then, "I am still becoming more mature, and learning by experience the difference between purity and maturity." He was first elected to the infamous New York General Conference of 1844 and served in the called Louisville Convention of 1845 which established the Methodist Episcopal Church, South, going on to serve in every General Conference the remainder of his life, except the one in progress at the time of his death. Rev. Evans died while Augusta Presiding Elder, passing away on May 18, 1886, in the home of G. M. Curtis, a parishioner in Thomson, while at the Quarterly Conference for the Thomson Circuit. He preached his last sermon in the same church at Thomson where Bishop George F. Pierce had preached his last. Evans' funeral was at Mulberry Street Church in Macon, and he was buried in Riverside Cemetery, Macon.

As the Georgia Conference entered its second decade following the separation from South Carolina, it still had only 111 preachers and eight districts, with 27,298 White and 8,358 Colored members. Athens

Grave of Rev. J. E. Evans
at Riverside Cemetery, Macon

was among only eight "station" appointments in the entire state, the others being Augusta, Savannah, Milledgeville, Columbus, Macon, Washington, and LaGrange/West Point. The rest of the conference within Georgia was served entirely by circuits, as the full Georgia Conference stretching from Blue Ridge to Key West covered great expanses of land still virtual wilderness.

Athens Methodist Church future and former clergy who were delegates to the 1840 General Conference of the Methodist Episcopal Church were Lovick Pierce, William J. Parks, Ignatius A. Few, and George W. Foster Pierce.

☙1841☙

Daniel Curry, Pastor, 1841, and Co-Pastor, 1842

Born near Peekskill, New York, on November 26, 1809, Pastor Daniel Curry graduated in 1837 from Wesleyan University in Connecticut. He first served as principal of New York's Troy Conference Academy, moving in 1839 to Wesleyan Female College in Macon. In 1841 he joined the Georgia Conference, was admitted on trial as deacon that year and was ordained an elder in full connection in 1843. During this formative period, he served his first appointment as minister at Athens. For his second year here the churches at Athens and Lexington were paired in a single charge, and Rev. Walter

Branham joined him as a co-pastor on the circuit. Curry was appointed to Savannah in 1843 and Columbus in 1844 before choosing to go home to the Northern church in the North-South split of 1845. He joined the New York East Conference, building a distinguished career in New York and Connecticut. He was elected to General Conference eight times, and was "always a prominent figure," according to his *New York Times* obituary. He made a speech at the 1848 General Conference repudiating the separation of the Northern and Southern churches. His further appointments were: 1845 27th Street, NYC; 1846-47 New Haven First; 1848-49 Washington Street, Long Island; 1850-51 Fleet Street, Brooklyn; 1852-53 Hartford First; 1854 27th & 37th Street; 1855-56 President, Asbury (now DePauw) University, Greencastle, Indiana; 1857 Sands Street, Brooklyn; 1858-59 Middleton; 1860-62 New Rochelle; 1863 37th Street, NYC; 1864 Presiding Elder, Long Island District; 1865-76 Editor of the *Christian Advocate*; 1876 six-month sabbatical in Europe; 1876-80 Editor, the *National Repository*

(8 volumes); 1881-87 assistant editor and then editor, the *Methodist Review*; 1882-83 Harlem and 82nd Street; 1884 Bethany Chapel, 123rd Street; 1885 Trinity, 118th Street. He was author and editor of several books. Curry died "of acute indigestion" on August 17, 1887, at his residence at 17 West 132nd Street in New York City. He had just returned home from five weeks in Ocean Grove, New Jersey, seeking to restore his health. His funeral was at St. James Methodist Episcopal Church, Madison Avenue at 126th Street in NYC, with Bishop Thomas Bowman officiating.

An aside on Bishop Bowman, who presided at Curry's funeral: Like Rev. Curry, Bowman served as president of

The New-York Times, Thursday, August 18, 1887.

DR. CURRY'S DEATH.

THE END OF THE LIFE OF A LEADER OF METHODISM.

The Rev. Daniel Curry, D. D., LL. D., died at his residence, 17 West One Hundred and Thirty-second-street, at 3 o'clock yesterday afternoon of acute indigestion. Dr. Curry was a native of New-York and was born Nov. 26, 1809 in what is now Cortlandville, near Peekskill His early education was acquired in White Plains, whence, in 1835, he matriculated in Weslyan University, in Middletown, Conn. graduating two years later, so close was his application and quick perception. In 1840 he went to Georgia to take charge of an academy at Macon. Two years later, while the Methodist Church was still undivided, he entered the Georgia Conference. The great conflict over the slavery question was then going on Dr. Curry was ever a fervent advoate of aboli tion, and when the Methodist Church South sprang into being he returned to the North and continued his crusade against slavery in the company of Garrison, Whittier, and Phillips.

Entering the New-York East Conference he held appointments from 1844 to 1855 as follows Twenty-seventh-Street Church, New-York, two years; New-Haven, two years; Washington street, Brooklyn, two years; Fleet-street, Brook lyn, two years; Hartford, Conn., two years and for the succeeding nine months again at the Twenty-Seventh-Street Church, resigning the Pastorate there in 1855 to take the Presidency of Asbury (now De Pauw) University in Indiana. In 1857, he returned to Brook

(Obituary NY Times, Aug. 18, 1887, p. 2)

Asbury College which became today's DePauw University. Bowman was chaplain of the U.S. Senate during the administration of President Abraham Lincoln and the two became friends and confidants. Bowman later reported having warned Lincoln that he was in danger from John Wilkes Booth, a well-known actor who was prowling the halls of the U.S. Capitol building and the White House. Lincoln laughingly made light of the warning. Lincoln was assassinated by Booth at Ford's Theatre just five days later.

☙1842 ❧

Walter R. Branham, Sr., Co-Pastor, 1842

Rev. Walter Branham joined Rev. Daniel Curry as a co-pastor of the Athens/Lexington circuit for the year 1842. Born in Eatonton November 18, 1813, Branham graduated from Franklin College (UGA) in 1835. He married Elizabeth Flournoy (1819-1904) of Eatonton. He was admitted on trial in 1836 and appointed to Watkinsville for 1836-37, where he was co-pastor with John W. Glenn. His further appointments were 1838 Augusta; 1839 Clinton/Monticello; 1840-41 Milledgeville. His year in Athens, 1842, was followed by: 1843 Lawrenceville; 1844 Madison; 1845-46 Eatonton; 1847-48 Vineville, Macon; 1849-50 Macon; 1851 Trinity, Augusta; 1852 Professor of history and moral philosophy, Wesleyan College; 1853-54 supply, Columbus mission; 1855-56 Oxford/Covington; 1857-59 Presiding Elder, Atlanta District; 1860-63 Presiding Elder, Griffin District; 1864-65 Presiding Elder, Atlanta District; 1866-68 Presiding Elder, Athens District; 1869-70 Presiding Elder, Griffin District; 1871 Washington; 1872-74

Rev. Walter R. Branham, Sr. and his elaborate
tombstone at the historic cemetery in Oxford, Ga.

Oxford/Social Circle; 1875-76 Covington/Mt. Pleasant; 1877-78 Social Circle; 1879 Jackson; 1880-81 Oxford; 1882 city missionary; 1883 supply. Rev. Branham died September 2, 1894 at Oxford, Ga., and is buried in the historic Methodist cemetery there. The oldest of the Branham's seven children, Junius, volunteered for the Confederate Army while a senior at Emory College in 1861, eventually making Colonel and serving in the same company as the poet, Sidney Lanier. Another son, Walter R. Branham, Jr., born in 1850, was an elder in North Georgia 1874-1916 and served as associate at Athens First 1878-79 with responsibility for the Oconee Street Mission, forerunner of the Oconee Street Church.

Of the original Athens Methodist Church trustees named by the General Assembly in 1828, Cicero Holt died in 1830, but his position inexplicably was not filled over the next decade. Trustee William Lumpkin died in 1840. By that time, James Meriwether apparently had moved from Athens. The remaining two trustees, Asbury Hull and Right Rogers, lacked a quorum and were unable to act. The Georgia General Assembly passed an act enabling the two remaining trustees to fill the vacant positions. At a meeting February 5, 1842, Hull and Rogers elected Daniel Grant, Francis Gideon and James R. Carlton.

Relatively little is known of trustee Daniel Grant. He is listed among Athens leaders who worked to bring the first railroad to town in 1831, and was among those who bought and improved the Prince's Mill on McNutt's Creek (forerunner of the former Puritan Mill in today's Princeton community). He apparently was removed from the board by the other trustees before 1845, when he and Right Rogers, who had moved from Athens, were replaced by Henry Hull and Ross Crane, Sr.

Likewise, little is known of trustee Francis Gideon, whose only mention in the record is at his election in 1842 and his apparent replacement by A.S. Hill sometime before 1866.

Trustee James Richardson (or Richeson) Carlton was a Virginia native and a contractor who came to Athens to rebuild New College after it was destroyed in an 1830 fire. His business partner was Ross Crane, Sr. Listed as a brick mason in the 1860 census, Carlton would be one of only two surviving trustees in 1866 who under a second special authorization of the General Assembly elected three new trustees, Marcellus Stanley, John W. Nicholson, and Reuben Nickerson. Among Carlton's twelve children, a son,

Henry Hull Carlton, became a Congressman from Athens, a trustee of the University of Georgia, a Captain in the Troup Artillery of the Confederate Army, and years later, in 1898 became a Major in the U.S. Army, dying in 1905. A second son, Benjamim Richard Carlton, died in the battle of Sharpsburg during the Civil War. The elder Carlton was contractor for the new Athens Presbyterian Church in 1855, and future trustee Ross Crane was contractor for the new Athens Baptist Church built in 1860. Carlton would resign from the board for health reasons in early 1888 and died in August of the same year.

꧁1843 ꧁

Alfred Turner Mann, Pastor, 1843

Pastor Alfred Mann was born near Augusta on November 1, 1815, son of John H. and Henrietta Mann, who throughout his formative years were active and prominent members of the Augusta Methodist Church. The family was wealthy, giving Alfred many opportunities including a fine education. He attended Richmond Academy, the Cokesbury School, Franklin College, and finally Randolph-Macon College in Virginia, where in 1837 at age 20 he graduated "with high class distinction." He later received his Doctor of Divinity degree from Randolph- Macon. While at Franklin College in Athens he was converted in the faith, and at Randolph-Macon joined the Methodist Church and became fully active in it. In 1838, he married Julia Pierce of Athens, the daughter of longtime Athens pastor and resident Lovick Pierce, making him brother- in-law to Bishop George Foster Pierce.

Rev. Alfred Turner Mann (from the Smithsonian Institution National Portrait Gallery)

Following her death, in 1854 he married Fanny Batty. Neither marriage produced children. Admitted on trial in 1836, he was ordained deacon in 1838 and elder in 1841. He would serve two appointments to Athens Methodist Church. His appointments were: 1836-37 McDonough Circuit associate under Pastor J. Dunwoody; 1838 Columbus associate under Rev.

Thomas Stanford; 1839 Washington; 1840 Quincy, Fla.; 1841 Macon; 1842 Milledgeville; 1843 Athens; 1844-45 Sparta; 1846-47 Wesley Chapel, Savannah; 1848-50 Presiding Elder, Marietta District; 1851-52 Athens; 1853-54 Presiding Elder, Macon District; 1855-56 St. John, Augusta; 1857 Columbus First; 1858 St. Luke (Columbus First renamed); 1859 Vineville and Macon Colored Mission; 1860 St. James, Augusta; 1861-62 Presiding Elder, Augusta District; 1863 Louisville and Concord Mission; 1864 Louisville associate to Rev. E. G. Murrah; 1865-66 transferred to Memphis Conference, Wesley Chapel, Memphis; 1867 Second Street, Memphis; 1868-70 transferred to North Georgia Conference, St. John, Augusta; 1871 Washington; 1872-75 Madison; 1876-79 transferred to South Georgia Conference, Presiding Elder, Savannah District; 1880-81 Presiding Elder, Macon District; 1882 St. Paul, Columbus; 1883-85 Americus; 1886-89 transferred to North Georgia Conference, Richmond Circuit, Augusta. He was elected to General Conference several times. Mann died at home during the last appointment at Augusta on February 2, 1889, and was buried at Magnolia Cemetery, Augusta. His obituary lauded "the best-known living member of the Methodist Conference" whose eloquence in the pulpit was exceeded only by that of his brother-in-law, Bishop Pierce. He had no children of his own but was survived by three children of his second wife. Mann Memorial Methodist Church of Augusta was planned in his memory in 1890 and merged with Mize Memorial United Methodist Church in 2016. In 2023, Mann-Mize disaffiliated from the UMC. *(Note: At times we are confounded by a one-year difference in listings of appointments from various sources, apparently because the appointments were made in December to be effective in January. This is apparent in Mann's listings, but occurs in those of other pastors, as well.)*

᧐1844 ᧐

William Justice Parks, Pastor, 1844-1845

Born in Franklin County on November 30, 1799, William was a son of Henry Parks, an "exhorter" who had been influenced by evangelists Humphries and Major. His mother was Martha Justice. Young William was converted at a camp meeting in Elbert County at age eight. Sent to Clarke County to study English grammar and board in the home of Rev. Joseph Tarpley, Presiding Elder of the Athens District, William received a "license to exhort" in 1820 and was licensed to preach in 1821. He assisted a Black Athens minister, preaching his first sermon in Powellton, Hancock

County, in 1822, and came to be known by the nickname "Uncle Billie." He was married four times, with each wife predeceasing him. There were nine children, all by the first wife, Naomi Prickett (1796-1856). A son, Harwell Hodges Parks, also would serve Athens Methodist as pastor. The elder Parks was admitted on trial in 1822, deacon in full connection in 1824, and elder in 1826. His appointments were: 1822 Sparta; 1823-24 Gwinnett Mission; 1825 Broad River; 1826 Grove; 1827-28 located; 1829 Gwinnett; 1830 Walton; 1831-32 Presiding Elder, Athens District; 1833 Apalachee; 1834-35 Presiding Elder, Milledgeville District; 1835-36 Presiding Elder, Macon District; 1837-40 Presiding Elder, Athens District; 1841 Agent, Emory College; 1842 Presiding Elder, Cherokee District; 1843 Conference Agent; and 1844-45 Athens. Pastor Parks in his own handwriting produced an updated membership list of the Athens church containing 268 names, but only the White members. His time here was followed by 1846-47 Greensboro; 1848 agent, Emory College; 1849 agent, American Bible Society; 1850-53 Presiding Elder, Athens District; 1854 Lexington Circuit and Oglethorpe County mission; 1865 supply. He was elected a clergy delegate to General Conference in 1832, 1840, 1844, 1846, 1850, 1854, 1858 and 1870. During his 1844-45 stay in Athens, Parks conducted an "unusually effective" revival bringing into membership "163 White and 97 Colored members." He served as a trustee of Wesleyan College. Parks died October 16, 1873, and was buried in the historic Methodist cemetery at Oxford, Ga.

The General Conference of the Methodist Episcopal Church included as delegates future and former Athens Methodist Church clergy George W. Foster Pierce, Lovick Pierce, William J. Parks, and James E. Evans.

☙1845☙

The Louisville Convention, a called session of Southern conferences of the Methodist Episcopal Church, became the organizational conference of the Methodist Episcopal Church, South, which split from the mainline denomination over the issue of slavery, in particular the ownership of three slaves by Bishop James Osgood Andrew. Some 462,000 members left with the Southern church, and 689,000 remained in the Northern church. Athens Methodist Church became part of the M.E. Church, South. The organizational conference of the M.E. Church, South voted to separate Georgia and Florida into separate conferences. A large swath of South Georgia from the Altamaha River to the Chattahoochee was made part of the Florida Conference while a section of Northwest Georgia became part of the Holston Conference. Athens Methodist Church clergy from over the years who served as delegates from the Georgia Conference were: Lovick Pierce, James E. Evans, and Samuel W. Anthony.

Athens Methodist Church trustees held an election December 18, 1845 to choose successors to Right Rogers, who was "removed" (perhaps meaning he moved out of the city) and Daniel Grant, apparently removed from office for absences. Joining Asbury Hull, Francis Gideon and James R. Carlton on the board were Henry Hull and Ross Crane, Sr. A. L. Hill also is listed as a trustee that year, but was not on the Board of Trustees, but rather on another group, such as the parsonage board.

Trustee Henry Hull was the second son of founding pastor Rev. Hope Hull. He would serve the Athens Methodist Church for many years, dying in 1881. A complete obituary is found at that point in this record.

Trustee John Ross Crane, Sr. was a contractor who came to Athens in 1830 to rebuild New College following a devastating fire. He likewise was the contractor who built the new Athens Baptist Church on Washington Street at College Avenue in 1860. Without access to the historical records since located and available to us, John Bondurant in his 1988 history mistakenly presumed it was John Ross Crane, Jr. who was the trustee, but the newly-recovered records reveal it indeed was Ross Crane, Sr.

9 1846 9

George W. Foster Pierce, Pastor, 1846-1847

Born in 1811 in Greene County, George Foster Pierce was son of Lovick Pierce, the first appointed pastor at Athens Methodist. In 1854, the younger Pierce would become the first of three former pastors of our church to be elected a Bishop. A teenager when his father moved the family to Athens, the younger Pierce was converted during a revival at Athens Methodist Church at age 16. He attended Franklin College, where he came under the influence of Athens Methodist Church pastor John Owen Andrew, whom he credited with counseling that helped him to accept his call to ministry. Pierce was admitted to the conference on trial in 1831, made deacon in full connection in 1833, and ordained elder in 1835. In 1834 Pierce married New York native Ann W. Waldron. His appointments were: 1831 Alcovy; 1832 Augusta; 1833 Savannah; 1834 Charleston; 1835 Augusta; 1836-38 Presiding Elder,

Augusta District; 1839-40 President, Georgia Female College, Macon. In 1840 he was among the Georgia delegation to the General Conference at Baltimore, where he saw trouble clearly brewing between the Northern and Southern churches over the issue of slavery and concluded that an inevitable separation was coming. His further appointments were: 1841 Agent, Georgia Female College; 1842 Macon; 1843-44 Augusta. In 1844, Pierce again was a delegate to the General Conference, this time held in New York City. Though only 33 years old, he became a chief spokesman of the Southern viewpoint, and in a rousing speech defended his friend, Bishop James Osgood Andrew, whose father had brought Pierce into the ministry. The younger Andrew's slave ownership caused the Northern delegates to seek to expel him. The next year, Georgia sent Pierce as a delegate to the called convention at Louisville, where Southern conferences voted to separate from the mainline church. Further appointments for Rev. Pierce were: 1845 Presiding Elder, Augusta District; 1846-47 Athens. The strongest revival to that date in Athens came during his pastorate, with 163 Whites and

Bishop George W. Foster Pierce

90 Blacks being added in one quarter that fall. During Pierce's two years in our pulpit, 201 White members and 132 Colored joined the church, with influence of the revival reaching throughout the city's population. In that same period, 36 White and 27 Colored were expelled. Pierce's further appointments were: 1848 Columbus, and 1849-54 President, Emory College. From that position, a fertile ground for producing bishops over many decades, Pierce was elected Bishop in 1854 and served until his

BISHOP
GEORGE FOSTER PIERCE
—(1811-1884)—

Born February 3 in 1811 near Greensboro. George Foster Pierce was converted while at the University in Athens. In 1830 he followed his father, Dr. Lovick Pierce, into the Methodist ministry. He was first assigned twenty-two preaching stations on the Oconee Circuit. Later he served pastorates in Augusta, Savannah, Charleston, and Columbus. He may have preached ten thousand times. His life with his family on his farm "Sunshine" near Sparta was idyllic.

He was in 1834 the first president of Wesleyan College, also editor of the "Southern Ladies' Book", then president of Emory (1848-1854). In 1844 at the New York Conference he defended Bishop Andrew as a slaveholder; and in 1845 at Louisville, Kentucky he helped organize the Methodist Episcopal Church, South. Elected Bishop in Columbus, Georgia, 1854.

He was without a peer as an orator. As a Methodist Bishop, he suffered with his people the hardships of the Civil War. He died in 1884 in Sparta and is buried there.

death in 1884. A preacher whose sermons were filled with emotion, Pierce once was back in Athens to preach the UGA commencement sermon, and stayed at the home of his old friend, Ferdinand Phinizy. He asked Phinizy if preaching a camp-meeting style sermon would be out of place for a UGA commencement. Phinizy encouraged him to preach as he wanted. His sermon on "The Power of the Gospel as Seen in the Cross of Christ" was reported to have "swept the learned audience before him." Bishop Pierce died in 1884 on his plantation at Sparta, and there he was buried. Of him, future Bishop Warren A. Candler wrote, "I have had the privilege of hearing many of the greatest preachers of the English-speaking world...And I affirm deliberately that I have never heard any preacher greater than George Foster Pierce."

Athens Methodist Church clergy from over the years who were delegates to the 1846 General Conference of the M.E. Church, South were: Lovick Pierce, William J. Parks, Samuel W. Anthony, James E. Evans, and George W. Foster Pierce.

໑1847 ໑

John M. Bonnell, Pastor of Athens Colored Mission, 1847

As with many larger churches across Georgia, the African-American membership at Athens Methodist grew to a size to warrant its own pastor. Such congregations came to be known as "Colored Missions." In 1847 the conference sent John M. Bonnell to be minister to the Black members of the Athens Methodist Church. Born in Bucks County, Pennsylvania, on April 16, 1820, Bonnell grew up in Philadelphia. He graduated from Jefferson College and moved to Georgia at age 18 to teach school in Greenville, Meriwether County. Trained as a Presbyterian, he was converted to Methodism in Greenville in 1842 and accepted a call to ministry. Admitted on trial in 1846, he was granted full connection with his appointment to Athens in 1847 and was ordained an elder in 1850. A year-and-a-half before he came to Athens, in December 1845, Bonnell married Cornelia Frances, who died less than five months later at the age of 29. Bonnell arrived at Athens during the pastorate of future Bishop George W. Pierce. Bonnell spent much of his life as a professor or president of educational institutions rather than in the pastorate alone. Following his first station in Athens, his appointments included: 1848 Washington; 1849-51 Professor, Emory College (then at Oxford, where a residence hall still bears his name); 1852-54 Professor, Madison Female

Rev. John M. Bonnell, D. D., died last Saturday night, in Macon, aged about forty-nine years. He had been a little unwell during the week, but thought it nothing serious. Saturday night, about 10½ o'clock, he felt a sudden pain in his chest, and before a physician could reach him he died.

For many years he was connected with the Wesleyan Female College as Professor and President, and was untiring in his labors for the institution. It was the privilege of the writer to know him well, and to know him well was to admire and love him. He held a high place in his profession, and was honored among men for his great mind; but greater than this was the Christian charity which crowned his life, and without which a man, though he understood all mysteries, were as "sounding brass and a tinkling cymbal." He lived an eminently useful life, loved and served God faithfully, and has gone to his reward. What more can be said of any man?

College; 1855 Professor, Wesleyan College; 1856 Frankfort-Lexington, Kentucky; 1857-59 Principal, Tuscaloosa Methodist Female High School, Alabama; 1860-71 President, Wesleyan College; 1864 Mulberry Street/Vineville, Macon. He authored numerous books, including textbooks on prose composition and a review of the Wesleyan hymn book. Bonnell died September 30, 1871, at age 51. He is buried in Rose Hill Cemetery, Macon. His conference memoriam describes him as possessing "a finely cultured intellect, a versatile talent, and a pure, gentle spirit."

The phenomenon of Colored Missions grew across the southern church through the 1840s and 1850s. By the time the Civil War began, there were some 60 ministers appointed across the Methodist Episcopal Church South to serve the 207,000 African-American members, almost all of them slaves. The White and Black members of a church would most often worship in the same room or sanctuary, with the Whites on the main floor and the Blacks separately in the balcony or at the back. One wonders how the pastors of that time did not perceive the irony of teaching the love of Jesus Christ to such an assembly of masters and slaves, though they did understand, it seems, that God loves all equally and without favor. At the conclusion of the Civil War, with the slaves freed, Blacks largely left the White churches to form their own churches, many in the new denominations African Methodist Episcopal Church (the AME Church), Colored Methodist Episcopal Church, today known as the Christian Methodist Episcopal Church (the CME Church), and the African Methodist Episcopal Church, Zion (the AME, Zion Church). In 1861 the Georgia Conference of the Methodist- Episcopal Church, South had 25,580 Black members. By 1872, the North Georgia Conference had only 176 Black members.

On June 12, 1847, a meeting of Athens Methodist Church leadership was called at the home of member David Holmes to address circus attendance by members of the church. The two pastors were present, Reverends Pearce and Bonnell, as were trustees Asbury Hull, Henry Hull and James R. Carlton, joined by Young L.G. Harris and eleven other leaders. Pastor Pearce sought a sense of the church leadership as to "attending circuses and such other amusements." A motion by Asbury Hull, as amended by Henry Hull, was adopted unanimously: "Resolved that we regard it very inexpedient and dangerous that any church member should attend a circus, and deem it no place for them; and therefore affectionately recommend our members to abstain from going to one." Future preachers assigned to the church were asked in an attached note to "take care that this foregoing is preserved and copied in every succeeding edition of the Church Book."

୨1848 ୧

Samuel Wesley Anthony, Pastor, 1848

Born in Abbeville, South Carolina on August 1, 1808, as a child Anthony moved with his family to Gwinnett County. Married in 1826 to Elizabeth Blalock, the couple had nine children. Following her death just a year after they left Athens, when the youngest child was not yet two years old, he remarried in 1854 to Sarah Rakestraw, only to see her die four years later. Anthony was licensed to preach in 1827, admitted on trial in 1832, made deacon in full connection in 1834, and ordained elder in 1835. His appointments were: 1832-33 Ocmulgee; 1834-35 Perry. In 1835, he reported having added 1,500 members to the church to that point in his ministry. 1836-37 Forsyth; 1838 Covington; 1839-42 Presiding Elder, Augusta District. As the newly appointed Augusta Presiding Elder, in 1839 Anthony preached a three-week revival in Washington, Wilkes County, making such an impression that the town undertook to build him a parsonage if he would make Washington the seat of the district, which he did for three years. Today it is the oldest home in Washington. Further appointments were: 1843 Macon; 1844 Agent, Wesleyan College; 1845 Macon; 1846-47 Presiding Elder, Athens District. In 1848, he moved to the pastorate at Athens Methodist Church and reported church membership to be 350. Then, 1849 Columbus; 1850-51 Presiding Elder, Columbus District; 1852 Macon; 1853 Presiding Elder, Macon District; 1854 Washington; 1855 Atlanta; 1856-58 Presiding Elder, LaGrange District (which at the time included the few new and relatively small Atlanta-area churches); 1859-60 Agent, Emory College; 1861-62 Cuthbert/Emmaus;

1863-64 Americus and Colored Charge. At the 1866 Georgia Conference separation, he went with South Georgia and was named Presiding Elder, Americus District; 1867 South Georgia Sunday School Agent; 1868 supply; 1869 Superintendent of Colored Churches; 1871-75 Agent, Orphan's Home, Altamaha; 1876 Perry; 1877 Quitman; 1878 Sunday School Agent, Dublin District; 1879-80 Presiding Elder, Americus District. A well- known preacher throughout Georgia during his more than three decades of service, Anthony drew unfortunate national headlines when in 1869 he was shot while performing a wedding. Scurrilous details became more distorted as they traveled. It seems the wedding was underway at Andersonville when the bride's uncle, who had been responsible for procuring the preacher, had too much to drink, almost missed the ceremony, and came wobbling into the in-progress wedding brandishing a bird-gun. Pastor Anthony tried gently to move the barrel of the gun aside, when it went off, shooting him in the abdomen. Rev. Anthony finished the ceremony and forgave the bride's uncle on the spot. He lived another decade, dying March 3, 1880, while serving in Americus, and is buried in Oak Grove Cemetery there.

Grave of Rev. Samuel Wesley Anthony, Oak Grove Cemetery, Americus

W. M. Crumley, Pastor of Athens Colored Mission, 1848

Our research did not reveal a service record for Rev. Crumley. Perhaps a future researcher can fill this gap in our history.

ᕱ**1849** ᕲ

Jesse Boring, Pastor, 1849

Rev. Jesse Boring was one of two pastors of Athens Methodist Church who were instrumental in taking Methodism to the new frontier in California, working together to found churches and establish the Pacific Conference. Boring served Athens in 1849, the year before he and Rev. Alexander Wynn

Rev. Jesse Boring

left for five years in California. They returned to Georgia in 1855, and Wynn came to Athens the next year. Born December 4, 1807, in Jackson County, Boring was converted in 1814 at age seven. In 1822, he served the Gwinnett Mission at age 15. He was licensed to preach in 1825, admitted on trial in 1827, made deacon in full connection in 1829 and ordained elder in 1831. Described as "exceedingly timid and sensitive," he was discouraged by early pulpit failures. He married Harriett E. Howard in 1833 when she was 17 and he was 26. They met when her father was converted by the

young pastor as he was riding his circuit through her hometown of Greensboro. His appointments were: 1827 Chattahoochee Circuit; 1828 Ocmulgee; 1829 Washington; 1830 LaGrange; 1831 Columbus; 1832 Milledgeville/Scottsboro; and 1833 Columbus. During his year at Columbus, the congregation outgrew its wooden sanctuary. Meetings were held outdoors while a larger brick building was constructed, the first brick Methodist church in Georgia and forerunner of today's St. Luke UMC. After Columbus, Boring went to: 1834 Augusta; 1835 a second tour at LaGrange; 1836-37 Columbus Colored Mission; 1838-40 supply, located because of failing health, he moved to Alabama. Regaining his health, he resumed itineracy in 1841 Tuskegee Circuit, Alabama; 1842 Jackson Street, Mobile; 1843-44 Presiding Elder, Mobile District; 1845 Agent, Centenary Institute; 1846 Presiding Elder, Mobile District; 1847 Columbus; 1848 Presiding Elder, Columbus District, and 1849 Athens.

In 1850, Boring and Wynn were sent by the Georgia Conference as missionaries to California, with the goal of founding churches and establishing a conference structure. They sailed March 1, 1850, from New Orleans to Panama, which they crossed by mule for 37 miles over land to the Pacific, and then on to San Francisco, all while Harriet Boring was pregnant with the couple's fourth child. His further appointments were: 1850-51 Superintendent, California Missions, where he helped found the Wesley Chapel Church in San Francisco, the first M.E. South church west of Texas, and helped found the Pacific Conference; 1852-53 Editor, *The Christian Observer*; 1854 Presiding Elder, San Francisco District. He attended the General Conference in Columbus, Georgia, that year and decided not to return to California. Instead, he sent for his family and applied for "location" in 1855. Boring began study for a medical degree, receiving the M.D. degree in 1857 from Atlanta Medical College. While in Atlanta, he and Rev. Samuel Anthony jointly served Trinity and Wesley Chapel churches. Further appointments: 1857 a third tour at LaGrange; 1858 Vineville, Macon and city mission. The family then packed up again, this time all possessions and seven children, traveled to Mobile, Alabama and took a ship to Galveston,Texas to take up a new appointment: 1859-60 San Antonio, Texas; 1861-62 Founding President, San Antonio Female College; 1863-64 Confederate military service in McCullough's Division. While he was away in the army, the family lost their home in San Antonio, auctioned by the sheriff as Harriet and the children watched. In 1865 they went to Goliad/ Middletown, Texas; 1866-68 medical faculty, Soule University, Galveston, where they lost two homes – the first to a defective title deed and the second to a hurricane. In 1869, the family returned to Atlanta and the pastorate at Wesley Chapel; 1870-72 Agent, Orphan's Home, Atlanta; 1873-74 supply; 1875-76 Washington; 1877 supply; 1878 Presiding Elder, Griffin District; 1879 St. John, Augusta; 1880-83 Presiding Elder, Atlanta District; 1884-85 Presiding Elder, Athens District; 1886 Trinity, Atlanta; 1887 retired supply. Rev. Boring is credited with the founding of Methodist Orphans' Homes in both Decatur and Macon. He continued to preach "happily and successfully" until two weeks before his death. His conference memoriam describes him as having a "massive brain, nervous temperament, shrinking disposition and delicate constitution," saying there was "no more illustrious name" than his "in the galaxy of Methodist genius and greatness." He died January 29, 1890, and was buried in Atlanta before being re-interred on the grounds of the Methodist Children's Home at Decatur.

Joseph Staunton Key,
Pastor of Athens Colored Mission, 1849

Future Bishop Joseph S. Key served the first appointment of his ministry at our church as pastor of the Athens Colored Mission. He would return as pastor of the Athens Methodist Church in 1854-55. See his full biography at that point in this timeline.

9**1850**9

Eustace Willoughby Speer, Pastor, 1850-1851

Rev. Eustace Speer was born December 1, 1826, in Columbia, South Carolina. Described in Hull's *Annals* as "a master of English," Rev. Speer served Athens Methodist Church as pastor over four widely spread years: 1850-1851, 1859, and 1871. In 1874 he was named *Professor of Belles Lettres* at the University of Georgia and made Athens his home. His sermons were "simple and helpful, never long, expressed in choicest language, chaste in thought and diction. He spake *ore rotundo*, his fine face full of expression, lighting with interest in his subject." He was admitted on trial in 1846; 1849 deacon in full connection; 1851 ordained elder. His first appointment was in 1847 to the Decatur/Atlanta Circuit, where he was one of two preachers. The

Eustace W. Speer

first wooden Methodist church in Atlanta was built that year, named Wesley Chapel, forerunner of today's Atlanta First UMC. From there his appointments were: 1848 Monticello; 1849 Lumpkin, Columbus District; 1850-51 Athens; 1852 Madison; 1853-54 Vineville, Macon; 1855-56 Columbus and Columbus mission; 1857 Covington/Oxford; 1858 St. James, Augusta; 1859 a second time at Athens, 1860 Trinity, Augusta; 1861-62 Americus and Colored Mission; 1863 St. Luke, Columbus; 1864 Mulberry Street and Vineville, Macon; 1865-67 LaGrange; 1868-69 Madison; 1870 Washington; 1871 his third time at Athens Methodist Church, followed in 1872-73 as Presiding Elder, Athens District; 1874 Atlanta First; 1875- 81 Professor, University of Georgia; 1882-83 Whitesburg; 1884 Houston, LaGrange District; 1885-86 Canton/Little River; 1887-88 Alpharetta; 1889-90 Whitesburg. Rev. Speer died October 29, 1899, and was buried in Oconee Hill Cemetery.

James Lovick Pierce, Jr., Pastor of Athens Colored Mission, 1850-1851

Rev. James L. Pierce was the son of the first appointed pastor at Athens Methodist Church, Rev. Lovick Pierce, and the brother of Bishop George Foster Pierce. Our research has not uncovered his complete service record.

At the 1850 General Conference of the M.E. Church, South, former and future Athens Methodist Church clergy delegates were: William J. Parks, Samuel Anthony, James E. Evans, George W. Foster Pierce, and Lovick Pierce.

The "Brick Church" and current steeple were constructed in 1852. It stood just more than 30 years, as a major project in 1884-1885 removed all but the steeple and built much of our current sanctuary structure.

9**1852** 9

Alfred Turner Mann, Pastor, 1852-1853

This was Mann's second appointment to Athens, the first coming in 1843. His wife was Julia Pierce, daughter of our first appointed pastor, Rev. Lovick Pierce. The church prospered under Mann's leadership over these two years, adding 60 White members and 13 Colored. Sunday School attendance was reported as lagging a bit, down to 75 from a high of 150 reached in 1846.

The small frame structure in place on the lot at Lumpkin and Hancock since 1825 and expanded in 1835 was removed, with its components used to construct a church for an African-American congregation on Hancock Avenue at Foundry Street. In its place, a brick sanctuary and the present steeple were constructed at a total cost of $6,500. Says Smith's *History*: "The old church did not meet the demands of the young city. It had been built when Athens was a village in the woods; now it was a thriving commercial and manufacturing town, and a handsome and commodious brick church was now erected." This church came to be known as the "Brick Church," as opposed to the previous wooden one. It would stay in place until the 1880s, when all was removed but the steeple, and a new structure built onto it. Also in the early 1850s, the church constructed a parsonage on the corner of its property at Washington (then Market) and Lumpkin Streets.

9**1853** 9

John H. Greghan, Pastor of Athens Colored Mission, 1853-1854

We were unable to find a service record for Rev. Greghan, a gap in our history to be filled by a future researcher.

9**1854** 9

Joseph Staunton Key, Pastor, 1854-1855

Future Bishop Joseph S. Key, who served in Athens for the year 1849 as pastor of the Athens Colored Mission, returned as pastor of Athens Methodist Church for two years 1854-55. Born in LaGrange on July 18, 1829, Rev. Key was the son of Methodist minister Caleb Witt Key , who was ordained elder in the conference in 1829 and retired in 1879, and the grandson of itinerant Methodist preacher Joseph Key. The younger Key would be the second former pastor at Athens Methodist Church to be elected a Bishop. Converting to Methodism in 1847 while a student at Emory College, Key graduated from Emory in 1848 with AB and MA degrees. He received the Doctor of Divinity degree from the University of Georgia. He was licensed to preach in 1848, admitted on trial in 1849, made full connection deacon in 1851, and ordained elder in 1853. He was elected a bishop in the Methodist Episcopal Church, South, in 1886. His appointment record: 1849 Athens

BISHOP JOSEPH S. KEY, D. D.

Bishop Joseph Staunton Key

Colored Charge; 1850 Columbus; 1851 Lumpkin; 1852 Talbotton; 1853 Madison; 1854-55 Athens; 1856-57 Trinity, Augusta; 1858-59 St. John, Augusta; 1860 St. Paul, Columbus; and in 1861-62 Key returned for a third tour at Athens. From 1862-65 he returned to St. Paul, Columbus. At the division of the Georgia Conference in 1866, he chose to go with the South Georgia Conference. His further appointments were: 1866-69 Mulberry Street, Macon; 1870 Agent, Emory College; 1871, Presiding Elder, Macon District; 1872-74, St. Luke, Columbus; 1875 Presiding Elder, Americus District; 1876-78 St. Paul, Columbus; 1878 Mulberry Street and Vineville, Macon; 1880-82 Mulberry Street, Macon; 1883 Presiding Elder, Macon District; 1884-86 Presiding Elder, Columbus District. Elected Bishop in 1886, Key retired in 1910. His first wife was Susie M. Snyder; they were married from 1851 until her death in 1891. In 1893 he married Lucy C. Kidd, a noted educator and founder of Kidd-Key College in Sherman, Texas. Bishop Key died in 1920 and was buried in Sherman, Texas

Of the 11 clergy delegates elected from Georgia to the 1854 General Conference of the M.E. Church, South, seven were former or future pastors of Athens Methodist Church: George W. Foster Pierce, Samuel W. Anthony, Lovick Pierce, William J. Parks, James E. Evans, Josiah Lewis, Jr., and Alfred T. Mann.

The church passed the 25th anniversary of its founding in 1850, and by 1854 the membership stood at 341 and total giving for the year was $583.

᠑1855 ᠑

The Athens Presbyterian Church moved from its original building on the UGA campus to its present location on Hancock Avenue between College Avenue and Lumpkin Street.

A. H. Palmer, Pastor of Athens Colored Mission, 1855-1856

We were not able to uncover a service record for Rev. Palmer, a task left to a future researcher of our church history.

᠑1856 ᠑

Alexander McFarlane Wynn, Pastor, 1856

Rev. Alexander Wynn joined Rev. Jesse Boring as two pastors of Athens Methodist Church instrumental in taking Methodism to the new frontier

Rev. Alexander McFarlane Wynn

in California, working together to found churches and establish the Pacific Conference. Boring served Athens in 1849, the year before he and Wynn left for five years in California. Wynn came to Athens in 1856 – one year after they returned to Georgia. Born in Charleston on January 20, 1827, Wynn was a son of Methodist preacher Thomas Lemuel Wynn, who died with three-year-old Alexander among family members at his bedside. His mother was Sarah Harriet McFarlane, sister of Bishop James Osgood Andrew's first wife. Following his father's death, Alexander Wynn was adopted and raised by Bishop Andrew

and his wife. Alex graduated from Emory College in 1848. He was licensed to preach and admitted on trial in 1849, became a deacon in 1850, and was ordained elder in 1851. His first appointment was in 1849 to Decatur/Atlanta (a circuit including the future Wesley Chapel), after which the conference sent him and Boring to California. There they organized Wesley Chapel Methodist Episcopal Church, South, in San Francisco, the first church west of Texas in the denomination. Wynn held that church's first services in the original San Francisco courthouse. He also was founding pastor of the first Methodist church in Stockton, California. Together, Wynn and Boring established the California mission and organized the Pacific Conference in 1852. Wynn's fluency in both French and Spanish was a great aide to the work. Wynn served as principal of Basom Institute in California, was Pacific Conference secretary 1852-53 and was elected by that conference as a delegate to General Conference in 1854. Wynn was appointed to San Jose church in San Francisco in 1852-53 and became Presiding Elder of the San Francisco District in 1854. The next year, he returned to Georgia with appointments as follow: 1855 Thomasville; 1856 Athens; 1857 Columbus; 1858 Columbus, Girard, and the Colored Mission; 1859-60 Talbotton; 1861-62 Eatonton; 1863-65 Trinity and Wesley Chapel, Augusta. At the 1866 separation, he continued with the South Georgia Conference, serving 1866 Trinity, Savannah; 1867 Isle of Hope and City Mission, Savannah; 1868-71 St. Paul, Columbus; 1872-73 Americus; 1874-77 Wesley Church and Mission, Savannah; 1878-80 Presiding Elder, Columbus District; 1881 Presiding Elder, Savannah District; 1882-83 Thomasville; 1884-85 St. Paul, Columbus; 1886 1st Street, Macon; 1887-90 Wesley Memorial, Savannah; 1891-93 Thomasville; 1894-95 Waycross and mission; 1896-98 St. Paul, Columbus; 1899 Rose Hill; 1900 Sandersville; 1901 Superintendent and Trustee, Wesleyan College. Wynn worked diligently to establish an Orphan's Home in Macon, which was approved by the South Georgia Conference in 1872. He was instrumental in planning and building the Wesley Monumental Church in Savannah. Wynn died August 17, 1906, in Columbus and was buried in Linwood Cemetery.

൭**1857**൭

Harwell Hodges Parks, Pastor, 1857-1858

Harwell H. Parks was born June 19, 1825, in Franklin County (now in Banks County), son of Rev. W. J. "Uncle Billie" Parks, a pioneer Methodist minister in Georgia who was pastor at Athens in 1844-45. His mother, Naomi Prickett, was a daughter of a Revolutionary War soldier. The younger Parks was converted at age 10 in a service at the Bold Springs Campground there. He was educated at the Oxford Manual Labor School, the year before it became Emory College. At age 19, he married Sarah Ann Quillian, the 17-year-old daughter of Rev. James Quillian. They became parents of eight sons and two daughters.Parks was licensed to exhort in 1847,licensed to preach in 1848, admitted on trial in 1850, became a full connection deacon in 1852, and was ordained elder in 1853. His appointments were: 1850 Gainesville Circuit; 1851-52 Lexington Circuit; 1853 Carnesville; 1854-55 Elberton;

1856 Presiding Elder, Atlanta District; 1857-58 Athens; 1859-60 Macon and Vineville; 1861 St. Luke, Columbus; 1862 St. Luke and Pierce Chapel; 1863-64 Trinity, Atlanta; 1865-68 Athens; 1869 Rome; 1870-72 St. James, Augusta; 1873-74 Trinity, Savannah; 1875 LaGrange; 1876 St. James, Augusta; 1877 Milledgeville; 1878-79 Atlanta First; 1880 Milledgeville; 1881-83 Presiding Elder, Augusta District; 1884-86 Presiding Elder, Atlanta District; 1887-89 Presiding Elder, Griffin District; 1890-93 Presiding Elder, Athens District; 1894-95 Edgewood, Atlanta. Spending 13 years of his ministry as a Presiding Elder, Parks was described as "wise in

Rev. Harwell Hodges Parks in the 1892 Conference Journal

counsel, fertile in resources and carefully considerate of all the interests of the church. Those serving in his districts found him always approachable, companionable and sympathetic." Said to have a tremendous verbal memory, he quoted long passages of scripture in his sermons verbatim and without notes, knew the hymns by heart, and did it in a "remarkably easy, colloquial and direct style." He is described as having a "straight, tall form, towering head and shoulders above his brethren." He was elected multiple times to the General Conference. Parks became the longest-serving pastor at Athens to that date with his two separate appointments totaling six years. He first arrived in 1857, and the church experienced a wonderful revival under his leadership. The revival grew out of a new movement in the community toward daily prayer meetings, organized by General Thomas R. R. Cobb, a member of the Presbyterian Church and founder of the Lucy Cobb Institute at Athens. Cobb was an Athens attorney who authored the Constitution of the Confederate States. Becoming a Confederate general, he died in the battle of Fredericksburg. The first "Brick Church" was new when Parks arrived. Hosting the Georgia Annual Conference that year, it boasted being among Athens' first buildings lit by gas lights. But the Gas Works located on Thomas Street occasionally had supply problems, throwing its customers into darkness. In Hull's *Annals*, Rev. Parks is quoted as telling the Annual Conference, "Dr. W. P. Harrison will preach tonight. There will be plenty of gas." The delegates applauded.

Parks died August 8, 1895, at the age of 70. His funeral was held at Oxford, conducted by Bishop Atticus Haygood and future bishop, Rev. Warren Candler. Parks was buried in the Oxford Historic Cemetery in Oxford, Ga.

John H. Harris, Pastor of Athens Colored Mission, 1857

Born June 7, 1830, Rev. Harris was son of Rev. West Harris and Martha Harvey Harris. He was converted at age 18 at Salem Campground in Newton County, and was licensed to preach in 1850. He was admitted on trial to the Georgia Conference meeting at Savannah, January 8, 1851. His appointments were: 1851 Watkinsville; 1852 Lexington Circuit; 1853 Carnesville Circuit; 1854 Elberton Circuit; 1855 Clarkesville Circuit, 1856 Columbus Colored Mission; 1857 Athens Colored Mission; 1858 Cuthbert; 1859 Fort Gaines; 1860 Lumpkin Circuit; 1861-62 Hamilton Circuit; 1863-65 medical leave; 1866 Fort Gaines; 1867 located; 1868 Blakely Circuit; 1869-72 transferred to North Georgia Conference, McDonough Circuit; 1873 Newton Circuit; 1874-76 Evans Chapel, Atlanta, where he died while serving on February 17, 1876, having spent the afternoon of the day he died in pastoral visiting. He first married in 1853 to Martha Banks, and following her death married Miss E. Parks in 1857. They had six children. She was the daughter of Rev. William G. Parks. Rev. Harris is described in his memoriam as "popular, with a bright and sunny disposition, making all happy about him." The McDonough Circuit "would have kept him for life," except that he had served out the four-year limitation of that time.

୭1858୭

Lucius Holsey, Bishop of the Colored Methodist Episcopal Church, 1873-1920

By 1858, with the erection of the new Athens Methodist sanctuary and the construction of a separate African-American sanctuary on Hancock Avenue at Foundry Street using elements of the former Athens Methodist building, there continued to be a close association between the White and Black congregations. Outstanding pioneer leaders of the Black churches came out of the Athens Methodist congregation as its Black members separated into their own church. At the time of the great revival at Athens Methodist during the ministry of Rev. H. H. Parks, there was a similarly great revival among the Black congregation under the preaching of evangelist Henry McNeal Turner, a free Black and an ordained minister in the M.E.

Bishop Lucius Holsey

Church, South, who later would become Bishop in the AME Church. Turner, who would serve as a chaplain in the Union Army during the Civil War and was with Sherman's Army on its march through North Carolina, would play a leading role after the war in recruiting Black members of congregations in the M.E. Church, South to move to the AME Church. Turner was elected from Macon to the Georgia General Assembly in 1868. In his congregation at the 1858 Athens revival was a slave boy named Lucius Holsey, a Black member of the Athens Methodist congregation. Holsey's mother was a slave.

He was fathered by a White slaveowner in Columbus. Holsey was raised at Sparta on the plantation of his father's cousin. As the slaveowner/cousin neared death, Holsey was offered a choice of new owners. Holsey chose Richard Malcom Johnston, owner of another Sparta plantation, who in 1858 accepted a position as professor of English at UGA and moved his family and slaves to Athens. This brought Holsey along with the entire Johnston family and entourage of slaves to Athens Methodist Church and Holsey's attendance at the Henry McNeal Turner revival. Holsey was converted and was taken under the wing and mentorship of the Athens Methodist pastor, Rev. H. H. Parks. Holsey followed this call into the ministry. When Civil War broke out and UGA closed, Johnston moved the family back to Sparta, where Holsey met Harriet Turner, a slave owned by Bishop George F. Pierce, who had a neighboring plantation. The young couple was married by Bishop Pierce in his home and Holsey was greatly influenced by Pierce in his progression toward the episcopacy. Freed after the war, Holsey received land from Johnston, and Pierce provided property to build a church which Holsey would pastor. A founding pastor of the CME Church when it evolved out of the M.E. Church, South, in 1870, Holsey was appointed to Trinity CME in Augusta. In 1873, Bishop Pierce and the one remaining Black bishop elevated Holsey to the CME episcopacy.

Holsey founded many CME churches. He built a record of interracial collaboration and was instrumental in the founding of Paine College at Augusta. He and Bishop Atticus G. Haygood traveled the South raising money for Paine College. The remainder of his life, he represented the CME at General Conferences of the M.E. Church, South. He lived in Atlanta's Sweet Auburn district where the King Center is located today and was a figure in cooperating with White pastors and city leadership in quelling the 1906 Atlanta race riots. His views on the efficacy of racial cooperation soured as the numbers of lynchings in Georgia soared in the early 20th Century. He went so far as to propose the federal government carve out of the Indian territories a separate state for Blacks, an idea which went nowhere. Yet Holsey continued to be a racial diplomat and a leader of the CME church as its bishop until his death in 1920.

William Asbury Parks, Pastor of Athens Colored Mission, 1858-1859

Rev. William A. Parks was born in 1834 in Alabama. He was baptized by his uncle, Rev. William Justice Parks, taught at the Ebenezer Methodist Church School in Forsyth County, and was ordained in the late 1850s. The Athens Colored Mission likely was one of his first appointments. He became a chaplain for the 52nd Georgia Regiment of the Confederate Army, was captured at Vicksburg and paroled. He later served as chaplain for the Georgia legislature. Parks died in 1910 in Hall County and is buried at Whitesburg, Carroll County, Georgia.

William Asbury Parks in the 1897 Conference Journal

The 1858 General Conference of the M.E. Church, South, had the following former or future Athens Methodist Church clergy elected as delegates from the Georgia Conference:

Samuel W. Anthony, William J. Parks, Lovick Pierce, Jesse Boring, Alfred T. Mann, James E. Evans, and Walter R. Branham, Sr.

૭1859૭

Eustace W. Speer, Pastor, 1859

This was Pastor Speer's second appointment to our pulpit, and his third of four total years served here over his distinguished career, which concluded as a professor at UGA.

ꝺ**1860**ꝺ

James Wooten Hinton, Pastor, 1860

Born in Wilkes County in 1826, Hinton attended Cokesbury Academy in Greenwood, S.C. He was admitted on trial in 1847, became a deacon in full connection in 1850, and was ordained elder in 1852. His appointments included: 1848 Decatur; 1849-50 Griffin; 1851 Marietta; 1852 Milledgeville; 1853-54 Talbotton; 1855 Macon; 1856-57 Americus; 1858-59 Presiding Elder, Columbus District; 1860 Athens; 1861-62 Rome and Colored Mission; 1863 Wesley Chapel, Atlanta; 1864 Presiding Elder, Griffin District; 1865 Cuthbert and Emmaus, Americus; 1866 Marietta; 1867 Eatonton; 1868-72 Presiding Elder, Savannah District; 1873-75 Presiding Elder, Macon District; 1876-78 Presiding Elder, Americus District; 1879- 80 St. Paul, Columbus; 1881-82 Presiding Elder, Columbus District; 1883 Mulberry Street, Macon; 1884-85 Presiding Elder, Macon District; 1886-87 Presiding Elder, Savannah District; 1888-91 Presiding Elder, Thomasville District; 1892-96 Presiding Elder, Sandersville District; 1897-99 Presiding Elder, Columbus District; 1900 Supply. In 1878, Hinton was editor of the *Methodist Review*. He was elected to five General Conferences from 1880-1896. His 31 years as Presiding Elder likely still hold the record for years served by Georgia clergy as Presiding Elder or District Superintendent. Hinton died July 16, 1903, and was buried in Riverside Cemetery, Macon.

Dr. J. W. Hinton Dead

Dr. J. W. Hinton, one of the oldest and best known Methodist ministers in Georgia, died Saturday morning at ten o'clock at his home in Macon. The news of his death was received in Columbus during the day and caused the deepest sadness among his many friends and admirers here. Dr. Hinton's last active work in the ministry was as presiding elder of the Columbus district of the Methodist church which he retired upon his superannuation, some three or four years ago.—Columbus Enquirer-Sun.

Obituary, The Macon Telegraph, and grave in Riverside Cemetery, Macon

Henry Crawford, Pastor of Athens Colored Mission, 1860

As with many others who served Athens as pastor of the Black members of the congregation, we have not been able immediately to uncover a service record for Rev. Crawford.

The Athens Baptist Church built a new sanctuary on Market (now Washington) Street east of College Avenue to replace their original building on the UGA campus.

⊝1861⊝

Joseph Staunton Key, Pastor, 1861-1862

Key previously was Athens' pastor in 1854-55. Returning here at the outbreak of the Civil War, in April 1861 he preached a farewell sermon and service at the church for members and others in the Troup Artillery, the first unit from Athens to depart for the Civil War. The company's captain, Marcellus Stanley, was son of our first pastor, Thomas Stanley. Marcellus Stanley would return from service to become a longtime leader of the church, serving as a trustee from 1866-1890. Rev. Key in 1886 would become the second former pastor of Athens Methodist Church to be elected bishop.

Bishop Joseph S. Key
in the 1902 Conference Journal

Cicero Augustus Mitchell, Pastor of Athens Colored Mission, 1861

Born October 3, 1832, in Athens, Mitchell was raised here and entered the University of Georgia as a "freshman, half-advanced" in 1847, graduating in 1851 with an A.B. degree, after which he immediately entered the Georgia Conference. He earned a master's degree from UGA in 1853. He married Elmira Clementina Smith of Greene County on May 23, 1858. His obituary reports that "he served in the active itinerancy for many years." He died in Athens February 7, 1910, his funeral held at Athens First Methodist Church with Rev. Marcellus Troutman officiating. Pallbearers were the trustees of the church. He is buried in Oconee Hill Cemetery. (Obituary in the *Weekly Banner*, February 8, 1910).

ᦉ1862ᦉ

William S. Turner, Pastor of Athens Colored Mission, 1862

There is disagreement between the Conference Journal and our own church records as to which pastor served the Athens Colored Mission in the year 1862. It is surmised that Anderson Joseph Jarrell was to have been appointed, as that is what was printed in the Conference Journal. Apparently a last-minute change in appointment resulted in Rev. William S. Turner being sent instead. A similar situation occurs later in our history with the senior minister position. The Conference Journal for 1919 shows C.O. Jones coming to Athens Methodist, when in fact Elam F. Dempsey came here that year. As with several others sent to Athens to pastor the Colored Mission, we found no service record for Rev. Turner.

ᦉ1863ᦉ

William J. Scott, Pastor, 1863

Born March 4, 1826, in the Salem Community of Clarke County, Scott was educated in Milledgeville Academy and began the practice of law at age 16 in Columbus and Rome. Described as studious and precocious, he received a call to the ministry in 1854, when he was admitted on trial at the age of 28. He became a deacon in full connection in 1856 and was ordained elder in 1858. His wife was the former Edna L. Bonner; they had a son and a daughter. His appointments were: 1855 Columbus;1856-57 Marietta; 1858-59 Americus; 1860 Milledgeville and Bethel, Macon; 1861-62 Wesley Chapel, Atlanta; 1863 Athens; 1864 St. John, Augusta. In an era when clergy and laity were brought up on charges more often than is usual today, in 1865 Scott was tried by a committee of Annual Conference on charges of slander and falsehood. Found guilty, he was suspended from the pulpit for one year, a matter described in his memoriam as "one year of forced inactivity." Interestingly, his first appointment upon return in 1866-67 was to a pulpit rapidly becoming one of Georgia's most prestigious, Wesley Chapel in Atlanta, the forerunner of Atlanta First Methodist, and to that church's "Colored Charge." His further appointments likewise carried little reflection that his career was negatively affected: 1868-70 Acworth; 1871-72 Presiding

Elder, Dalton District; 1873-74 LaGrange; 1875 Trinity, Atlanta. A stroke of paralysis during a revival at Trinity led to five years of appointments to accommodate his condition: 1876-77 Supply; 1878-80 Agent, Orphan's Home. He then returned to the pulpit in 1881 Acworth; 1882 Ringgold; 1883-84 Carrollton; 1885 Atlanta First. His memoriam references that he lost a young daughter and saw his "brilliant only son go down in hopeless insanity." During his year at Athens amid the Civil War, Athens Baptists were without a pastor, and many Baptists attended the Methodist church, pushing total collections for the year to a record $8,000. A prolific writer, Scott had many articles published over the years in the *Methodist Quarterly Review* and the *Wesleyan Christian Advocate*. Among a few select titles: "Christian Polemics," "Cromwell and His Times," "Mormanism: What Is It?", a review of Smith's "Life and Letters of Bishop Andrew,""Story of the Magna Carta," and "Transubsantiation." He died May 2, 1899, and was buried in Oakland Cemetery, Atlanta.

George Wesley Yarbrough, Pastor of Athens Colored Mission, 1863

Rev. Yarbrough was appointed pastor of the Athens Colored Mission for the year 1863 and would return to Athens First as pastor in 1879-80. See his full biographical information at that point in this timeline.

෧1864෧

Patrick Arminius Wright, Pastor, 1864

Born in 1829 in Columbia County, Arminius Wright was converted in 1843 at a revival in Macon. In 1845 at age 16, he was licensed to preach by the Quarterly Conference of Mulberry Street Church in Macon. He was admitted on trial in 1846, became a deacon in full connection in 1847, and was ordained elder in 1850. His appointments included: 1846 Covington and Oxford (age 17 in a full appointment - granted, it was a college campus church); 1847 Carnesville; 1848 Jeffersonville; 1849 Oglethorpe County Mission; 1850 Jeffersonville; 1851 Canton; 1852-58 no appointment by request. He was then 23 years of age and had been married since age 19. He and his wife had five children before she died in 1861. He was appointed 1859-60 to Griffin; 1861-62 St. Paul, Columbus; 1863 LaGrange. By the time Wright came to Athens Methodist Church in 1864, he was age 35, was remarried and had five children under the age of seven. It was the darkest time of the Civil War. Wright's further appointments were: 1865 Presiding

Elder, Columbus District; 1866-69 St. John, Augusta; 1870 Griffin; 1871 Atlanta First; 1872-74 St. Paul, Columbus; 1875 Mulberry Street and Vineville, Macon; 1876 Mulberry Street, Macon; 1877 Supply; 1878 Broad Street, Columbus; 1879 Supply. The two supply appointments during his last three years likely reflect failing health. Wright died of tuberculosis in 1879 at the age of 50 and was buried in Linwood Cemetery, Columbus. A significant collection of Wright's papers, family Bible, genealogical records and correspondence is held at Columbus State University.

Even as the Union Army advanced through Georgia from northwest to southeast laying waste to a swath of the state, Annual Conference was planned to be held in the sanctuary of Athens Methodist Church in November 1864. The conditions of war caused the meeting to be postponed to January 1865, by which time Sherman's March to the Sea was concluded and Savannah had fallen. Having been optimistic about the Confederate military prospects to the very end, Bishop George Foster Pierce was crestfallen as he opened the Conference saying, "Methodism never presented a gloomier aspect than at this Conference."

William P. Pattillo, Pastor of Athens Colored Mission, 1864-1865

Rev. Pattillo is the last pastor of record appointed to the Athens Colored Mission. Following the Civil War, African-American members of Athens Methodist Church quickly left to form their own congregations in what became the CME and AME Churches. A large segment of the Black membership of our church already had left to form their own church on the corner of Hancock Avenue and Foundry Street (where the Classic Center is today) beginning in 1852, using components of the former Athens Methodist Church sanctuary after it was removed for construction of a new brick building. From time to time over the next decade discussion ensued in the Athens Quarterly Conference to have the trustees "perfect the title of the church in which the Colored people worship to the Methodist Episcopal Church, South," but there is no report on whether that ever occurred or whether that church instead became titled to the CME church.

Through the three decades of the 1840s through the 1860s, Athens Methodist Church proved a fertile ground for producing clergy. Church records over those years show fifteen men licensed to exhort, three of these coming from the Black membership, and thirteen licensed to preach.

Harwell Hodges Parks, Pastor, 1865-1868

Having served an earlier tour as Athens' pastor 1857-58, Parks returned to our pulpit for another four years. In earlier days, pastoral appointments normally were for one year, being extended to two years in exceptional cases. By the mid-19th century, appointments were limited to four years. Rev. Parks became the first to serve Athens Methodist Church for four consecutive years, and with his previous pastorate, six years total. A revival of note occurred during his pastorate in fall 1866. Begun and carried on in the Methodist Church, it spread into the community and resulted in 151 Whites and seven Colored converts joining the church. These seven were the last African- American members reported joining Athens Methodist Church for more than a century. Sunday School attendance reached a new high, averaging 200 per Sunday in 1866. Rev. Parks is referenced in Hull's *Annals* as preaching ardently against attendance at a circus which came to town just at the close of the Civil War.

Grave of Rev. Harwell Hodges Parks at Oxford Cemetery

The Atlanta Journal
Thu, Aug 08, 1895 ·Page 8

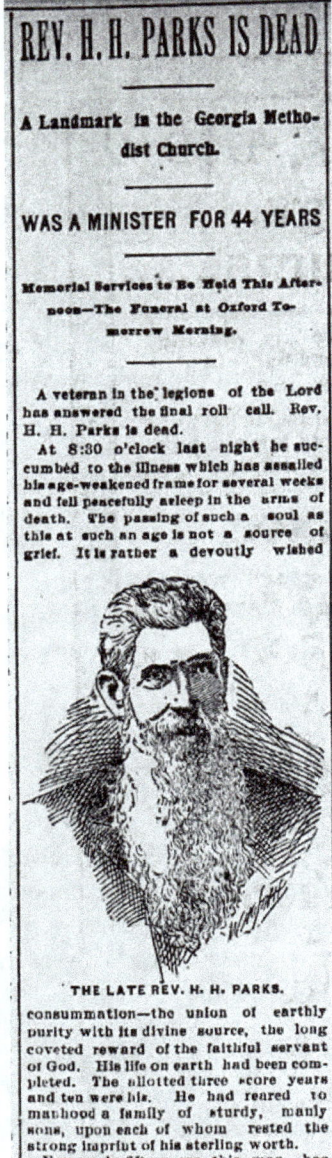

REV. H. H. PARKS IS DEAD

A Landmark in the Georgia Methodist Church.

WAS A MINISTER FOR 44 YEARS

Memorial Services to Be Held This Afternoon—The Funeral at Oxford Tomorrow Morning.

A veteran in the legions of the Lord has answered the final roll call. Rev. H. H. Parks is dead.

At 8:30 o'clock last night he succumbed to the illness which has assailed his age-weakened frame for several weeks and fell peacefully asleep in the arms of death. The passing of such a soul as this at such an age is not a source of grief. It is rather a devoutly wished

THE LATE REV. H. H. PARKS.

consummation—the union of earthly purity with its divine source, the long coveted reward of the faithful servant of God. His life on earth had been completed. The allotted three score years and ten were his. He had reared to manhood a family of sturdy, manly sons, upon each of whom rested the strong imprint of his sterling worth.

For nearly fifty years this man has consecrated himself to the Master and the seventy years of his life show a blameless, beautiful record. Of him all men said in passage, "There is a Godly man." Naught had anyone to say against him.

A SERMON DECRIES CIRCUS ATTENDANCE

TRANSCRIPT OF REV. HARWELL H. PARKS'
SERMON NOTES OF OCTOBER 20,
1867:

"Why have all churches in which there is any spirituality from time immemorial forbid their members attending circuses? Those who own them are ungodly men and follow the business for the sole purpose of making money. They are adventurers who feel no interest in the welfare of the country, and are consuming of its substances, and make no returns except to corrupt and demoralize the people.

"The vilest, corrupt, and most mischievous part of the population are sure to be present at such places, such persons as no decent man or woman ought to come in contact with. Their very breath is poison. The songs that are sung and the coarse, vulgar and profane language used, to say nothing of the low evil and buffooning which are the chief attractions of the place are objectionable on the highest degree and are either disgusting or demoralizing.

"The money you thus spend ought to be laid out in a better way and for more praiseworthy objects. You are God's stewards and He holds you accountable for its use."

The people, desperate for a diversion after the terrible war, ignored his exhortations and went to the circus in droves, so much so that during the circus show the clown thanked Rev. Parks by name for the advertisement.

⁹1866⁹

A General Conference of the M.E. Church, South, was held for the first time in eight years, delayed by the Civil War. Clergy who had served or would serve Athens Methodist Church elected to the delegation from the Georgia Conference were: Samuel W. Anthony, Lovick Pierce, Weyman H. Potter, James E. Evans, James W. Hinton, and Joseph S. Key.

The Georgia Conference meeting at Americus voted to divide into the North and South Georgia Conferences. The portions of southern Georgia south of the Altamaha River, previously in the Florida Conference, were moved to the new South Georgia Conference. Portions of northern Georgia previously served by the Holston Conference moved to the North

Georgia Conference, except for Dade County, which remains in the Holston Conference today. As of 2025, discussions are underway to merge the North and South Georgia Conferences into one Georgia Conference after having been separate since 1866. The Conferences shared a bishop for all but 22 years, 1992 to 2024.

In January 1866, church trustee Asbury Hull died, followed that spring by the death of trustee A. S. Hill. At its July meeting, the Quarterly Conference nominated Marcellus Stanley and John W. Nicholson to succeed them, but because trustee Ross Crane was ill, the trustees apparently could not have a meeting with quorum to ratify the nominations. Note that Ross Crane is not to be confused with his son, John Ross Crane, who lived 1842-1887. No formal election had been held by the time the senior Crane died on October 20, 1866, leaving the board again in the position of having only two surviving members, Henry Hull and James R. Carlton *(pages 13 and 20, Quarterly Conference record book 1866-1877)*. The church obtained special legislation again by the Georgia General Assembly allowing the two remaining trustees to act. Hull and Carlton named Marcellus Stanley, John W. Nicholson and Reuben Nickerson to fill the three vacancies.

Trustee Marcellus Stanley was a son of the first pastor of Athens Methodist Church, Rev. Thomas Stanley. He was born in the Stanley home in the Salem community of Clarke County (in what is now Oconee County). He became Captain of the Troup Artillery in the Confederate Army. Upon returning from the war, he lived in the home of his mother-in-law, Mrs. Burwell Pope, on the east side of College Avenue between Washington and Hancock, before buying the home in which he spent the rest of his life on the north side of Dearing Street between Finley and Pope Streets, known today as the W. L. Jones house. After the Civil War, he taught at the University of Georgia before briefly becoming head officer of Centenary College in Summerfield, Alabama. Returning to Athens, he became president of University Bank and a director of Southern Mutual Insurance Company. He would serve as trustee until his death in 1890.

Trustee John W. Nicholson was an Athens merchant who first lived on Jackson Street at the corner of Hoyt Street, before buying the home of a wealthy planter, Thomas Wray, on Hull Street. This historic home is known today as the Wray-Nicholson House and serves as headquarters of the UGA Alumni Association. He also managed some thirty tenant farms in the vicinity, his obituary stating that he was known for balancing the accounts of tenants in arrears at the end of the year, in addition to inquiring what they had for Christmas, providing what was needed without charge from his store. He served as trustee until his death in 1886. Of his nine children, a son, Madison Gartrell Nicholson, also would serve as an Athens First trustee from 1920-1959.

Trustee Reuben Nickerson was a Maine native who, with an engineering degree from the Rensellaer Institute, came to a position in Athens as agent of the Iron Foundry. His home faced Thomas Street between Clayton and Washington Streets, near the Foundry at which he spent his career as superintendent. He also opened a hardware store which became Athens Hardware Company. He served on Athens City Council and was for a time president of the Bank of the University. He was involved in organization of the Union Sunday School on the Factory grounds, which later moved into its own home on Baldwin Street, where he was its superintendent. Nickerson resigned as a trustee at Athens Methodist Church in 1873, his being one of the families that left to form the new Oconee Street Methodist Church. He served that church as Sunday School superintendent for 29 years. He died in 1913 and is buried in Oconee Hill Cemetery.

Henry Hull stepped down as secretary of the Quarterly Conference after 22 years in the position and was succeeded as secretary by Young L.G. Harris (who had the most elegant handwriting – all the church minutes of that era were, of course, kept by hand). Henry Hull lived until 1881, throughout his life serving as an active leader and symbolic connection to the founding of Methodism in Athens by his father, Hope Hull.

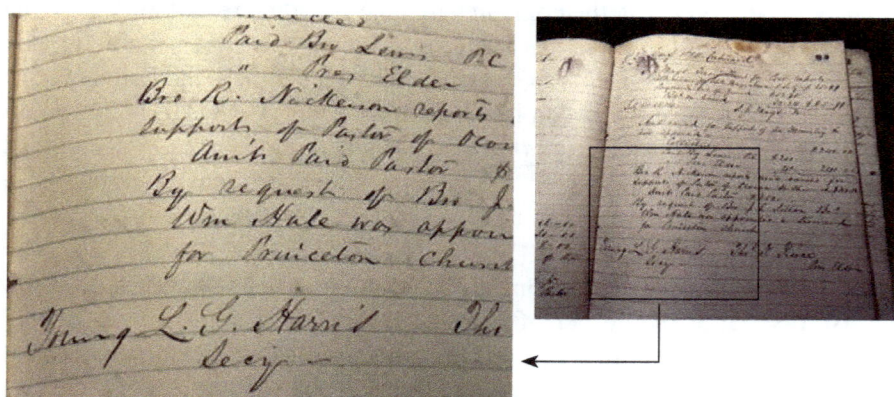

The elegant handwriting of Judge Young L. G. Harris is seen in a minute book of the Athens Methodist Church Board of Stewards from September 1874. Harris served as the church's Sunday School Superintendent and on the Board of Stewards for 40 years.

The year's expenses for repairs are listed as $53.75, which covered repair to a portion of the sanctuary floor which was deemed unsafe, and repair of the fence around the parsonage. "Attention is called to the unseemly condition of the floor and benches in that part of the church occupied during religious service by the male members of the congregation," the Quarterly Conference opined. "A suitable Sunday School room is much needed and it is hoped that the time is not distant when it will be practicable to erect one." It would be the 1884 renovations before this was accomplished.

❧**1867**❧

For several decades following the Civil War, Athens Methodist Church finances were on a shoestring. A typical quarterly report is this one for the second quarter (April-June) of 1867: Total collected $991.85, pastor's salary paid $862.50, share of Presiding Elder's salary paid $60, sexton's pay $60, repair bill $5.30, treasurer's balance $4.05.

❧**1868**❧

In the first quarter of 1868, Walter B. Hill, a University of Georgia student from Talbotton, Georgia, transferred church membership to Athens Methodist Church. Hill would graduate with his bachelor's degree in 1870, a master's degree in 1871 and a bachelor's degree in law that same year (at the time, law at UGA was a one-year course). He practiced law with his father in Macon and became a founder of the Georgia Bar Association, before returning to Athens and church membership here. He was named chancellor of the University of Georgia in 1899, becoming the first UGA alumnus to head the institution. He contracted pneumonia in December 1905 and died in office. Noted accomplishments at UGA include expanding the law curriculum to two years and greatly investing the university in public service and outreach to the state. His memorial service in the UGA

Walter B. Hill 1851 – 1905
(Hargrett Rare Book and Manuscript Library, The University of Georgia Libraries)

Chapel drew the governor and many others in state and higher education leadership. The service was conducted by Athens Methodist Church Pastor Isaac Stiles Hopkins, who ironically was a former president of both Emory and Georgia Tech.

ᦇ1869ᦉ

Clement Anselm Evans, Pastor, 1869-1870

Clement A. Evans carries one of the more extraordinary biographies of any pastor to serve Athens Methodist Church. Born February 25, 1833, in Stewart County, Evans attended school in the county seat, Lumpkin. He was converted and joined the Methodist church there at age 13. He read law under Colonel B. S. Worrill beginning at age 17 and that same year left for law school, graduating from Augusta Law School and being admitted to the bar at age 18. Evans practiced law in Lumpkin, where Colonel Worrill accepted him as a law partner. He was elected Judge of the Inferior Court at age 22, in 1859 at age 25 he was elected to the State Senate, and in 1860 was an elector for Democratic Presidential candidate John C. Breckinridge. With the outbreak of war, Evans entered the Confederate Army, becoming Brigadier General in Company E, 31st Georgia Regiment (later the Second Army Corps). He led his own "Evans' Brigade" at Gettysburg and in the battles of Marye Hill, Morton's Ford and Appomattox, where his Georgia brigade reportedly fired the last shot and made the last charge of the war (although some straggler battles occurred elsewhere after the surrender, as news of it travelled slowly). By the end of the war, he was commanding the Division as acting Major General. Evans was a colleague and friend of fellow generals J.E.B. Stuart, Stonewall Jackson and Robert E. Lee. Wounded in battle five times, Evans became Commander-in-Chief of CSA Veterans in 1908. At the war's conclusion, General Evans answered a call to the ministry, being admitted on trial in November 1865, as deacon in 1866, and as elder in full connection in 1867. Three staff from his unit also went into ministry, one an Episcopal minister, one a Baptist, and another a Methodist. Evans' appointments included: 1866-67 Manassas Circuit covering Bartow County (one cannot help but note that the former Confederate general's first church battle was at Manassas); 1868 Cartersville; 1869-70 Athens (still only 36 years of age when he arrived in the Athens pulpit with a lifetime of experience); 1871-74 Trinity, Atlanta; 1875-78 St. John, Augusta; 1879 Rome; 1880-83 Atlanta First; 1884 St. James, Augusta; 1885 Richmond Circuit; 1886 St. James, Augusta; 1887 St. James and Chapel, Augusta; 1888-89 Broad

Street Mission, Augusta; 1890 Merritts Avenue, Atlanta; 1891 Presiding Elder, Griffin District; 1891-1911 Agent, Preachers' Aid Society. That first appointment to Manassas was a twelve-point circuit he rode on the horse he rode at Appomattox. At first he preached in full Confederate uniform complete with the cloak. A colleague advised him that the scarlet red cloak and his mustache made him appear "too warlike" for the pulpit. Evans heeded the brother's advice, put away the uniform and shaved. He ultimately considered that appointment among the best times of his life. According to the *New Georgia Encyclopedia*, Evans was offered the position of Chancellor at the University of Georgia in 1888 but declined, choosing to continue in the ministry. He offered as a candidate for Governor of Georgia in 1894, but discerned he would not prevail and withdrew from the race in favor of the ultimate Democratic nominee, William Y. Atkinson. Evans was named a prison commissioner and later also was named state Adjutant General by a subsequent governor, James M. Smith. In great demand as a speaker, Evans made many addresses across the South. His Conference memoriam asserts glowingly that he made speeches "ably, forcefully and convincingly, presenting the Confederate cause, its leaders and soldiers in their true light, and rendered valuable service in correcting many erroneous impressions relating to Democratic President candidate Breckenridge." He was an author and editor of *Confederate Military History: a library of Confederate States history,* a 12-volume collection written by distinguished men of the South. In 1854 he married a hometown girl from Stewart County, Mary Allen "Allie" Walton, they had eight children, three of whom died in infancy.

Brigadier-General Clement A. Evans in 1864 and as Pastor of
Athens Methodist Church 1869-70
(right photo courtesy Hargrett Rare Books and Manuscript Library, UGA Libraries)

The couple would become grandparents of U.S. Representative Robert G. Stephens of Athens and great-grandparents of today's Western Circuit Superior Court Judge Lawton Stephens. Allie died in 1884 and Evans next married in 1887 to Sarah Avary Howard of Augusta, who died in 1902. They had one daughter. Evans died July 2, 1911, in Atlanta. His body lay in the State Capitol rotunda and the General Assembly adjourned for a day to attend his funeral. He is buried in Oakland Cemetery, Atlanta. Evans County, Georgia, is named for him. Judge Stephens recounts that his great-grandfather, surveying the aftermath of the battle at Fredericksburg in 1862, declared to God that he would dedicate himself to the church and teaching lessons of humility, brotherly love, and Christian forbearance when the war was over. Gen. Evans survived the war and indeed dedicated the remainder of his life to the church in a notable way. Late in life, Evans was quoted as asking that he be remembered more for his connection to the church than anything else.

The annual report by Athens Methodist Church to the North Georgia Conference showed 507 members, an increase of 27 over the previous year; 18 baptisms during the year (3 infants, 15 adults); and an annual budget of $12,685, of which $11,100 was salary of the pastor and staff.

୨1870୨

The 1870 General Conference of the M.E. Church, South, was the first to include lay delegates alongside clergy. When Athens first had a lay member elected as delegate is unknown because of incomplete membership rolls. Our first confirmed lay delegate to General Conference was State Normal School Dean Jere M. Pound in 1918, followed by Dr. Nat G. Slaughter who was first elected in 1930, Dr. Tom Jackson first elected in 1988, and Chancellor Henry M. "Hank" Huckaby first elected in 2008. Slaughter, Jackson and Huckaby each would go on to serve multiple terms. Our past and future clergy who were in the 1870 delegation were: Jesse Boring, William J. Parks, Weyman H. Potter, and Alfred T. Mann.

Sylvanus Morris' *Strolls About Athens During the Early Seventies* (1870s) describes the intersection of Lumpkin Street and Hancock Avenue as the reader "strolls westward" along Hancock Avenue: At the northeast corner of Hancock at Lumpkin [site of today's Post Office and federal courthouse], "Next to the [Presbyterian] church the home of Mr. A. M. Scudder is today but little changed in appearance from its early seeming. Scudder's

School for Boys was for many years one of the institutions of Athens. Even today many elderly men in the community have feeling recollections of his ministrations...." "On the [northwest] corner of Lumpkin and Hancock Avenue [site of today's Saye Building] stands the old Hancock Tavern. It looks today much as it did when the stroller first saw it, barring the need of repairs.... The tavern fronted the side yard of the Scudder house [facing across Lumpkin toward the side of today's Post Office].The front on Hancock Avenue was added after the tavern days.... Mr. Thomas Hancock, the grandfather of Miss Sarah Frierson, so long the University librarian, kept the tavern. He donated the land for the Methodist church [across Hancock from the tavern]. He took particular interest in a blue-eyed student boarder and used to say, 'Some day you will be President of the United States.' That boy was Benjamin H. Hill [future U.S. Senator from Georgia].... On the block between Lumpkin and Hull we find on our left the Methodist church, much changed and enlarged. That gallant soldier and strong man, Gen. Clement A. Evans, was pastor. It was an inspiration to any man to hear him. M. Myers' house was on the Hull Street corner [site of today's AFUMC Family Life Center.]. It has been moved back from the street and improved."

Excellent growth led Athens Methodists to begin several mission congregations, one resulting in construction of Oconee Street Methodist Church. Several families withdrew from the Athens Methodist Church to begin the new congregation. Among them was Ferdinand Phinizy, who opposed plans at Athens Methodist to install its first organ. Phinizy promised a larger contribution to Oconee Street than his giving to the existing church, so long as the new church had no musical instrument. An initial Board of Trustees and Board of Stewards for the Oconee Street Church was elected by the Athens Methodist Church Quarterly Conference in March 1870. The Oconee Street church was organized and began regular meetings on July 2, 1871. A new Oconee Street church building was constructed on land donated by Athens Methodist trustee John W. Nicholson and was furnished with a loan of one thousand dollars. Other "factory mission" congregations were operating by this time at Stanley Chapel and at Princeton. Stanley Chapel reported 120 in Sunday School with 16 teachers, and Princeton reported one person converted by grace and "a sound improvement in the tone of the congregation," although eleven of its members chose to move to the new Oconee Street church. Our church downtown was routinely referred to as "the Brick Church," distinguishing it from the satellite congregations. For some years, Quarterly Conference minutes carried regular reports from all the Athens area congregations, including the Brick Church (the downtown church which is now known as Athens First), Oconee Street Church, Princeton Factory, Georgia Factory, and Stanley Chapel congregations.

The Sons of Lovick Pierce

Although he was not a pastor of Athens First Methodist Church, Rev. Thomas F. Pierce served twice as Athens District Presiding Elder, from 1869-71 and from 1874-77. He was one of the three prominent sons of our first appointed pastor, Rev. Lovick Pierce. Thomas's brothers were Rev. James L. Pierce, who came to Athens First 1850-51 as pastor of the Colored Mission, and George Foster Pierce, who was pastor at Athens Methodist Church from 1846-47 and went on to distinguished service as president of Emory and as Bishop.

Rev. Thomas F. Pierce twice served as Presiding Elder of the Athens District from 1869-71 and 1874-77.

Born at Greensboro on April 13, 1825, Thomas Pierce was an infant when his father first pastored the Athens church, but outlived both his brothers, dying July 20, 1904, at Gainesville. He graduated from Emory College in 1845, was converted at the Hancock Camp Meeting in 1846, and joined the Georgia Conference that same year. He married Ann Dickey Malone of Augusta and had five children. Following her death, he married in 1863 Susie Sinquefield of Madison and had ten children. His appointments were: 1847 Wilkes Circuit, associate to Josiah Lewis; 1848 Augusta, associate to James E. Evans; 1849 Hamilton Circuit; 1850 Waynesboro Circuit; 1851 Burke Circuit; 1852 Savannah; 1853 Hancock Mission; 1854 Richmond Circuit; 1855-56 Madison; 1857 Thomaston; 1858 Louisville Circuit; 1859-60 Washington; 1861 Covington; 1862 Presiding Elder, Sandersville District; 1863 Rome; 1864, Chaplain, Confederate Army; 1865-66 Greensboro; 1867 White Plains; 1868 Presiding Elder, Atlanta District; 1869-71 Presiding Elder, Athens District; 1872 Rome; 1873 Presiding Elder, Rome District; 1874-77 Presiding Elder, Athens District; 1878-80 Presiding Elder, Augusta District; 1881-81 Cedartown; 1883 Walker Street,

Atlanta; 1884-87 Presiding Elder, Rome District; 1888-89 Presiding Elder, LaGrange District; 1890-93 Presiding Elder, South Atlanta District; 1894- 97 Presiding Elder, Rome District; 1898-1901 Greenville and Trinity; 1902- 03 Woodlawn, Augusta. He served as trustee at both Emory and Wesleyan Colleges. Bishop Warren A. Candler later described Thomas Pierce as "a man of child-like simplicity, candid and cordial, tender and true. His soul was a stranger to greed for gain or ambition for place." Candler poignantly recalled, "When my father died, he [Pierce] walked five miles to console and pray with my broken-hearted mother." Less known than his distinguished father or more famous brother, he nonetheless was elected to General Conference in 1890, but did not enjoy it. "I do not wish to go again," he said, "It does not suit me."

Athens Methodist Church proceeded with plans to install a new pipe organ, a Johnson Organ of one manual and 15 stops. Much discussion was devoted to the fact that the trustees would "own" the organ while the church conference would "operate" it, including selection of the music and of the choir. Two ladies of the church, Miss Clara Barrow and a Miss Sawyer, were appointed volunteer organists, but they moved out of town the next spring and were succeeded by Mrs. William King as organist, whom we presume to be the former Augusta Clayton, wife of church trustee Dr. William King. Miss Belle Hardeman and Miss Sallie Stanley were named as associate organists to serve in Mrs. King's absence. The choir was to be "not less than ten nor more than twenty persons" who were "to receive careful instruction in singing." The Quarterly Conference of June 18, 1870 elected the current choir to be the choir for the coming year, including the director, Miss Susie Still. She stepped down the next April, and the Quarterly Conference named Miss Belle Hardeman to succeed her. Only authorized tune books were to be used, music was to be congregational, and "chants" were prohibited. Three choir members were to be instructed in playing the organ, in addition to the two organists. A "boy" was to be employed to work the bellows. It is not clear how long the church conference continued this deep interest in managing the quotidian details of choir membership and music selection.

Trustee William King had come to Athens from Savannah, as a student at UGA, graduating in 1871 and marrying Augusta Clayton, daughter of Athens judge Augustin Clayton, an outstanding layman in Athens Methodist Church. The couple moved first to Savannah, where King's father, William King, Sr., was a successful cotton factor who acted as mediary between his personal friend, General William Tecumseh Sherman, and Georgia Governor Joseph E. Brown during Sherman's taking of Savannah late in 1864. William and Augusta soon moved to Philadelphia where he finished his medical degree, before returning to Athens to open a medical practice. King soon became mayor of Athens and was elected a trustee of Athens Methodist Church. Dr. King and his wife first lived on the north side of Clayton Street between Thomas and Jackson Streets. They later moved to "the old Baynon house" facing south on Hancock at the Hull Street corner, between Lumpkin and Hull. In 1879, reportedly facing health difficulties, he resigned the church trustee position to relocate to Atlanta to be nearer the couple's daughter, Julia King Grady, and her husband, the noted journalist Henry W. Grady. King's health improved in Atlanta and he accepted a position in the federal revenue department under the Cleveland Administration, a position he still held at his wife's death in 1901. Augusta King became somewhat of an anonymous Atlanta celebrity, writing in her son-in-law's paper, the *Atlanta Weekly Constitution*. Under the pseudonym "Aunt Susie," she served as editor of the women's and children's section of the paper for two decades and is recognized as the first female journalist of the South. King's grandfather, Roswell King, and his uncle, Barrington King, were pioneer settlers of Cobb County and the community of Roswell.

918719

Eustace W. Speer, Pastor, 1871

This was Rev. Speer's third appointment to Athens and marked his fourth year as our pastor. At the time, the Methodist parsonage was on the corner of Lumpkin and Washington Streets, but Washington at the time was known as Market Street. The Town Hall was located in the center of Market Street at College Avenue at the top of the hill to the east, beside where today's City Hall stands. Regular sales of farm goods, particularly fresh beef, would be held at the market there, thus the street's name. Sylvanus Morris' *Strolls About Athens* credits the street's name change to Rev. Speer, who thought when the market at the old Town Hall was discontinued, the name of the Father of Our Country would be a more fitting and dignified name for so significant a street in our city. Following his time in our pastorate, Speer was on the University faculty 1875-81 as *Professor of Belles Lettres*.

For the third time, the Athens Methodist Church hosted the Annual Conference in its sanctuary, with Bishop Wightman presiding. In its annual report for the year, Athens Methodist Church reported membership exceeding 500 for the first time.

MINUTES

OF THE

""IFTH SEssi9N

OP THE

North Georgia Annual Conference

OF THE M, E. CHURCH, SOUTH,

HELD AT

ATHENS, GEORGIA.,

BEGINNING NOV. 29-ENJJIXG DEC. 5, 1"7·.

———

MACO , GA.:
J, W, BURKE & CO., PRINTERS AND BINDER*
1872.

ᵍ**1872**ᵍ

Josiah Lewis, Jr., Pastor, 1872-1874

Born December 31, 1808, in White Plains, Greene County, Josiah Lewis, Jr. was one of 13 children of Rev. Josiah Lewis, Sr. and Elizabeth Moore. The younger Lewis was converted in a service in 1823 at Union Church. He graduated Emory College in 1859 and studied law before entering the Confederate Army, where he served as a Private in the 6th Georgia Regiment. He married Rosie Hubert in 1866 in Warrenton, the same year he was admitted on trial. He became deacon in 1867 and was ordained elder in full connection in 1868. His appointments were: 1867-71 Professor, Emory College; 1872-74 Athens; 1875 Eatonton; 1876 Located; 1877-79 Greensboro, Alabama, and 1878-79 Professor, Southern College. In 1880-81 Lewis served as President of Southern, a Methodist college founded in Greensboro, Alabama in 1854. Southern would merge with another Methodist college at Birmingham in 1918 to form Birmingham- Southern University, which operated for 106 years until closing because of financial exigency at the end of the 2023-24 academic year. In 1882, Evans returned to North Georgia with an appointment to the church at Rome and served 1883-84 at LaGrange. In 1885, apparently ill, he took Supply status and died June 11, 1885, in Sparta, where he is buried in the city cemetery.

When Josiah Lewis arrived as Athens' new pastor, the Board of Stewards voted to pay him the same salary as his predecessor, $1,500 per year. The church's contribution to the salary of the Presiding Elder was maintained at $160 for the year. The pastor was authorized to hire a sexton at $75 per year. The church raised very little money for operations beyond these salaries over a year's time. Much of the money was collected by individual stewards calling in person on church members to make contributions in support. Those members who contributed usually gave $10 to $20 for the year. A few gave as much as $60 or $75. Three members contributed $100 for the year, and one gave $200.

P. A. Heard, Associate Pastor, 1872-1881

Rev. Heard was a retired elder in the conference who served as associate at Athens First for ten years.

᧐**1873**᧐

By vote of the Quarterly Conference on January 3, 1873, the church was named First Methodist Church of Athens. Originally known as Athens Station or Athens Methodist Church, it more recently had been referred to as the "Brick Church" to distinguish it from its various mission churches being established around the community.

Augustus L. Hull's *Annals* mentions the town's noted shoemaker, a Methodist layman, William Stark. His leg had been crushed by a falling horse, requiring its amputation. Yet he was "an artist in making boots which fit every undulation of the foot and never rubbed the heels." Stark is described as "a kindly man" yet "an active exhorter in the Methodist church who made a fervent prayer."

Athens First trustee Reuben Nickerson resigned the post to join Oconee Street Church,

Augustus Longstreet Hull

where he would serve as Sunday School Superintendent for the next 29 years. Dr. John Atkinson Hunnicutt, Sr. (his obituary lists his first name as James) was elected to succeed him. A native of Coweta County, Hunnicutt served in the Confederate Army and was with Lee's army during the surrender at Appomattox. He returned home to receive a medical degree from Emory College. After practicing for some years in Coweta County, he moved to Athens to establish a practice. His home was at 325 North Milledge Avenue, on the northwest corner of Milledge at Hancock Avenues "across from St. Mary's Hospital." He also served as president of the Bank of the University. He joined many Athens First trustees as members of the board of Southern Mutual Insurance Company. He was a member of Athens City Council and the Board of Education. He was a trustee of the Lucy Cobb Institute and a director of the Athens Foundry. He served until his death at age 91 in 1930 and is buried in Oconee Hill Cemetery.

᧐**1874**᧐

The North Georgia delegation to the General Conference of 1874 included these former and future Athens First clergy: Weyman H. Potter, Jesse Boring, James E. Evans, and Eustace W. Speer.

FORWARD *through* THE AGES

BICENTENNIAL
ATHENS FIRST UNITED METHODIST CHURCH

The Second Half-Century

1875 - 1924

ᕼ1875 ᕽ

Weyman H. Potter, Pastor, 1875-1878

Born in Laurens County, South Carolina on April 11, 1828, Weyman Potter was converted at age 12 in a service at Salem Campground. An 1849 graduate of Emory College, he taught school in Jasper, Ga. in 1850, and married Sarah Julia Bettison on December 23, 1851 in DeKalb County. They had five children. He was admitted on trial in 1853, became deacon in 1855, and was ordained an elder in full connection in 1857. His appointments were: 1854 Cuthbert; 1855 Cuthbert and Emmaus; 1856 President, Andrew Female College, Americus; 1857 Hamilton; 1858-59 Trinity, Augusta; 1860 Rome; 1861-62 St. John, Augusta; 1863 Georgia Relief and Hospital Association; 1864 Asbury Church and Trinity Mission; 1865 Superintendent, Georgia Relief and Hospital Association; 1866 St. John, Augusta; 1867-71 Presiding Elder, Augusta District; 1872- 74 Presiding Elder, Atlanta District; 1875-78 Athens.

Quarterly Conference met at Athens First on January 2, 1875, beginning Potter's appointment here. In his remarks to the church leadership, Rev. Potter noted that having recently arrived in the city, he had not yet ascertained the condition of the church. He asked some pointed questions: "I would like to know how many families in the city do not attend church at all, and who they are? How many and who are the families in which there is no church membership? How many and who are the adult Whites who are not members of any church?" At the subsequent Quarterly Conference in April, Potter reviewed his study of the church roll, which carried 348 names. He reported "18 of them are reported to be walking more or less disorderly, nine are known to have been gone from the city for more than twelve months, and 44 are dead or are in a state of uncertainty as to their relationship to the church." He counted 277 members "whose location and relation to the church are known and whose lives are reported to be consistent." A book of church members then on roll, added, removed, baptized and died, created in meticulous hand, apparently in 1876, is likely work done by Potter himself, or certainly at his direction. It was maintained only through 1884. It is transcribed in its entirety in the appendices of John Bondurant's 1988 history, and was microfilmed in 1960 by the UGA Libraries at the behest of the church historian at the time, Dr. Robert C. Wilson. The original is in the church archives.

After his three years' service at Athens, Potter's further appointments were: 1879-81 Presiding Elder, LaGrange District; 1882 Rome; 1883-90 Editor, *Wesleyan Christian Advocate*; 1891 Conference Missionary Secretary. He was a trustee of Wesleyan College and Emory College. A sermon Potter delivered at Trinity Church, Atlanta, is credited with moving Laura Askew Haygood, principal of Girls High School in Atlanta, to go as a Methodist missionary to China from 1884 until her death in 1900. Her notable career there included founding a girls' school in Shanghai which still operates today. She was a native of Watkinsville and sister of Bishop Atticus Greene Haygood. Haygood Memorial UMC in Atlanta is named for them both. Rev. Potter died October 11, 1891, in Austell, at age 64. He is buried in Magnolia Cemetery in Augusta.

A hotly contested proposal to move the Clarke County seat from Watkinsville to Athens ultimately resulted in state legislation doing so. But the hot dispute was not ended, as in 1877 the southern

Dr. W. H. Potter Dead.

A great and good man has gone to his reward. Dr. Wayman H. Potter died last Sunday night, at Austell Ga. Dr. Potter has been one of the leading lights in Southern Methodism for a quarter of a century, and probably no man has had a greater influence in shaping the destinies of the Church than he. He was for many years editor of the Wesleyan Christian Advocate, his connection with the paper having only been severed at the last annual conference.

Magnolia Cemetery, Augusta

part of Clarke County withdrew to establish Oconee County and placed its county seat back in the courthouse at Watkinsville. This author, who has lived back-and-forth on each side of this county line over the past 50 years, regrets that there are those who are still fighting this battle now nearly 150 years hence.

৯**1876**৯

The year after Athens First Methodist celebrated the 50th anniversary of its founding, membership stood at 363 and total giving for the year was $4,155. This membership made Athens the fourth-largest church in the Athens District, with Watkinsville (708 members), White Plains (406), and Morgan (378) being larger. A report to the April 1877 Quarterly Conference found "the number of boys attending the Sunday School is lamentably small." At the close of the year, it was noted that all obligations of the church had been paid, except for a balance on the gas bill. A special collection was taken during the worship service one Sunday to make up the shortfall. The pastor's salary for the coming year was reduced from $1,500 to $1,200, to be paid $100 per month, "in advance, if possible." The church apparently was not insulated from the national economy and effects of "the Long Depression" which began with the Panic of 1873 and lasted through 1885. The $1,200 salary for the pastor, a $200 annual contribution for the Presiding Elder's salary, and $8 per month for the sexton, who was responsible for cleaning the church building and pumping the organ bellows at services, remained the rate of pay for at least the next decade.

ᕱ**1877**ᕱ

Hull's *Annals* references Athens First member Peter A. Summey and his wife: "A better or more kind-hearted pair than Mr. and Mrs. Summey never lived. Mr. Summey prospered until the war and afterwards, but crediting farmers who staked their all on cotton ruined him." For some years, Mr. Summey had been on the Board of Stewards and was one of the larger contributors to the church budget. But having lost their home to financial ruin, the Summeys began operating the boarding house in Old College, where "the boys imposed dreadfully on the Summeys and disorder reigned supreme." And this final note: "Mr. Summey for a long time sang bass in the Methodist choir – at least he was supposed to do so since he stood with the basses and his lips moved in unison with theirs." Summey would be named a trustee of the church in 1888, three years before his death in 1891.

ᕱ**1878**ᕱ

Walter R. Branham, Jr.,
from the
1879 Conference Journal

Through the 1860s and '70s, associate pastors were appointed to Athens First to serve the Oconee Street and Factory Mission churches, as mission outreach of the parent church. The last person appointed in this manner to Oconee Street was Walter R. Branham, Jr., in 1878-79. His father had been pastor at Athens First in 1842 and served as Athens District Presiding Elder 1866-68. From 1880 forward, Oconee Street and the Factory Mission (later known as Princeton) became their own appointments within the conference.

The North Georgia delegation to the 1878 General Conference included these former and future Athens First clergy: Weyman H. Potter, Jesse Boring, and James E. Evans.

Funds reported raised for missions beyond the basic church budget: for Yellow Fever sufferers $150, for the poor $193.29, to aid Judge Young Harris in his travels to and from China $50, for Orphans' Home $100.

<h1 style="text-align:center">◙1879◙</h1>

George Wesley Yarbrough, Pastor, 1879-1880

This was Rev. Yarbrough's second tour at Athens First, having served the year 1863 as pastor of the Athens Colored Mission. He was born March 10, 1838, in Jefferson County, Florida, when it was not yet a state "and the Indians were still in the land." He was the eldest child of Rev. John Wesley Yarbrough and Amanda Lane. He was converted at Mount Gilead Campground in DeKalb County (today in Fulton County) in 1848 at age 10. He graduated from Emory College in 1857, the same year being licensed to exhort, to preach, and admitted on trial. He was ordained deacon in 1859. His appointments during this period included: 1858 Lexington; 1859 Waynesboro; 1860 Isle of Hope; and 1861 Oxford. As the Civil War erupted that year, he entered the Confederate Army, serving as chaplain to the 35th Georgia Regiment, French's Brigade (later Pettigrew's), Smith's Division of the Army of Northern Virginia. He became a full connection elder in 1861 by vote of the conference even while he was away at war in Virginia. Leaving the service because of poor health, he was appointed in 1863 to the Athens Colored Mission. That year he married Mary Boyce Morris of Cobb County, their wedding officiated by Rev. Atticus G. Haygood. The couple would have eight children. In 1864 Yarbrough returned to the Confederate Army as chaplain to Wofford's Brigade in the Army of Northern Virginia. He was appointed in 1865 to Milledgeville; 1866 Milledgeville and Bethel; 1867 Lumpkin and Green Hill; 1868 Washington; 1869 Presiding Elder, Marietta District; 1870 Dalton; 1871-72 Greensboro; 1873-74 Presiding Elder, Elberton District; 1875-77 Presiding Elder, Griffin District; 1878 Rome; 1879-80 Athens; 1881 Newnan; 1882-83 Presiding Elder, Athens District; 1884-85 Barnesville; 1886 Cedartown; 1887-90 Presiding Elder, Oxford District; 1891 St. James, Augusta; 1892-94 Presiding Elder, Augusta District; 1895 Athens First; 1896 Gainesville; 1897-98 Grantville; 1899 Sparta; 1900 Barnesville; 1901-02 Cartersville; 1903 Thomson; 1904 Epworth, Atlanta;

1905-06 Oxford, Midway, and Mission; 1907 Jonesboro; 1908 The Rock; 1909 Supply. A prolific writer, Yarbrough had 106 different columns published in the *Wesleyan Christian Advocate* over the years. His book, "Boyhood and Other Days in Georgia," was published by the Methodist Episcopal Church South Publishing House in 1917. Rev. Yarbrough died October 17, 1922, in Chattanooga, having preached three services on the Sunday before he died on a Tuesday. He was buried in Marietta city cemetery.

G·W·Yarbrough

The Chattanooga News
Wed, Oct 18, 1922 -Page 2

DALTON PASTOR PASSES AWAY

Dr. George W. Yarbrough Dies in Local Hospital—Funeral at Marietta.

Stricken Monday afternoon at the terminal station, Dr. George W. Yarbrough of Dalton, Ga., one of the best known ministers in North Georgia, passed away in a local hospital Tuesday night. He appeared to be slightly improved Monday night, but complications set in Tuesday. Dr. Yarbrough was en route from Trion, Ga., to his home in Dalton at the time he became ill.

The body was removed to Wann's and later sent to Dalton. It will be taken to Marietta for funeral services in the First Methodist church in that city at 1 o'clock Friday morning. Bishop Warren A. Candler, J. H. Hakes, Dr. L. G. Johnson and the Rev. H. C. Emory will officiate.

Dr. Yarbrough was 84 years of age and one of the oldest preachers in point of service in the North Georgia conference of the Methodist church. He had answered rollcall of the conference sixty-four times. Aside from his work as a pastor, he spent a great deal of time in writing, being the author of two books as well as a large contributor to church periodicals. He was loved throughout North Georgia. For the past four years he had resided in Dalton.

Surviving him are seven sons: The Rev. John S. Yarbrough, presiding elder of the Dalton district, M. E. church, south; Dr. J. H., of Milledgeville; Dr. W. F., of Millasooka, Fla., Haygood, of Huntington, W. Va.; George, of North Augusta, S C.; T. W., of Sarasota, Fla., and Mack Yarbrough, of Atlanta.

in Chattanooga

The monthly report of Pastor Yarbrough for January 1879: 4 sermons, 2 prayer meetings, 12 pastoral visits, attended 2 Sunday Schools, no expulsions, none received, none withdrawn, 1 died. "The kind attention of the Church to the Pastor and his family are held in high appreciation and it is hoped that for the present year our hearts will be filled with peace and our labors crowned with success." In March he reported a "decided improvement in the Sunday School, both in respect of punctuality of teachers and scholars and the interest taken by all in the work." And in May: "There is a falling off in the attendance of our male members, especially at our weekly prayer meetings. The great body of our membership (including members of the Official Board) never attend." And in September: "Some of our young people have engaged in forbidden worldly amusements. The Pastor will endeavor to hold them to their allegiance to the Church."

Trustee William King, whose daughter was married to Henry W. Grady, resigned the post to move to Atlanta. He was succeeded by Manasseh B. McGinty, a local contractor and North Carolina native whom Hull's *Annals* credits with building UGA's Moore College, the old Clarke County Courthouse on

Prince Avenue which later became Athens High School, and other important business and residential buildings in the community. McGinty was building a new courthouse in Rabun County at the time of his death in 1899. He served as a church trustee until his death.

ꙅ1880ꙅ

In February 1880, the Board of Stewards was faced with Conference requests to support special offerings. The board resolved "that our pastor, Rev. George W. Yarbrough, be informed of the amount collected and paid out for the past conference year and that it is the opinion of this board that the stewards of the church cannot be relied upon for the Missionary Conference and Bishop's Collections for the present year and that he had better take such steps as he deems proper to raise the money." At the same meeting, the stewards voted to continue a $15 monthly payment "to the poor of this church," who are noted as three female members receiving five dollars per month each. The first evidence of a fundraising campaign beyond the personal contacts of the stewards appears, as member S. J. Mays was contracted to distribute envelopes to the membership for annual pledges and to collect the envelopes, turning them over the the treasurer and receiving a three percent commission on the amount collected.

A view of UGA North Campus in 1880

"Sister Linton" presented the church with a handsome Bible for the pulpit. It is not the one in use in the sanctuary or chapel today.

Through this period, the Sunday School was thought of by church leadership quite literally as a school that the church happened to sponsor on Sundays. The Sunday School had a separate board of managers and a budget completely separate from that of the church. Pastor George Yarbrough told church leadership as he neared his departure that he thought the church should "strive to have the school identify more directly with the church."

918819

Willard W. Wadsworth, Pastor, 1881

After two years as Athens First pastor, Rev. George Wesley Yarbrough was named Athens District Presiding Elder. Rev. Willard W. Wadsworth

Rev. Willard W. Wadsworth

succeeded him in our pulpit. Admitted on trial in 1871 and ordained deacon in 1872, Rev. Wadsworth became an elder in full connection in 1873. His appointments included: 1872-73 Covington and Mount Pleasant; 1874 Monticello Circuit; 1875 Milledgeville; 1876-77 Columbus, Mississippi; 1878 Gainesville; 1879 Madison; 1880 LaGrange; 1881 Athens; 1882-85 Newnan; 1886 Presiding Elder, Newnan District; 1887-89 Presiding Elder, South Atlanta District; 1890-93 St. John, Augusta; 1894 Washington; 1895 Conference Missionary Secretary; 1896-99 Presiding Elder, Griffin District; 1900 Marietta; 1901 Rome First; 1903-04 Church Street, Knoxville, Tennessee; 1905 Hartwell/suspended; 1906 located. His dedication sermon for the new sanctuary at Forsyth was printed in full in the *Monroe Advertiser* newspaper, March 31, 1894. His book,"The Coming Kingdom," was printed by the M.E. Church South Publishing House in 1889 and still is widely available online. Without explanation, records indicate Rev. Wadsworth was suspended for the year 1905 and located in 1906, apparently ending his career.

For the fourth time of record, the Annual Conference met in the sanctuary of Athens Methodist Church, with Bishop Holland Nimmons McTyeire presiding. Athens First raised funds to support hosting of the conference, which primarily involved providing sacramental elements and feeding the guests' horses.

Pastor W. W. Wadsworth reported to Quarterly Conference, "We are in the midst of a gracious revival," as some 60 persons from both within and outside the church had been converted. "We believe that the moral sentiment of the church is being raised to a higher plane." Rev. Wadsworth noted that early in the year he had emphasized the church's requirements against participation in and attendance upon dances, social

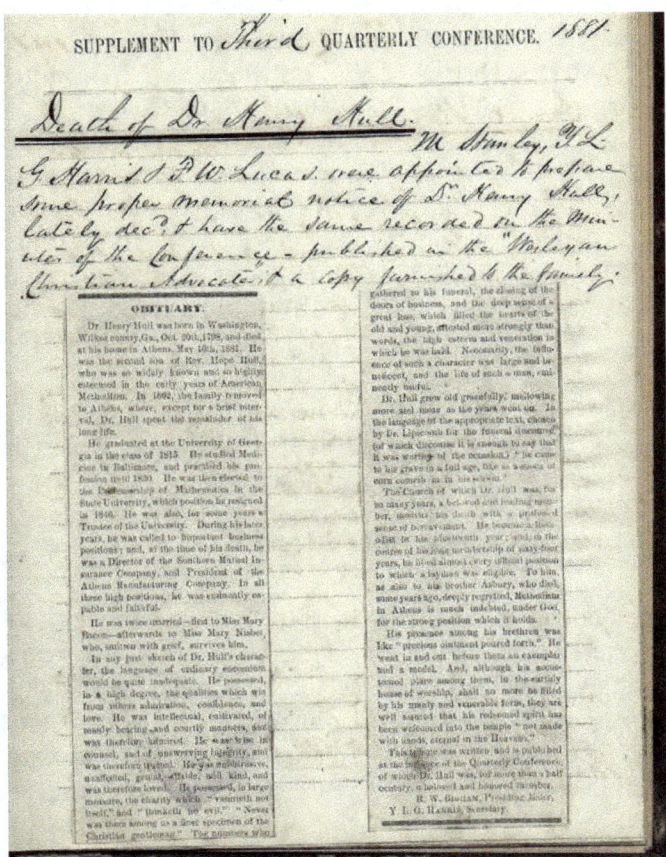

card playing and attending the theater, but the warnings were largely ignored. "But we hope that the royalty of the precious revival we are now enjoying will correct all the difficulties and allay the necessity of resorting to discipline." By his year-end report, he reported the conversion of at least 100 souls, and could say his goal was making progress "to elevate the standard of Christian living among the Methodist people, and by an earnest and aggressive effort to pluck sinners out of the jaws of death."

९1882९

John Dennis Hammond, Pastor, 1882-1884

Rev. Hammond was born May 12, 1850, in Franklin, Heard County, and was raised in Newnan, son of Judge Dennis F. and Adeline E. (Robinson) Hammond. He graduated from the University of Georgia with the A.B. degree in 1870, Drew University B.D. in 1875, and Central College of Missouri D.D. in 1886. In 1879 he married Lily Hardy, and they had three children. He was admitted on trial in 1871 and readmitted to trial in 1875. He became a deacon in full connection in 1877 and was ordained elder in 1878. His appointments were: 1872 Roswell; 1873 discontinued; 1876 Dahlonega and Jones Chapel; 1877 Dahlonega; 1878 Oconee Street, Athens; 1879 Edgewood, Atlanta; 1880-81 Forsyth; 1882-84 Athens First; 1885 Presiding Elder, Athens District; 1886 Milledgeville; 1888 First Church, St. Louis, Missouri; 1889-96 President, Central College (now Central Methodist University), St. Louis, Missouri; 1897-98 President, Wesleyan College; 1899-1910 Secretary, Conference Board of Education (based in Nashville, Tennessee); 1911 Professor, Missionary Training School, Atlanta; 1912 Professor, Paine College; 1913-15 President, Paine College; 1916-18 Dalton First; 1919 Madison. Rev. Hammond was elected a General Conference delegate seven times from 1886-1910. He died December 11, 1923.

The North Georgia delegation to the General Conference of 1882 included these former and future Athens First pastors: Weyman H. Potter, Jesse Boring, Harwell H. Parks, and James E. Evans.

९1883९

Pastor J. D. Hammond reported on the state of the Sunday School: "The working machinery of the School seems to be all that could be asked, except some irregularity on the part of a few of the teachers and a continuous indifference on the part of many parents to the whole subject." He reports average attendance of 125 with 17 teachers. "A large majority of those who have joined the church during the past two years have come in from the Sunday School."

Because of delinquent pledge payments, the church was unable to meet the pastor's salary for the month of July 1883, and the sexton had not been paid for two months. Brother S. J. Mays, who for years had been responsible for the annual pledge drive and was commissioned based on pledges paid, was urged by the Board of Stewards to make collections diligently so that the church could bring the payroll up to date. Through this period the Trustees, the Board of Stewards, and the Sunday School Department each kept discrete budgets and apparently there was little interaction among them. This would explain how the church might be behind on meeting its payroll at the same time it was undertaking a major construction project.

A report of the Board of Trustees in 1883 lists the members as Marcellus Stanley, James R. Carlton, John W. Nicholson, John A. Hunnicutt, and M. B. McGinty. (Quarterly Conference Record Book 1882-1885). McGinty was the contractor hired to undertake the complete rebuilding and renovation of church facilities the following year.

In 1885, a new sanctuary building was completed surrounding the steeple which has stood since 1852.

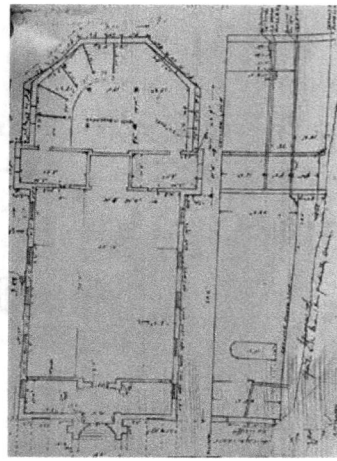

Above are exterior and interior photos of the new sanctuary completed in 1885. At right, plans drawn by architect W. W. Thomas, for which he was paid $50.

୨1884୨

A remodeling amounting to a virtually complete rebuilding and addition to the sanctuary building on the west end provided a new sanctuary and new Sunday School space. This project removed the entire 1852 "Brick Church" building except for the steeple, with the new facility built back onto it. The additional square footage provided the first dedicated Sunday School space, bringing the sanctuary building nearer its present size and shape, except 30 feet narrower than the present nave, and a rounded west wall. The cost of the project was $10,107 plus $346.98 for a new furnace. The total was underwritten by the membership beginning in 1882 and was completely paid by 1885. During the reconstruction work, the church met in the Clarke

A postcard of the Clarke County Courthouse on Prince Avenue at Finley Street, where the church met during the construction work.
(photo courtesy Hargrett Rare Book and Manuscript Library, University of Georgia Libraries)

County Courthouse then located on Prince Avenue.

୨1885୨

Rev. Anderson Joseph Jarrell, Pastor, 1885-1886

Born in Jones County on March 28, 1840, Jarrell grew up on his father's plantation, graduating from Emory College in 1861, though sadly there was no commencement ceremony with the Civil War underway. As a young schoolboy, he attended his first Methodist protracted meeting and was converted there, soon joining the church. He called that conversion experience "the crowning event of his life." The same year he graduated, Jarrell married Elizabeth Ann "Lizzie" Smith, daughter of Rev. George G. Smith, who was wounded in 1862 while serving as a Chaplain in the Confederate Army and was confined to a wheelchair for the remainder of his life. Rev. Smith was a prolific author, including writing two significant histories of Methodism in Georgia and Florida. Anderson Jarrell (to whom some sources refer as "Addison") was admitted on trial in 1861, became a deacon in full connection in 1863, and was ordained elder in 1865. His appointments included:

Rev. Anderson Joseph Jarrell

1862 Watkinsville and the Athens Colored Mission, as associate to elder-in-charge Atticus G. Haygood; 1863 Whitfield Circuit, from which he left to join the army; 1864- 65 Chaplain, Confederate Army. He came home to his father's plantation following the surrender, working with the local Methodist circuit until Conference could again assemble and make appointments; 1866 Cave Spring and Cedartown; 1867-69 Sparta; 1870 Marietta; 1871-74 Milledgeville and chaplain, lunatic asylum (later more gently known as the State Mental Hospital); 1875-76 Cartersville; 1877-80 St. James, Augusta (and Jones Chapel in 1877); 1881-82 Cartersville; 1883-84 Gainesville; 1885-86 Athens First; 1887-90 LaGrange. At special appointment by Bishop Haygood, Jarrell was sent out of the conference in 1891-93 to Trinity, Savannah, and then by the full College of Bishops was sent 1894-95 to First Church, St. Louis, Missouri, before returning to North Georgia in 1896 to Cartersville. He died August 1, 1896, while still in active service at Cartersville and only age 56. He was buried in the historic Methodist cemetery at Oxford.

Pastor A. J. Jarrell started his term at Athens exhibiting a much brighter view of the state of the Sunday School than did his predecessor. "The pastor rejoices to say that it is a deeply religious school and has often had to deplore the opposite in schools elsewhere." However, by later in 1885 he is concerned about the same issues as was Rev. Hammond before him: "The pastor fears the work of saving the children is not being pressed as it ought to be by teachers. The children are not looked up by the teachers when they are absent. Those who are not in school are not looked up and brought in. The teachers are not uniformly punctual as they ought to be for the highest efficiency."

The salary of the pastor-in-charge, which had been reduced from $1,500 to $1,200 per year in 1876, was restored to $1,500. The church also employed an organist for $100 a year and a person to operate the organ bellows at $24 per year, or two dollars per month. While continuing the envelope system of pledging, their use by the members was made optional and the fundraising commission arrangement with S. J. Mays was discontinued. Stewards were asked to announce aloud at their meeting the amount they would be pledging. They were urged to pay their pledges quarterly in advance and to urge the members on their lists to do the same.

The Georgia Holiness Association held its spring session in the Athens First sanctuary. As a result, 69 persons were reported as joining the church on profession of faith.

At the Fourth Quarterly Conference of the year a resolution was passed admonishing two members of the Board of Stewards for having reported no collections during the entire year. Stewards were responsible for obtaining pledges from the list of members appointed to them, and for collecting payments on those pledges through the year. The two Stewards were given a week to report back on what they had done about the matter.

෧**1886**෧

The North Georgia delegation to the 1886 General Conference included former and future Athens First pastors Weyman H. Potter, William D. Anderson, Harwell H. Parks, and John D. Hammond.

S. P. Thurmond was elected to the Board of Trustees to fill the vacancy left by the death of John W. Nicholson. (Minutes of Third Quarterly Conference of 1886) Thurmond died just a year later, in July 1887, and was succeeded as trustee by Rufus K. Reaves. (Minutes of Fourth Quarterly Conference of 1887). Thurmond was born in 1820 in Morgan County, but grew up in Coweta County, where he participated in the wars to expel the Cherokees. In 1840 he moved to Watkinsville, working in the mercantile business of his uncle, H. H. Sheats, while borrowing books to learn to read, and being tutored in the law by attorney Green B. Hagood. Admitted to the bar in 1843, he opened a law practice in Jefferson, but

Rev. S. P. Richardson, Presiding Elder of the Athens District, 1886-89.

moved to Athens in 1860. His wife, Elizabeth Long, was sister to Dr.

Crawford W. Long of Jefferson. In Athens, the Thurmonds lived on the south side of Dearing Street between Church and Harris streets. He was elected to the state legislature and was chosen Solicitor General of the Western Judicial Circuit. Said in his obituary to be "worth more than one hundred thousand dollars," he was noted for "grim humor backed by sense and shrewdness." Likewise, he "wielded a strong pen...with power in controversial correspondence." Colonel Thurmond served as church trustee only briefly, dying in 1887, the year after he was appointed. His successor, Rufus Reaves, was an Athens alderman who was mayor 1887 and 1888. A Confederate soldier, he came home after the surrender with less than $50 to his name, but through shrewd business acumen soon was worth $150,000, primarily through his Reaves Warehouse Company. He married a daughter of Isaac Powell of High Shoals, a prominent farmer, and after her death, he married her sister. His home faced south on Washington Street between Thomas and Foundry Streets. Reaves later served many years on the city board of education and held that position until his death in 1917. He resigned as a church trustee for an unrecorded reason in 1901.

୨1887୨

William D. Anderson, Pastor, 1887-1890

Rev. Anderson was born in Marietta on June 24, 1839, son of Superior

Rev. William D. Anderson

Court Judge George D. Anderson and Jane Holmes Anderson. He graduated with distinction from the University of Georgia in 1859 and entered the practice of law in his hometown. Anderson took a non-traditional path to the ministry. At age 22, he and four friends traveled to Charleston to enlist in the Palmetto Guards, 2nd South Carolina Regiment, where he was a private. He saw extensive action including the battles of Bull Run, First and Second Manassas, Yorktown, Millersburg, Richmond, and Cold Harbor, where he was wounded. Following recovery, he transferred to Phillips' Legion as a first lieutenant and saw further action at Mechanicsville, Gaines' Mill, Savage Station, Fair Oaks, Frazier's Farm,

90

Malvern Hill, Fredericksburg, Chancellorsville, Boonesboro, Harper's Ferry, Sharpsburg, and Gettysburg. Following the war, in April 1865 he returned to the practice of law in Marietta. He married Louise J. Latimer, and they had two children. He first joined the church in 1867, serving as a Sunday School superintendent, steward, and trustee. He was elected to the Georgia General Assembly from Cobb County in 1868 and served four years as Speaker Pro Tem. Louise died in 1875. William, then age 36, answering a call to the ministry, stepped aside from his lucrative law practice and resigned from the General Assembly. The moves astounded his friends and colleagues, which many considered "the climax of folly." He was admitted on trial in 1875, became deacon in full connection in 1877, and was ordained elder in 1879. In 1877, Anderson married his first wife's sister, Lula H. Latimer, and they had seven children. His appointments included: 1876 Eatonton; 1877-78 Cedartown; 1879-80 Marietta; 1881-82 Presiding Elder, Elberton District; 1883 Rome; 1884-86 Presiding Elder, Marietta District; 1887-90 Athens First; 1891 Atlanta First; 1892 LaGrange; 1893-94 Presiding Elder, Oxford District. He served on the board of trustees at Emory, which awarded him an honorary Doctor of Divinity degree. Anderson also was a trustee at Wesleyan, LaGrange and Young Harris colleges, and chairman of the board of managers of the *Wesleyan Christian Advocate*. He died of pneumonia at his home in Marietta on February 19, 1894, while still in the active ministry as Presiding Elder at Oxford, and only age 54.

At the first meeting of the Board of Stewards for the year, each of the 14 men present announced his pledge for the coming year. They ranged from $25 to $200, with an average of $68.57.

U.S. President Grover Cleveland visited Athens and the University of Georgia in 1887 as part of a tour while in the state for the Cotton States Exhibition.

ꙮ1888ꙮ

In late 1887, organist Mrs. T. C. Hampton resigned and action to secure a replacement was deferred for several months. In early 1888, apparently for the first time, the church employed a choir director to assist the organist in leading church music. The choir director, Mrs. Emma Mell, was paid $180 per year and the organist, Mrs. Mary Nicholson, was paid $100 per year. By the time of the Second Quarterly Conference in June 1888, Mrs. H. N. Wilcox had resigned as organist, succeeded by Miss Furlow Anderson. Three months later, Mrs. Anderson had resigned and a committee was working to find her successor. By the beginning of 1891, Mrs. Mell was organist at $150 per year and there apparently was no longer a choir director.

Trustee James R. Carlton apparently resigned his position, likely due to failing health, in late 1887 or early 1888. He died in August 1888. By the time of the First Quarterly Conference held March 21, 1888, the roll lists his former position as being held by Peter A. Summey, a prominent Athens merchant in his early years and one of the church's largest contributors, who had fallen on hard times when cotton failed, but nonetheless had been a longtime faithful member of the church. He had been operator of the town's leading hardware store, served on the founding board of the Bank of Athens, and was a founder of Athens Steam Company. In 1878 he even lost his home, which faced north on Washington Street between Thomas and Foundry Streets, and he and his wife were reduced to running the boarding house in

Separate records were maintained for the church's support of maintenance of the Athens District parsonage, such as this receipt for the annual property insurance premium and another for purchase of a coffee pot. Note the signature of the Southern Mutual Insurance Company president, Judge Young Harris, who also was chair of the Board of Stewards at Athens First Methodist.

Old College. Nonetheless, he remained a faithful member of the church and sang bass in the choir. Finally appointed as a church trustee in 1888, he died just three years later in 1891.

A committee was appointed "to look into the title to this church and the relation it sustains to the Quarterly Conference." As to the state of the church, Pastor W. D. Anderson reported, "There is nothing like revival manifestation, still there is much for which to thank God and take courage."

ම**1889**ම

At its August 6, 1889 meeting, the Quarterly Conference urged Pastor W. D. Anderson to take a one month's vacation, "assuring him that the money will be forthcoming with which to pay his expenses to any point he may desire to go." The Conference also voted to seek the reappointment of Pastor Anderson to Athens First for a fourth year, which by rules of the Conference at that time was the limit a person could serve in one appointment.

ම**1890**ම

The North Georgia delegation to the 1890 General Conference included the current Athens First pastor, William D. Anderson, and former and future pastors W. P. Lovejoy, Weyman H. Potter, Willard W. Wadsworth, and Harwell H. Parks. A committee of stewards was appointed to secure guest preachers for the Sundays Rev. Anderson was away at General Conference.

In his written report on the state of the church made to the Quarterly Conference on March 17, 1890, Pastor Anderson discussed attendance at Wednesday evening prayer meeting: "The attendance is good generally, the sisters in fair numbers, the numbers of the brethren much smaller." At that same meeting, a resolution was adopted asking City Council to place a light at the corner of Meigs and Church Streets, though it is not clear what interest they had in that particular intersection.

Trustee Marcellus Stanley died May 10, 1890, having served since 1866. He was succeeded as trustee by Edward R. Hodgson, who would serve until his death in 1920. Hodgson served in Lumpkin's battery in the Confederate Army, after the war graduating in the UGA class of 1868. Among his Athens businesses, he was president of Hodgson Oil Company, noted manufacturer of cooking oil, and also was a long-time director of Southern Mutual

Insurance Company. He was on the original board of trustees of Georgia Tech, served on the Athens Board of Education, was treasurer of Rabun Gap School, and served as an Athens firefighter. In 1891, he was head of the Athens Prohibition Club, which led a successful campaign to turn Clarke County dry. The eighth of Hodgson's nine children, Nell, married the noted Atlanta businessman and philanthropist Robert W. Woodruff.

୨1891୨

Thomas Rogers Kendall, Sr., Pastor, 1891-1892

Born on February 16, 1846, in Bellwood, Upson County, Thomas Kendall attended Collinsworth Institute in Talbotton before serving as a Captain in the Confederate Army in his late teen years. He surrendered at Greensboro, North Carolina on April 26, 1865, at just age 19. After the war, he attended the Military College in Marietta and graduated in 1869 from Atlanta Medical College. In 1869 he married Julia Wright Thomas. Following her death, he married Mary Lovelace in 1886. Admitted on trial in 1874, he became a deacon in full connection in 1876 and was ordained elder in 1878. His appointments included: 1875-76 Culloden; 1877-78 Hampton; 1879-81 Griffin; 1882-84 Trinity and Pierce Chapel, Atlanta; 1885 Trinity, Atlanta; 1886-87 Rome; 1888-90 Mulberry Street, Macon; 1891-92 Athens First; 1893-96 Grace, Atlanta; 1897 Presiding Elder, LaGrange District; 1898-1900 St. John, Augusta; 1901 transferred to the Louisville (Ky.) Conference, appointed in 1902-04 to Settle Chapel,

At left, Thomas R. Kendall, Sr.
Above, his grave at Oakland Cemetery, Atlanta

Owensboro, Ky.; 1905-06 Walnut Street, Louisville, Ky.; 1907-10 Lander Memorial. He returned to North Georgia, appointed 1911-12 to St. James, Augusta; 1913-16 Gainesville First; 1917-18 Milledgeville; 1919-22 Inman Park, Atlanta; 1923 Cartersville; 1924 Supply. He died on October 5, 1936 in Decatur and was buried in Oakland Cemetery, Atlanta. A son, Thomas Rogers Kendall, Jr., born in 1872 in Thomaston, also served as an elder under appointment in North Georgia 1899-1940 and died in 1947.

In his first year at the church, Rev. Kendall termed the Sunday School to be "one of the very best.... It is very rare to find such intelligence, practability and spiritual quickening among the children." His assessment of the congregation at large was equally effusive: "We have some of the most faithful, consistent and consecrated men and women to be found in all the earth." In the first six months, there was a great revival in the city, which meetings "were almost entirely supported by the Methodists." An impressive 80 new members were reported that January through June, with 31 baptized. By the end of 1891, the year's total stood at 153 new members, compared with 25 the previous year, only one of which was on profession of faith (termed "accession" in those days).

☙1892☙

Minutes of the Quarterly Conference list eight persons as Trustees at the opening of the year 1892, but there were only six trustees of the church: F. W. Lucas, R. L. Moss, J. A. Hunnicutt, E. R. Hodgson, R. K. Reaves and M. B. McGinty. Also listed were A. H. Hodgson and H. Cobb Davis, but they were trustees of the District Parsonage alone.

F. W. Lucas was a dry goods merchant in Athens, but little is known of his service as a church trustee except that he took office sometime before 1892 and served until after 1911.

Likewise, the precise date is not known for the appointment of Rufus LaFayette Moss as trustee, but is believed to be about 1872. He served until his death in 1912. Moss's first wife, Mary Alice, was daughter of former Athens Methodist pastor Samuel W. Anthony. They married in 1848 while her father was pastor here, but she tragically died while on their wedding journey one month to the day after they were married. Moss remarried six years later and his second wife, Elizabeth, survived him. His obituary described him as one of Athens' oldest and wealthiest citizens and among its largest property owners, saying "His departure is one of the most notable that Athens has known in many years." First elected a Steward of the church at age 18, Moss held church leadership positions continuosly for 70 years. At various points in his career he was a cotton merchant, superintendent at Princeton Cotton Factory and Pioneer Paper Mill, and oversaw the building of the Northeast railroad into Athens. He was noted for "frankness of manner and speech" and was remembered as "quick to adopt the essential and abandon the useless."

Early in the year, Pastor Kendall had a disagreement with the Board of Stewards over responsibility for utility bills in the parsonage. The board determined these were private expenses of the pastor and "should be paid by the occupant of the parsonage at the time such indebtedness was incurred."

At its final meeting of 1892, the Board of Stewards renamed the parsonage the "Anne Hodgson Parsonage" to commemorate the devoted work of the recently deceased church member as president of the parsonage committee. Miss Julia Moss was elected to succeed her. At the same meeting, church member L. A. Shackelford was elected church treasurer "with a compensation of 7.5 percent on all funds collected including basket collections." Salary for the outgoing pastor, Rev. Kendall, was $1,400. For the incoming pastor, Rev. Lovejoy, it was set at $1,800 per year.

᱑1893᱑

William P. Lovejoy, Pastor, 1893-1894

At his first meeting with the Board of Stewards in early 1893, Rev. Lovejoy told them it was apparent he should preach on the importance of members contributing to the support of the church. The Stewards asked that he do so "at an early date." Lovejoy brought numerous innovations to Athens First, including printed worship programs, an expanded assistance program for poor within the church, addressing "lack of organization and leadership in the choir," a regular order of business for the Board of Stewards, and the use of regular ushers in worship services. He set as an early goal to organize the church membership into teams for "thorough, systematic and continuous house-to-house work." Born September 26, 1845, in Meriwether County, he was one of twelve children of Rev. Anderson R. Lovejoy, who became an elder in the Georgia Conference in 1861 and died in 1890. The younger Lovejoy was converted at age 11. He was licensed to preach in 1866, graduated from

Courtesy: Hargrett Rare Book and Manuscript Library, University of Georgia Libraries

The sanctuary as it appeared from the 1884 renovation to the next one in 1910. Here it is decorated
for the October 13, 1892 wedding of Miss Birdie Moss to Emmet J. Bondurant.
The west wall stood about where today's pulpit and lectern are.

Emory College in 1869, was ordained deacon in 1870 and elder in 1873. In
1871, Lovejoy married Anna M. Lowe, daughter of Rev. Gideon Harris Lowe
of Ashland City, Tennessee. Lovejoy's appointments included: 1872
Oostanaula Circuit; 1873-74 Eatonton; 1875-76 Summerville; 1877-80
White Plains; 1881 Financial Secretary, Emory College; 1882 Agent, Emory
College; 1883-86 Presiding Elder,Elberton District; 1887-90 Presiding Elder,
Augusta District; 1891-92 Presiding Elder, Rome District; 1893-94 Athens
First; 1895-97 Presiding Elder, Athens District; 1891-1901 Presiding Elder,
South Atlanta District; 1902-04 Presiding Elder, Athens District; 1905-06
Marietta; 1907-10 Presiding Elder, Dalton District; 1911 Presiding Elder,

Rev. W. P. Lovejoy
from the 1892 Conference Journal

LaGrange District; 1912-14 Presiding Elder, Atlanta District, where Lovejoy died in office. Of his 42 years of appointments, 30 years were administrative. The two years at Athens First were among only twelve years he was in a local pulpit. He followed the two years in our pulpit with three years as Presiding Elder of the Athens District. Lovejoy wrote numerous columns in the *Wesleyan Christian Advocate* and published three books: "A Short History of Methodism in the United States," Macon: J.W. Burke, 1884; "The Mission of the Church," Nashville: Methodist Episcopal Publishing House, 1894; and "The Greatest Responsibility in the World," Atlanta: Foote & Davies, 1899.

Pastor Lovejoy conducted a "protracted service" in the evenings for a week or longer in May 1893, with special committees in charge of music and for lighting the church with an arc light. His stated hope was for a revival, but it also could have had something to do with the church being one to two months behind in paying his salary since his arrival in January. He requested that the members of the Board of Stewards be seated on the front bench of the church at all services as an example to the membership.

A meeting of the Quarterly Conference found a report from Pastor Lovejoy so compelling that they voted to have it published in the local newspaper. In it, Lovejoy pointed out that the public schools of Athens, including the University, were not as Godless as some might portray them. There was a concerted movement at the time by leaders of church-related colleges in Georgia to allow them to benefit from taxpayer funding, calling the lack of it an unfair competitive advantage for the public schools.

An annual "reading of the roll" was conducted in September, a practice for many years in the Methodist church that has fallen away in most larger churches in recent decades. The entire roll was read at a meeting of the Board of Stewards with the pastor present, and if no one in the room knew who the person was, their name was removed from the church roll. In the latter part of the 20th century this practice evolved. Such a reading still was held every year, but a person had to be "lost" for three years before being removed. Rolls at larger churches generally have not been read in this manner for the past two decades or longer, primarily because bishops put a premium on having enrollment numbers increase, and new apportionment formulae no longer placed a great emphasis on enrollment. We note that the resulting bloated rolls proved detrimental to some churches in the disaffiliation votes of 2023-24, as long-absent members suddenly reappeared to cast ballots and swing the vote in a direction perhaps not favored by the majority of active members.

At the final meeting of the year of the Quarterly Conference, the Trustees were authorized to install lights in the Sunday School room. From Pastor W. P. Lovejoy's report at the same meeting of October 25, 1893: "We have a few members who are said to be bad. Committees have been appointed to see them with the purpose to save them, if possible: failing in this, to save the church by cutting them off. The bulk of our membership are at least moral. A large number are deeply devoted to the church." Following his report, 30 members were "dismissed by order of the church conference."

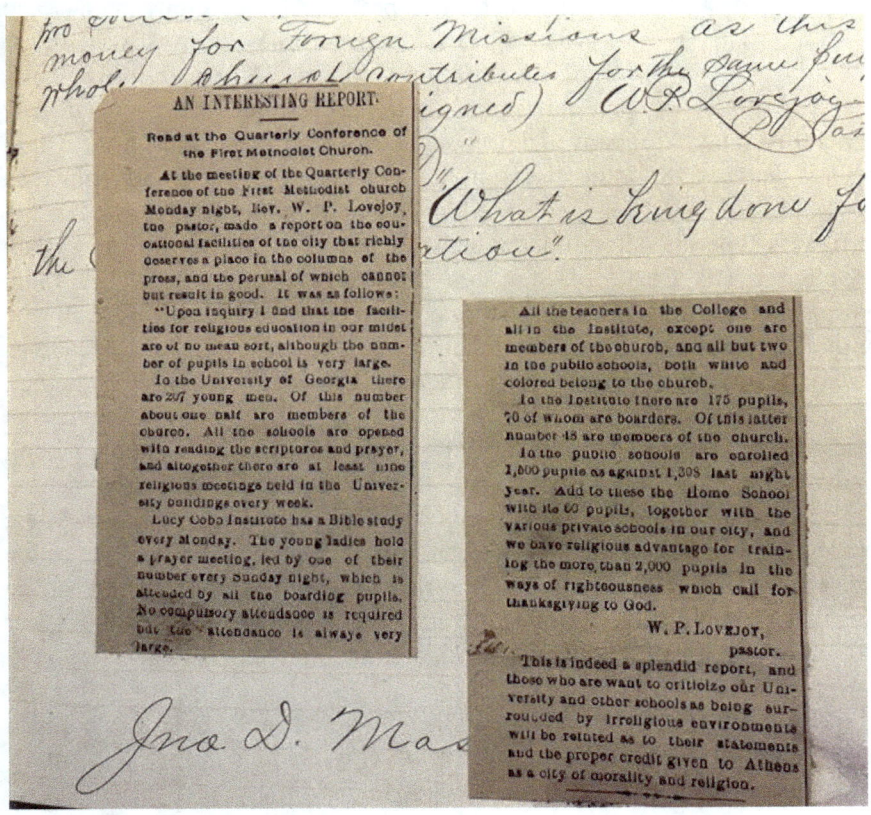

9**1894**9

Judge Young Loftin Gerdine Harris 1812 - 1894

Judge Young Loftin Gerdine Harris, a prominent member of Athens First, died April 28, 1894. He gave funds to erect the First Methodist Church

Judge Young Loftin Gerdine Harris 1812 - 1894

of Shanghai, China as one of the last of his many acts of benevolence. Over the years, his gifts purchased a President's Home at Emory College in Oxford, Georgia, and built two dormitories there, one of which later burned. He built a large hall and dormitory at McTyeire Institute in Brasstown Valley, in honor of which the college and the town both were renamed Young Harris. He represented Elbert County in the Georgia House of Representatives in 1841, then moved to Athens and was elected to represent Clarke County in 1847 and 1849-52. An Athens attorney, he was local Judge of the Inferior Court in 1849 and in 1853-57. Harris was among the founders of Southern Mutual Insurance Company and became president in 1866, a position he held until his death in 1894. Income from that venture was the primary source of his wealth. He was a trustee of the University of Georgia 1873-84. Young Harris was superintendent of the Athens First Sunday School for forty years and chair of its Board of Stewards for nearly that long, resigning the chairmanship at the age of 80 just two years before his death, though he continued on the Board the remainder of his life. In Harris's last decade as Sunday School Superintendent, Professor David C. Barrow was named associate superintendent. Few in the church and the community, even his closest friends, were aware of the full extent of Harris's charitable giving around the state and world, contributing to small churches, building ministers' homes, and supporting the YMCA. His wife of 53 years, Susan Bevel Allen, died in 1888. The couple had no children. Their burial monument is one of the largest in Oconee Hill Cemetery, featuring intricately carved figures of the three theological virtues, Faith, Hope and Charity, principles his biographer said guided his life and which he considered the meaning of life.

The North Georgia delegation to the 1894 General Conference included the current Athens First pastor, W. P. Lovejoy, former pastor William D. Anderson, and future pastor John Wesley Heidt.

As the church continued to run behind on its finances, the Board of Stewards accepted an offer from Pastor Lovejoy that he be paid $1,500 for the year rather than the established salary of $1,800. The Board reluctantly accepted his offer, saying they would pay him the remainder if it could be raised. Stewards were urged to press the collections from those members assigned to them. By December of that year, the pastor indeed had been paid his full salary, but the Board voted to set the salary of the incoming pastor for 1895 back to $1,500. For the year, the church had collected $2,468.65 against disbursements of $2,463.75 for a year-end surplus of $4.90.

Citing "a determination on the part of the Official Board to cure those that can be cured and to cut off those members of the body that cannot be cured," Pastor Lovejoy oversaw a vote to dismiss two more members "by order of the Church Conference" at its March meeting and another four at the November meeting.

In 1894, a proposal arose to plant a missionary congregation in the Milledge Avenue area, or "the southwestern part of the city." Discussion at the Quarterly Conference was for a chapel to be constructed near the terminus of the streetcar line on South Milledge Avenue. "But for the fearful monetary stringency this enterprise should be undertaken now," wrote Pastor W. P. Lovejoy. At a subsequent meeting on July 2, 1894, Rev. Lovejoy proposed a more specific location: "near the intersection of Baxter and Bloomfield Streets." Perhaps it was Lovejoy's championing of the idea that caused it to become a part of the appointment of Athens First's senior ministers for some years to come, even though it would be the 1950s before the idea finally would come to fruition in the chartering of St. James Methodist Church.

9**1895**9

George Wesley Yarbrough, Pastor, 1895

This was Rev. Yarbrough's third appointment to Athens First, having been at our church in 1863 as pastor of the Athens Colored Mission, and returning in 1879-80 as pastor. He also was Athens District Presiding Elder for 1882-83. In his report to the June 26, 1895, Quarterly Conference, Rev. Yarbrough lamented poor attendance at the three evening services held each week: on Wednesday, Thursday, and Sunday evenings. He noted "no men at our Wednesday evening prayer meetings" and "Would not our church do better to close on Sunday night than seek to impress the community by such an attendance as we have?" He added, "Our women are setting the men of our church an example in zeal and devotion that we would do well to follow."

ᵜ1896ᵜ

William Robert Foote, Jr., Pastor, 1896-1897

Rev. Foote was born May 7, 1854, in the Methodist parsonage at West Point, Ga., son of Rev. William Robert Foote, Sr., who served appointments in the conference from 1849-80. His mother was daughter of a Methodist preacher, the Rev. James Jones. Foote, Jr. graduated from Emory College in 1873 at age 19. He was admitted on trial that same year, became a deacon in full connection in 1875, and was ordained elder in 1877. He married Margaret F. Whittaker in 1878. His appointments were: 1874 Resaca Circuit; 1875 Lexington or Senoia (sources conflict); 1876-77 Baldwin Circuit, Augusta; 1878 Jones' Chapel, Augusta; 1879-80 Dahlonega; 1881 Lexington; 1882 Hogansville; 1883 Thomaston; 1884 Sparta; 1885 Edgewood, Atlanta; 1886 Douglasville and Salt Springs; 1887-88 Newnan; 1889 Eatonton; 1890-91 Carrollton; 1892-93 West Point; 1894-95 St. John, Atlanta; 1896-97 Athens First; 1898-99 Presiding Elder, LaGrange District; 1900-02 Presiding Elder, Oxford District; 1903-04 Presiding Elder, Rome District; 1904-05 Suspended (no explanation); 1906 Dahlonega; 1907-08 Commerce; 1909-10 Warrenton; 1911-14 Dalton First (1911 and Dalton

REV. W. R. FOOTE YIELDS TO STROKE

SERVED AS PASTOR OF JACKSON METHODIST CHURCH A FEW YEARS AGO. HAD BEEN AT FORSYTH 2 YEARS

Forsyth, Ga., April 22.—Dr. W. R. Foote, one of the best known and most honored members of the North Georgia conference of the Methodist Episcopal church, South, and for the past two years pastor of the Forsyth Methodist church, died suddenly at his home here early Saturday morning.

Dr. Foote left Atlanta Friday night, arriving here at midnight. A few hours later he sustained a stroke of appoplexy and died.

News of his death will bring grief to hundreds of his friends throughout Georgia. He was noted for his splendid Christian character and for the power and eloquence of his ministry.

The funeral will be held at the Methodist church here Sunday morning at 9 o'clock, with Presiding Elder Luke Jonson officiating. Interment will be at Milledgeville Sunday afternoon.

Dr. Foote is survived by his widew and one son, W. O. Foote, of Decatur, Ga. Walter O. Foote, president of the Atlanta Chamber of Commerce and president of Foote and Davies, of Atlanta, is a brother of Dr. Foote.

Dr. Foote had many friends in Jackson and Butts county who were grieved to learn of his death. He served as pastor of the Jackson Methodist church a few years ago, being succeeded by Rev. S. R. England, now presiding elder of the Marietta district, who in turn was succeeded by Rev. J. R. Jordan. Dr. Foote was a splendid gentleman in every way and commanded the respect of his congregation and the general public.

Top left, W. R. Foote in the 1892 Con...
Bottom left, Pastor William Foote's gravestone at Memory Hill Cemetery, Milledgeville.

Mills); 1915-16 Washington; 1917 Jackson; 1918-20 Hartwell; 1921-22 Forsyth. Rev. Foote died April 22, 1922, while pastor at Forsyth, retiring for a usual evening with no sign of discomfort, yet passing away during the night. He was buried in Memory Hill Cemetery in Milledgeville. His conference memoriam notes, "His style of sermonizing was unique. He seemed to have followed no accepted standards, but to have made his own model. This was not due to any desire to strain after the unusual, but in simple obedience to the unconstrained processes of his own thought. He was a distinct individuality, and this showed in his preaching as elsewhere."

Athens First had attempted to start an Epworth League, or youth program, for the past several years, but upon his arrival as pastor, Rev. Foote found that the roll was lost and he needed to start over. By April he could report 58 regular members in attendance at the Sunday evening sessions. "It is being wisely, shrewdly and religiously cultivated and developed. The young men and ladies work as requested quite well. I think it not improbable that a force for revival will be generated from this League."

Through this period, it was the practice of the Board of Stewards to appoint one of its members to be responsible for making announcements to the church at each worship service, including a financial report. Brother E. D. Sledge, who was first appointed in 1895, asked to be relieved of the duty "as it was impossible for him to be prompt in attendance." The Stewards appointed instead Hatton Lovejoy, the 19-year-old son of former pastor William P. Lovejoy. By then a UGA student, Hatton showed an early gift for public speaking and made the weekly announcements while he worked on an engineering degree, which he received from UGA in 1896 and a law degree in 1897. The younger Lovejoy would go on to a notable career, beginning the practice of law in LaGrange. He became Troup County School Superintendent and served in the Georgia General Assembly. He gained the confidence of industrial magnate Fuller E. Callaway, Sr., becoming his legal counsel. He obtained the charter for the Callaway Foundation of LaGrange and served as its legal counsel and later its vice president for decades until his death in 1964. Lovejoy gave the annual UGA Alumni Day Address in 1951. The courtroom in the UGA School of Law bears his name. Your author was a boy in LaGrange when Mr. Lovejoy was quite elderly. If one was riding his bicycle down a street and saw Mr. Lovejoy's car coming, you should get out of the way, as no one in town had the gumption to inform him that it was time to give up his keys.

ᴐ**1897**ᴐ

The annual budget for Athens First Church for the year 1897 was set by the Board of Stewards at their meeting on December 7, 1896. The total budget was $2,800, including pastor's salary $1,500, contribution to presiding elder salary $220, coal $100, lights $75, Sexton salary $100, wine and bread $10, organ boy $24, taxes $50, insurance $20, printing $20, and incidentals $681. It seems the music program must have returned to an entirely volunteer basis, as no salary is listed for a choir director or organist. For the first time in the church's 72-year history, the meeting minutes were typed rather than handwritten.

A new Sunday School class was formed by members of the church who attended the State Normal School on Prince Avenue.

A committee chaired by E. R. Hodgson was appointed to investigate purchase of a lot near Rock College for construction of the anticipated mission church that had been discussed. Today, Rock College is on the UGA medical campus on Prince Avenue, but clearly is not in the South Athens area that was the focus of the venture.

The North Georgia Annual Conference met in late November 1897 in the Athens First sanctuary with Bishop Charles Betts Galloway presiding, the fifth time Annual Conference had met in Athens as far as records are available. Emory President Warren Candler was elected head of the clergy delegation to General Conference, and the evangelist Sam Jones as head of the laity delegation. Jones twice preached rousing sermons to packed houses in the sanctuary, one of those sessions being on Thanksgiving Day. Candler made a speech adamantly opposing state funding of public education to the detriment of private schools such as Emory, yet he was gracious in welcoming UGA Chancellor William E. Boggs to bring words of greeting to the Conference. A resolution to split the North Georgia Conference into two was laid on the table by a narrow margin.

ᴐ**1898**ᴐ

John Wesley Heidt, Pastor, 1898-1900

Born July 12, 1841, in Macon, Heidt was the second son of Rev. Emmanuel Heidt and Frances Grayson Heidt. He attended Springfield

Academy and graduated from Emory College in 1859 with a bachelor's degree. He further completed a master's degree at Emory. He graduated from the University of Georgia School of Law in 1861 and immediately entered the Confederate Army, serving in the Chatham Artillery. In 1864 he married Eliza Villard. They became parents of six children. He was admitted on trial in 1866, became deacon in 1867, was granted full connection in 1868, and was ordained elder in 1869. His appointments were: 1867 Cave Spring; 1868-70 Broad River, Athens; 1871-74 Griffin; 1875-78 Presiding Elder,

LaGrange District; 1879-81 Trinity, Atlanta (during which time he served as Chaplain of the Georgia Senate – the State Capitol is across Washington Street from Trinity Church); 1882-85 President, LaGrange College; 1886-90 Regent, Southwestern University, Georgetown, Texas; 1890 Trinity, Atlanta; 1891-94 Presiding Elder, North Atlanta District;

John Wesley Heidt

1895-97 Presiding Elder, South Atlanta District; 1898-1900 Athens First; 1901 Presiding Elder, Rome District; 1902 Assistant Editor and Business Manager, the *Wesleyan Christian Advocate*; 1903-06 Presiding Elder, Oxford District; 1907-09 Presiding Elder, Augusta District. A key figure in the North Georgia Conference, Heidt served as Conference Secretary for 33 years. He was editor of the Conference minutes and yearbook from 1895-1908. He received a Doctor of Divinity degree from Trinity College in North Carolina, and was a trustee of Wesleyan, LaGrange, and Reinhardt Colleges. He died January 23, 1909, and was buried in Westview Cemetery, Atlanta.

The Athens Baptist Church built a new sanctuary at the corner of College Avenue and Washington Street, next door to its existing sanctuary. The brick building with a large, imposing steeple dominated Athens' skyline a block east of the Methodist church steeple.

At the 1898 General Conference of the M.E. Church, South, the North Georgia delegation included these Athens First clergy from over the years: John D. Hammond, W. P. Lovejoy, and Willard W. Wadsworth.

♀1900♀

As Athens First observed its 75th anniversary, membership was 684 and total giving for the year was $4,725.

♀1901♀

Joel T. Daves, Jr., Pastor, 1901-1902

Born while his father, Rev. Joel T. Daves, Sr. (lived 1833-1897), was a pastor in Louisiana, Joel Jr. moved with his family to North Georgia in 1891 when the elder Daves was named pastor at Marietta First. The younger Daves married Sophie Pauline Wright in 1894 and they became parents of five children. Daves was admitted on trial in 1891, became a deacon in full connection in 1893, and was ordained elder in 1895. His appointments included: 1892 Waleska; 1893-94 Epworth; 1895 Covington; 1896 St. John, Atlanta; 1897 St. John and Nellie Dodd Memorial, Atlanta; 1898-1900 Park Street, Atlanta; 1901-02 Athens First; 1903 Elberton First; 1904-06 Milledgeville and Conference Missionary Secretary; 1907 Presiding Elder, Griffin District; 1908-11 Presiding Elder, Atlanta District; 1912 Presiding

Elder, Marietta District; 1913 Located. He was editor of the conference minutes 1893-94.

Joel T. Daves, Jr. from the 1892 and 1895 Conference Journals

Rufus K. Reaves, a trustee of the church since 1886, resigned his post in 1901, and was succeeded by Emmet J. Bondurant, who also served many years as the church Sunday School Superintendent and as a teacher. President of the UGA Class of 1888, he established Bondurant Hardware Company and the Georgia Plow and Foundry Company and was a trustee of the State Normal School. Three of his children died young, a son at age three, and daughters at ages 26 and 16. His two youngest children grew up to be respected leaders in our church in their own rights. John P. Bondurant II was on the trustees from 1943 to 1985 and published a history of the church and its trustees in 1988 (copies remain available through the church office as of this writing). Birdie Moss Bondurant married E. J. "Sandy" Clower, and both served in church leadership positions.

At the same meeting, Thomas H. Dozier resigned as trustee. He had been named church treasurer in 1894, a position he held until 1914. Dozier was Clarke County Superintendent of Schools for more than forty years. As a Confederate soldier, Dozier was wounded and captured at the Battle of Sharpsburg, where his brother and almost their entire company were wiped out. Dozier survived only by being protected by a Union soldier who realized he was a fellow Mason. Dozier was exchanged instead and returned to the service. After Lee's surrender, Dozier walked from Virginia to his home in Lexington, Georgia. He was succeeded as a trustee by James S. King.

❥ 1902 ❧

Athens First removed its old Johnson organ to install a new one which had a large bellows activated by a hydraulic pump. The trustees also had a new furnace installed to heat the sanctuary. The cost was $150 to be paid $75 when the work was completed and the final $75 "when it has been proven that the furnace will heat the building."

Former Athens First pastors John D. Hammond and John Wesley Heidt were elected to the North Georgia Conference delegation to the 1902 General Conference of the M.E. Church, South.

❥ 1903 ❧

Isaac Stiles Hopkins, Pastor, 1903-1906

Rev. Hopkins' biography rivals that of Gen. Clement Anselm Evans as unique among the many pastors of Athens First Methodist. Born in Augusta on June 20, 1841, Hopkins graduated from Emory College in 1859 and Augusta Medical College in 1861. He married Emily Gibson of Augusta in 1861; she died in 1873. A second wife, Mary Hinton, died in 1896. Hopkins served briefly in the Confederate Army. He later received master's and doctoral degrees from Emory and a Doctor of Divinity degree from Central College in Missouri. Admitted on trial in 1861, he became a deacon in full connection in 1863 and was ordained elder in 1867. His appointments were: 1862-63 and 1865 Columbia County and the Augusta Colored Mission; 1864 Richmond County and the Augusta Colored Mission; 1866 St. James; 1867 Harrisburg

Dr. Isaac Stiles Hopkins

Mission, Augusta; 1868 Waynesboro; 1869-74 Professor, Emory College; 1876-78 Professor, Southern University, Greensboro, Alabama; 1880-84 Professor, Emory College; 1885-88 President, Emory College (including in 1888 being pastor of the Oxford Circuit); 1889 Atlanta First; 1890-94 Merritts Avenue, Atlanta; 1890-95 Founding President, Georgia Institute of Technology; 1896-97 Atlanta First; 1898 Located; 1899-1901 St. John, St. Louis, Missouri; 1902 Centenary, Chattanooga, Tennessee; 1903-06 Athens First; 1907-08 LaGrange First; 1909 Supply. According to biographer Elam F. Dempsey, Hopkins was "tall, well proportioned, of elastic step, with a large head set well upon the column of his neck – hair abundant, auburn, lustrous, somewhat curly, crowning a massive white dome-like brow, an aquline nose, and well-modeled chin and mouth...a handsome, richly gifted man, both graceful and vigorous, the beau ideal of the orator of the Old South." At Emory, Hopkins taught natural sciences, Latin, English, and tool-craft and design, which program was formalized as the School of Technology at Emory. As president of Emory 1885-1888, Hopkins taught mental and moral science. During his presidency, the chair of the Emory trustees was Atticus G. Haygood. Hopkins left the Emory presidency at the end of 1888 and was succeeded by Warren A. Candler. Hopkins took appointment to Atlanta First in 1889 and to Merritts Avenue Church in 1890, adjacent to the site chosen for the new Georgia Tech campus. Hopkins helped organize the new institute and in 1890 was named founding president of the Georgia Institute of Technology, a position he held until 1896. He stepped down from the Tech presidency, determined to return to fulltime ministry. For three years beginning in 1899 he pastored St. John's Church in St. Louis, then spent a year at Centenary Church in Chattanooga before returning to North Georgia where he was appointed pastor of Athens First for four years beginning in 1903. He had the unique experience of conducting in the UGA Chapel the 1906 memorial service for Athens First member and

UGA Chancellor Walter B. Hill, who died in office the previous autumn. As such, Hopkins was the former president of both Emory and Georgia Tech speaking as pastor of the UGA chancellor, recounting Hill's deep involvement in the Methodist church at-large and at Athens First. Hopkins concluded his illustrious career with two years at LaGrange First before taking supply status in 1909. He died in Atlanta on February 3, 1914. A funeral train carried his body to Covington, with an entire car of the train being devoted to the many floral arrangements. A large contingent met the train for a procession to the historic Methodist cemetery at Oxford, including current and former college trustees, former church parishioners, Georgia Tech and Emory officials and faculty, and virtually the entire Emory student body. The service was conducted by retired Atlanta pastor William Fisk Glenn and Emory President and future Bishop James E. Dickey (great-grandfather of this author). The gateway dedicated in 1937 as Emory's "front door" in Atlanta is the Haygood-Hopkins Memorial Gateway, recognizing Hopkins alongside Atticus Haygood as "builders of the New South."

9**1905** 9

UGA Chancellor Walter B. Hill (the position today known as President) died in 1905 and was succeeded by another long-time Athens First member, David C. Barrow, an 1874 UGA graduate. An active member of the the the church Board of Stewards since 1890, he continued in this role while UGA chancellor. He was a popular professor of mathematics and engineering, a department head, and served as a dean under Chancellor Hill. Barrow would serve as UGA Chancellor until his retirement in 1925. He died in 1929. His namesakes include Barrow County, Barrow Elementary School in Athens, Barrow Hall at UGA, and the Barrow Chair in Mathematics there. UGA students knew him affectionately as "Uncle Dave."

9**1906** 9

The original Athens First parsonage was replaced by a new one constructed on the same site adjacent to the church at the corner of Lumpkin and Washington Streets at a cost of $6,000. The trustees

David C. Barrow, Jr. (1852-1929)

109

"Uncle Dave" Barrow
(photos from Hargrett Rare
Book and Manuscript
Library, University of
Georgia Libraries)

also voted to improve a further portion of the sanctuary basement for use as an infant classroom.

Former Athens First pastors John D. Hammond and John Wesley Heidt were elected members of the North Georgia Conference delegation to the General Conference of the M.E. Church, South for a second quadrennium.

୨1907୨

Luke G. Johnson, Pastor, 1907-1908

Born June 22, 1859, in Oglethorpe County, Johnson was admitted on trial and was licensed to preach in 1881, became a deacon in full connection in 1883, and was ordained elder in 1885. His first appointments were in the Little Rock Conference: 1882 Saline; 1883 Gurdon Circuit; 1884 Gurdon; and 1885 Amity Circuit. Transferring to North Georgia, he was appointed: 1886 Royston; 1887-88 Located at own request; 1889 Decatur and Clarkston; 1890 Decatur. He moved to North Alabama Conference for two years, appointed in 1891 to Sheffield and in 1892 to Florence. Returning to North Georgia: 1893 Bethlehem; 1894 Presiding Elder, Athens District; 1895-96 St. James, Augusta; 1897-1900 Dalton First; 1901-04 Park Street, Atlanta; 1905-06 Rome First; 1907-08 Athens First; 1909 St. John, Augusta; 1910-13 Presiding Elder, Gainesville District; 1914 Trinity, Atlanta; 1915-17 Grace, Atlanta; 1918-19 Newnan; 1920-23 Presiding Elder, Griffin District; 1924 Supply. Rev. Johnson died June 2, 1948, in Atlanta.

ꙮ**1908**ꙮ

Trustee James S. King died after only seven years on the board, during which time he oversaw the construction of the new parsonage. A noted Athens merchant, at the church he chaired the Board of Stewards, the Board of Trustees, and the North Georgia Conference finance committee. He was a faithful teacher of a children's Sunday School class for many years. He was succeeded as trustee by Augustus Wylie Dozier, who owned a lumber company with his brothers. Dozier was on the city board of education and served 40 years on the church Board of Stewards. His homes were at 594 Hill Street and 760 Meigs Street. He was a trustee until his death in 1948.

In September 1908 the Trustees increased the size of the board to seven in accord with a change in the Discipline of the Methodist Episcopal Church, South, electing Thomas Fletcher Johnson "Tom" Comer and David F. Miller. Comer was a fourth-generation member of Athens First and ran a grocery store on Clayton Street. Miller, a native Pennsylvanian, was a cotton merchant.

The trustees approved adding a water closet to the basement level under the sanctuary near the new infant classroom, but before the work commenced it was decided to delay pending larger renovations to the church which were being discussed. A major renovation to the sanctuary would come in 1910.

ꙮ**1909**ꙮ

Marcellus Littleton Troutman, Jr., Pastor, 1909-1912

Pastor Marcellus L. Troutman was born August 23, 1861, at Oxford, Ga. His mother was sister to our 1842 pastor Walter R. Branham, Sr., making Troutman a first cousin to Walter R. Branham, Jr., associate pastor in charge of Oconee Street Mission in 1878-79. Troutman attended Emory College in his hometown for two years before transferring to the University of Georgia, where he earned Bachelor of Law and Doctor of Divinity degrees. He married Elizabeth "Bessie" Batty in 1883, and they were parents of five children. Having been converted in a service at Morrison's Campground in Floyd County, Troutman was licensed to preach in 1893, admitted on trial in 1894, became a deacon in 1895, was granted full connection in 1896, and was ordained elder in 1898. His appointments were: 1895-96 Harlem; 1897-99 Lyerly; 1900 Harmony Grove, Elberton; 1901-02 Conyers; 1903 Conyers and Factory Mission; 1904 Gainesville First; 1905-08 Park Street,

Atlanta (and in 1908, plus Bonnie Brae, Atlanta); and 1909-12 Athens First. While he was at Athens, UGA conferred upon him the degree Bachelor of Law in recognition of his three years of law study. UGA further granted him an honorary Doctor of Divinity degree. The "Georgia boys" were said to hold him in high regard. Rev. Troutman was ill most of the month of June 1912, and finally succumbed July 5, 1912, to an attack of appendicitis at only age 50. Athens mourned him greatly, with most buildings, public and private, closing during the time of his funeral. Rev. Troutman's daughter, Grace Troutman, married Dr. Robert C. Wilson, a member of Athens First and founding dean of the UGA College of Pharmacy, who died in 1981 at the age of 102. Dean Wilson was great-great-grandson of Rev. Lovick Pierce, the church's first appointed pastor. Their children included a daughter, Grace Wilson, and sons, Troutman Wilson and Robert Wilson. Grace Wilson married Dr. Kenneth Waters, who succeeded his father-in- law as dean of the UGA College of Pharmacy in 1948, serving until 1977. Dean Waters died in 1996 and his widow, Grace Wilson Waters, remained an active member at Athens First until her passing in 2008. Troutman Wilson, an Athens banker, succeeded his father as a trustee of Athens First Church, serving until his death in 1998. Troutman Wilson's two daughters, Jody Warner (and husband Richard) and Beth Lowrey (and husband Mack), are lifelong members of Athens First UMC today. Jody and Beth not only are great-great-granddaughters of Rev. Marcellus Troutman, but through their Wilson line are four-great-granddaughters of founding pastor Lovick Pierce. The next two generations are here, as well, including Jay Boling, Jo and Lee Sullivan and their children, and Will and Marcie Cochran and their children.

Grace Wilson Waters and
Dean Kenneth Waters

FIRST METHODIST FAMILY OF THE YEAR
THE TROUTMAN WILSONS

A LONG FAMILY LINE OF MEMORIES

JODY WARNER

Like many other Athens First families, my family has worshipped and served this church for generations. As I sit in the sanctuary on Sunday mornings, I can feel the warm presence of my parents, grandparents, and my ancestors. Some of my family members have served as pastors, going back to Lovick Pierce, who in 1825 became the first appointed pastor of the church. My parents and grandparents considered it a privilege to serve with their time and their talents. I am awash with memories of growing up in the church—of sitting in the same pew, third row from the front, every Sunday, next to my grandfather. He had an endless supply of mints to keep a restless little girl quiet while we listened to the sermons of a long line of outstanding ministers. These are cherished happy memories and I reflect on how many Sundays my family and I have looked at the beautiful stained glass windows. This church has been the site of the most important events in my family's life—births and baptisms, communions and confirmations, rehearsals and weddings. I think about my loved ones who have gone on before me and my long-gone ancestors who preceded

Jody and Richard Warner

them—we are bound together by family ties and our love of Athens First. It is with gratitude and blessing that I call Athens First my home church and hope that my children and grandchildren will continue to worship and serve the church.

YOUNG HARRIS CHURCH

A second mission church grew out of the Athens First, named for prominent Athenian and Athens First member Young L.G. Harris. Originally located on the eastern side of Chase Street at Nantahala Avenue, the church had 112 charter members in 1909 and built a parsonage at 685 Boulevard. In 1912 the church moved to a a handsome wooden building on Boulevard at Chase Street. The building was remodeled in 1922 when George Acree was pastor. He later would serve as pastor at Athens First. An annex was built in 1930. Mr. Eustace W. Lampkin gave the church $10,000 for remodeling and repairs, but rather than spend the funds on the existing physical plant, the Young Harris Methodist Church leadership determined to sell that property in 1945-46 and purchased the home of Judge E. K. Lumpkin on Prince Avenue at Prince Place. The home was remodeled to provide a sanctuary, classrooms and a kitchen. Ground was broken for a new, permanent sanctuary building which was completed in 1949 next door to the former Lumpkin home. The Young Harris congregation disaffiliated from the United Methodist Church in 2023 and re-named itself The Bridge Community Church.

ᔈ1910 ᔇ

The Athens First sanctuary building was completely remodeled, with the pulpit being moved from the west end to the Lumpkin Street end and additional Sunday School rooms added at a total cost of $25,000. The Board of Trustees approved issuance of $10,000 in bonds which were paid off over the next twelve years to finance the balance on the work. The steeple, standing since 1852, received a new ornament at its pinnacle - a six-foot weathervane, the arrow fabricated by church trustee Emmet J. Bondurant and mounted on a bicycle hub to rotate freely.

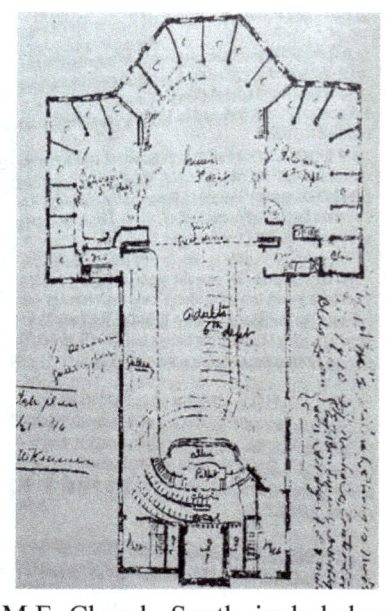

The newly remodeled sanctuary of Athens First for the sixth time hosted Annual Conference, Bishop John C. Kilgo and Bishop Luther B. Wilson presiding.

The 1910 General Conference of the M.E. Church, South, included as delegates from North Georgia two former Athens First clergy: John D. Hammond and W. P. Lovejoy.

114

Sunday School Superintendent Emmett J. Bondurant noted that the church's very large and growing Sunday School program lacked a class for men. He delegated Nat G. Slaughter to form such a class. With an initial group of ten men, it was decided to have four teachers rotate. But after just eight weeks (two rotations) it was determined that one of them, Col. H. C. Tuck, should be the permanent teacher. Col. Tuck would teach the class for more than 25 years, considering it "the crowning achievement of his life." The class eventually was named for Tuck. A native of Clarke County and a graduate of the

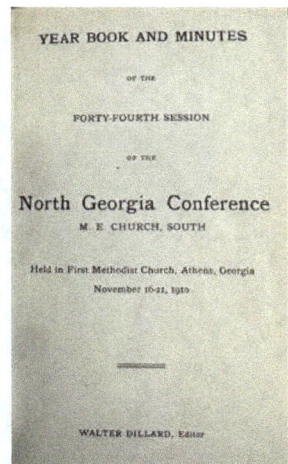

University of Georgia, Tuck was an Athens lawyer who was elected the youngest mayor in Athens history and was elected to the General Assembly. In 1927, Governor Lamartine G. Hardman appointed him Judge of City Court of Athens, a position he held the remainder of his life. Tuck was succeeded as teacher by Thomas Walter Reed, also a UGA graduate and editor of the *Athens Daily Banner* newspaper. In 1910, Reed was named Registrar and Treasurer of the University of Georgia, a position he held the rest of his life. He was close friend and biographer of UGA Chancellor

The photo above appears to be from the 1910 dedication of the newly renovated sanctuary, or it could be from the session of the North Georgia Annual Conference held in the sanctuary that year, the sixth time our church had hosted the conference.
The area shown is occupied today by our sanctuary's balcony.

The Tuck Class meets in the sanctuary, approximately 1930s. Howard Jordan was the teacher.

The Tuck Sunday School Class about 1983

Archie Patterson teaching the Tuck Class in 2000, when it was located in the sanctuary building basement where the choir offices and robing rooms now are located.

David Barrow. The Tuck Class celebrated its 100th anniversary in 2010, and at this writing, continues to meet weekly as the longest-running Sunday School class at Athens First by far.

❥**1911** ❥

The Board of Trustees at the first session of 1911 comprised Emmett J. Bondurant, Thomas Comer, A. W. Dozier, E. R. Hodgson, John A. Hunnicutt, D. F. Miller and R. L. Moss, Sr.

The House, Heating and Light Committee of the church was responsible for building a fire in the boiler each Sunday in time to warm the church for Sunday School and worship. The church remained uncomfortably chilly in winter, with the water-hammer from the pipes drowning out the service at times. The boiler was not started for Wednesday evening choir practice, so the members stayed in their overcoats throughout. Meetings of church committees such as the Board of Stewards rarely were held in the church building during the winter, as it was too cold. They would meet instead in the offices or home of one of the board members, and occasionally in the parsonage.

THE TUCK CLASS
BY BOBBY POSS

The Tuck Sunday School Class taught me the most powerful way you can influence people is to lead them closer to Jesus. I started at Athens First UMC in 1968 and had the opportunity to learn about God's word from Rev. Bill Britt, Rev. Chuck Hodges and now Rev. Jeremy Lawson. These gentlemen have helped me to grow closer to the Lord each day.

Bobby Poss

I didn't find my way to the Tuck Class until after my dad, Bob Poss, Jr., had passed. He was a longtime Tuck member. When I arrived in 1999, I was by far the youngest young man in the class. It was then on the bottom floor of the sanctuary building [where the choir robing rooms and offices are today]. I came into that first class – all men – and had to move out of the seat I had chosen three different times because I was in a member's seat – Fred Birchmore's and two others. Each member comes in, puts their offering in the little handmade wooden bowl on the table, and finds his seat.

For many years it's been my task in Tuck to pick out the hymns we sing each Sunday. I write the numbers on the board before members arrive. I always add a good memo on the board, such as "When I focus on God, I can weather any storm." And one of my favorites is, "We cough to clear our throats; we sigh to clear our hearts."

We always sing first and last verse of each hymn, and on the last song we all stand up "as you are able," and close with the Lord's Prayer. Our hymn books are the Cokesbury and Spiritual Life – we like oldies and goodies.

Tuck's class president asks for concerns or business, and then there is a roll call – each name is called and it's obvious when someone is absent.

We've always had outstanding teachers. To name a few: Cal Logue, Bob Carson, Al Hawley, Coach Jon Ward, and Dianne Morrison. And let's not forget our wonderful piano players: Claire Swann, Marianna Miller, Pam Ward, and Jack Merrill. And I want to name some unforgettable members over the years: Ed Benson, Lamar Wansley, the Birchmores - Fred and Boots, M.O. Phelps, Clyde Harris, Charlie Burch and Bucky Redwine. John Bondurant wrote a history of the Tuck Class in 2000.

I love my church. "The one who does the will of God lives forever." (1 John 2:17) Wth the strength of God and my church, I am fully capable and up to whatever faces me.

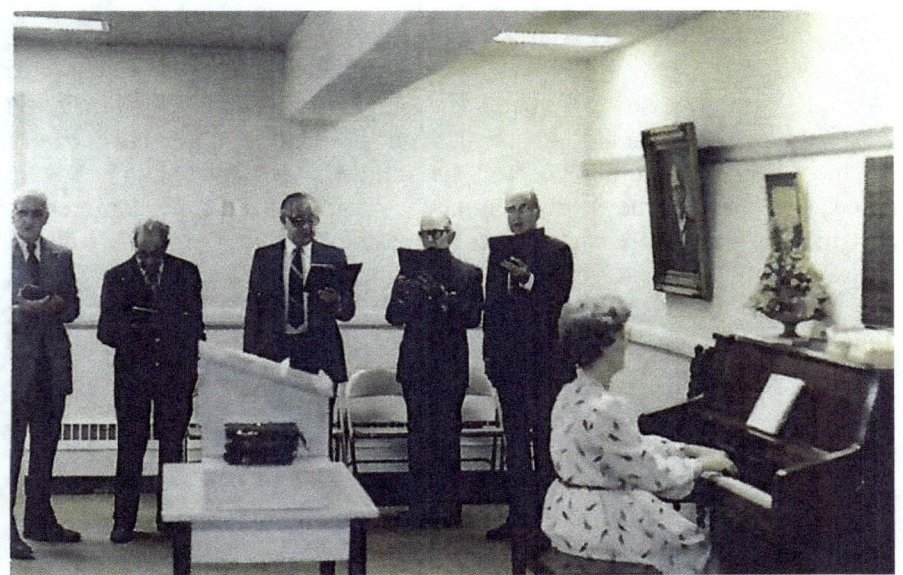

The Tuck Class song leaders about 1987

The first Quarterly Conference report of 1911 showed 599 students in the Sunday School taught by 74 teachers. Pastor Marcellus Troutman reported, "The Sunday School is growing steadily and has the best organization and is doing the most efficient work in its history. I know of nothing in the bounds of the conference its equal in the classwork and the enthusiasm of every member." He noted that the Epworth League (forerunner of what came to be known as the Methodist Youth Fellowship, or MYF) had been absorbed into two Sunday School classes serving that age group. Church membership stood at 1,121. The preacher's salary was $3,000 and the total church budget for the year $7,226. The recent renovations to the sanctuary building left the church with a debt of $12,000.

A report later that year showed eleven church members were away at college: one at Emory and the other ten elsewhere. Quarterly Conference held November 10, 1911 at Athens First was presided over by the resident bishop of North Georgia, Luther B. Wilson.

ම1912 ම

James C. Morris, Interim Pastor, July-December 1912

Upon the death of Rev. Marcellus L. Troutman in July 1912, mid-year of his appointment, Rev. J. C. Morris was sent to Athens First as interim pastor. *The Athens Banner* of July 19, 1912 announced the arrival at First Methodist Church of its new pastor: "He will be accompanied by his wife and they will take up their residence at the parsonage on Lumpkin Street.... He is one of the most distinguished preachers in the Southern Methodist church, having filled a number of the most prominent appointments in the conferences in which he has labored, including the pastorate of the largest Methodist church in St. Louis, and has been for a number of years president of Central College." In doing so, he followed a path set by two of his predecessors: John Dennis Hammond who had served at St. Louis First and as President of Central College, as well, and Anderson Joseph Jarrell, who also served at First Church, St. Louis. Morris served six months until the appointment of Rev. C. C. Jarrell to Athens for the new conference year of 1913. During that brief period, Morris reported 19 baptisms (five infants, 14 adults), and the reception of 43 new members, all by transfer from other churches. The Quarterly Conference adopted a resolution requesting the bishop to appoint Morris to Athens First permanently, but that did not happen.

The Board of Stewards authorized E. J. Bondurant, chair of the Board of Trustees, to sell at half price the asbestos pipe coverings left from the recent renovation project.

Trustee Rufus LaFayette Moss died and was succeeded by Edward Deloney Sledge, Sr. Sledge was an Athens native whose wife, Mary Newton Cobb, was daughter of Howell Cobb. Sledge ran a hardware store on Washington Street at the site of the current county courthouse parking lot. He was on the Athens Board of Education and a founder of Athens Savings and Loan Association, From his obituary: "He was a reserved person who never intruded his ideas, and this quality served only to lend more weight to his opinions when they were voiced."

๑1913 ๑

Charles Crawford Jarrell, Pastor, 1913-1916

Born November 14, 1874, in Milledgeville, Charles Jarrell graduated from Emory College in 1894, was licensed to preach and admitted on trial that same year, granted full connection as a deacon in 1898, and was ordained an elder in 1901. He married Margaret Moore on July 2, 1901. Rev. Jarrell graduated from Emory College with honors. At a time when advanced

A CENTURY'S WORTH OF STORIES TO TELL
FRED BIRCHMORE

Fred Birchmore was a fixture in Athens First for a full century. Born in 1912, his childhood home was two blocks from the church on Dougherty Street. Quite the raconteur, he told many stories of his interesting life. One of his favorites was of how when he was a young boy his bedroom window faced toward the church. With his windows open to let in the fresh air, and the morning sun gleaming in, he would awake each morning to a view of the church steeple – the first thing he would see every day. Athens First became a cornerstone of his life physically, emotionally, spiritually, a reminder every waking morning of its close presence in his life.

Willa Deane and Fred Birchmore in 1990

Fred indeed led a storied life, beating a very serious cancer and becoming the first person ever to circumnavigate the globe on a bicycle. He walked down all 896 steps of the Washington Monument on his hands, and late in his life he was likely to flip up into a handstand at a moment's notice, just to show that he still could.

His estate at the end of Milledge Terrace backed up to Memorial Park, for which he donated 25 acres years ago and where the Birchmore Trail bears his name. He called his home "Happy Hollow," and around it he built a massive rock wall by hand, hauling huge boulders he found all over Georgia in the back seat of his family car. He tore up the car seat, to his dear wife Willa Deane's chagrin, but he had a magnificent rock wall, twice as tall as Fred, dubbed "The Great Wall of Happy Hollow."

At the church, he was often the song leader – in the Tuck Class, in Administrative Board meetings, in worship services, it was Fred who would be up front encouraging everyone to sing. He was named an honorary lifetime member of the Administrative Board.

The church held a grand celebration of Fred's 100th birthday in November 2012, but sadly he was hospitalized on the big day and missed the party. He died in March 2013, four months beyond his 100th birthday milestone.

education was unusual in the Methodist ministry, he studied further in science, philosophy and theology at the University of Berlin, Germany, under Adolph Harnack, a leading scholar in historical theology. He was described as "scholarly in habit but a pastor at heart." His appointments were: 1896 Madison; 1897-99 Professor, Emory College; 1900 Student, Vanderbilt; 1901 Young Harris, Marietta; 1902 Jasper; 1903-05 College Park (and Factory Mission in 1904); 1906-08 Grace, Atlanta; 1909 Rome First; 1910-11 Rome First and Pansy Chapel; 1912 Student, Glasgow, Scotland; 1913-16 Athens First. In March 1916, with the decision to relocate Emory College to Druid Hills and create Emory University, Rev. Jarrell was named Conference Secretary of Education, also known as Commissioner of Emory University. Rev. J. C. Morris, who preceded him at Athens as an interim pastor, came to Athens First again to fill the unexpired term. Upon Jarrell's departure, a resolution by the Athens Board of Stewards said, "He leaves the church with a largely increased membership, full of zeal and determination, and, as we believe, consecrated to its good work." Jarrell continued his service at Emory through 1919, followed by these further appointments: 1920-23 St. John, Augusta (and Broadway, Augusta in 1921); 1924-34 Secretary, General Hospital Board; 1935-38 Presiding Elder, Athens-Elberton District; 1939- 41 St. John, Augusta; 1942-43 Monroe; 1944 Agent, Methodist Children's Home; 1945 Supply. Of his two appointments to St. John, Augusta, 16 years apart, future Bishop William R. Cannon wrote in Jarrell's conference memoriam that this was "unusual in the accomplishments of any Methodist preacher. Even the most effective of ministers dare not begin again where they left off." He was a delegate to General Conference seven times 1918-39. He served on the boards of trustees at Paine, Reinhardt and Wesleyan colleges. Jarrell retired in 1944, residing in retirement at Oxford, but continuing to offer active service throughout the conference. At the time of his death on November 26, 1961, his 63 years on the roll of the North Georgia Conference made him its longest-serving member. He was buried in the historic cemetery at Oxford.

Pastor C. C. Jarrell reported the communion service held May 4, 1913 to be "the largest ever held in Athens. It was certainly the largest I have ever seen in my ministry." In that same report, he noted the Sunday School had its largest attendance ever at 800, with so many students that one class was meeting in the church kitchen. The year's offering for missions was $3,500, raised in an "every member canvass," including $750 from the Moss family to support a missionary in a foreign field in memory of the late Athens First member R. L. Moss, Sr. And as to church attendance, "We have a house full every Sunday. The night congregations have increased to about 200. We have a great church teeming with power and full of talent."

Given this report, it did not follow that the church continued having difficulty making timely payments of the pastor's monthly salary. Members of the Board of Stewards were given lists of names of church members on whom to make personal calls seeking additional contributions. Additionally, the ladies of the church agreed to undertake a fundraising campaign among themselves to pay the $80 for recently purchased hymn books, thereby freeing those funds for the pastor's salary. The finance committee was directed to mail a statement to each church member in arrears on their pledge payments. If these methods failed, the church treasurer was authorized to take out a loan rather than miss the salary payment. From October to the end of the year, the finance committee met every Tuesday at 8 p.m. to manage the cash flow of the church. At the first meeting of November, an additional meeting was set for the coming Friday evening, "and the treasurer will be asked to bring his books for the purpose of going over the names of delinquent members." That meeting determined a report to the full congregation on the financial condition of the church was necessary at services on the following Sunday. At its next meeting, the finance committee learned "the financial status is reassuring in that funds are in sight to meet all obligations of the conference year."

The Quarterly Conference of Athens First endorsed a plan from the District Conference to erect a large tent on the property of the Seaboard rail depot for the purpose of conducting a "meeting" to start a new Sunday School to be sponsored by the District. It is not clear whether the proposal was implemented. Whether it is connected is not apparent, but on an adjacent page in the same report, Pastor C. C. Jarrell wrote of Athens First's own Sunday School, "We are on the brink of the biggest work our School has ever seen. We call on this Board to pray and pull for the School."

The City of Athens contacted the church about plans to pave Lumpkin and Washington Streets and Hancock Avenue bordering the church property, part of a plan to pave all downtown streets for the first time. The impact on the church would be significant as adjacent property owners would be assessed based on street frontage, which for the church at that time was a full block on Lumpkin and a half-block each on Hancock and Washington. For some years the church made payments on its share of this project, at least until 1917, although the amount of its obligation is not clear.

The church asked that the city deny an application for a beer license for an establishment at the corner of Hull and Washington Streets. The city denied the license.

1914

Former Athens First Pastor W. P. Lovejoy was a member of the North Georgia delegation to the 1914 General Conference of the M.E. Church, South.

In January 1914, Pastor C. C. Jarrell reported congregations "have been remarkably fine, filling our auditorium, galleries and all, with chairs in the aisles at times. The large numbers of students is noticeable."

The Board of Stewards adopted "a resolution of thanks to the church choir for the excellent services rendered" while expressing regrets that the choir director, Mrs. Richardson, had tendered her resignation.

The downtown Athens churches conferred over what could be done "to reduce the noises on the streets during regular hours of worship." One might imagine what it was like to hold worship services with the windows wide open.

The church continued to have cash flow concerns, at times having to contact members directly during a given week to update their pledge payments so that the payroll could be met. In the summers of 1913 and 1914, it was determined to suspend printing of Sunday bulletins for June through August to save money. In February 1915, a further motion failed which would have done away with printed bulletins altogether. A revival planned for October 1914 was approved, but the pastor was informed any expenses needed to be paid from collections taken at each evening's services. A proposal to set up an index card system to track each church member's giving was deferred until the costs of the cards could be ascertained. For the almost 90 years of the church's existence to that point, individual giving was collected and tracked by the Steward to whom that member was assigned. Through these years, members made specific pledges to various parts of the church budget: pastor's salary, general budget, and conference collections. The Sunday School also had significant collections and operated under its own board and budget, at times being called upon to help the Stewards pay the church's bills. The Trustees maintained a third, separate budget.

In October 1914, Captain Thomas Dozier asked to step down after twenty years as the church treasurer. In accepting his retirement from this extended volunteer duty, the Board of Stewards adopted a resolution authored by UGA Chancellor David C. Barrow and UGA Registrar Thomas W. Reed noting Dozier's "exactness" and his "cheerful hopefulness" which they found to be "inspiring." Barrow and Reed were the closest of friends, and Reed later became Barrow's biographer.

◉1915 ◉

At the beginning of 1915, membership at Athens First Methodist was 1,227, and Sunday School enrollment was even larger at 1,588. The pastor's salary was $2,400 per year and the total funds raised for the year were $14,345. At a March meeting, the Board of Stewards was so concerned at the $10.20 electric bill for the month that they shifted the janitor's hours to daytime, and in April they voted to change all the light bulbs in the building to tungsten or mazda lights to be more enegy efficient. Subsequently, the electric bill for May and June combined was $4.72. The church stewards in November agreed to pay the interest on a bank loan taken out by the pastor while the church was behind on his salary. It was agreed that no longer would the church be late on meeting the payroll and would borrow money if necessary to pay the pastor and staff their due in full. Emmett J. Bondurant submitted his resignation as Sunday School Superintendent for the coming year, but by unanimous vote the Quarterly Conference refused to accept the resignation.

◉1916 ◉

James C. Morris, Interim Pastor, March-December 1916

In a November 8, 1915 telegram from Birmingham, former interim pastor Rev. James C. Morris wrote Dean Jere Pound, Athens First layman, "Should be happy to see my dear people once more but have been under physician's care for a month, not in bed but unfitted for work. We send message of sincere love. You are ever in our prayers." Within four months, Rev. Morris indeed was back in Athens for another round as interim pastor following the mid-term appointment of Rev. C. C. Jarrell as Conference Secretary of Education (also called "Commissioner of Emory University"). Thus, Rev. Morris's interim appointments bookended Rev. Jarrell's time at Athens First. His service was well-received, with a significant contribution being a revision of the church register, the official roll book. *The Athens*

Banner-Herald of December 21, 1928 reports the death of Rev. Morris, and while replete with praise gives no details of the date and place of his passing.

The Stewards routinely took up offerings among themselves to assist the poor and needy of the church. In February 1916, for example, they raised $17 after determining the following needs among members:

- A mother with five children, whose husband was gone looking for work $2.50
- A family with four children, and the husband very sick $3.00
- Husband out of work, wife very sick, and two children with diphteria $5.00
- Four orphan children, the the two oldest becoming sick $2.00
- A mother not well, caring for a crippled child $2.50
- Parents with four children, entire family sick $2.00

Apparently beset with staff and church members buying items from local merchants and charging them to the church without prior approval, the Board of Stewards adopted a requisition system. Purchases were not to be made without written approval (in duplicate) from the appropriate committee chair of the board, and local merchants were to be notified not to extend credit to the church without such an approved purchase order.

At the October 17, 1916 meeting, the Board of Stewards discussed a proposed resolution from T. W. Reed specifying a particular clergy member of Annual Conference that the church would refuse to accept as a pastoral appointment. Upon discussion, Reed withdrew his motion pending a committee to draft a more acceptable resolution. A committee of three, J. D. Moss, R. E. Park and E. D. Sledge, brought to the October 24th meeting a resolution that a committee of three be appointed to go to Annual Conference the following month to secure an acceptable pastoral appointment, in that the interim pastor, Rev. James C. Morris, again would not assent to being appointed permanently. The resolution was adopted, but not before Reed attempted to amend it to include the name of the clergy member he did not want appointed to Athens. The proposed amendment lost, with only Reed voting in favor. Another steward then made a motion to strike from the minutes the clergy name that had been under discussion, but the vote was 5-4 to leave the name in the minutes. It remains there if any reader ever wants to look it up, but we choose not to place it here. The following week,

Reed tried again, which resolution likewise was not adopted. A motion to expunge his proposed motion from the record lost on a vote of 9-3. In the end, the person Reed did not want to accept was not appointed to Athens.

∋1917 ∋

Samuel Robinson Belk, Pastor, 1917-1918

Born March 21, 1857, in Union County, North Carolina, Belk was consecrated for the ministry by his mother before his birth. She promised God that if her unborn were a son, she would dedicate him to ministry, name him

for the prophet Samuel and for her pastor, Rev. D. P. Robinson. Belk joined the Presbyterian Church near his home at age 11. He attended Jackson Forest Academy and graduated with a master's degree from Rutherford College, North Carolina in 1882. He earned a Doctor of

Rev. Samuel Robinson Belk

Divinity degree from the University of Georgia in 1909. In 1886, he married Joanna Catherine Council and the couple had five children. He joined the Methodist Church at Pleasant Grove, N.C. in 1884, and that same year was admitted on trial and licensed to preach by the North Carolina Conference, being appointed in 1885-86 to Carver's Creek Circuit in Wilmington. He became a deacon in full connection in 1886 and transferred to the Denver Conference, appointed to Pueblo, Colorado. He was ordained elder in 1888. He transferred to the North Georgia Conference in fall 1889 and served these appointments: 1890 Villa Rica; 1891-92 Payne Memorial, Atlanta; 1893-94 Gainesville First; 1895-98 Rome First; 1899-1900 Elberton; 1901-02 Marietta; 1903-06 St. James, Augusta; 1907-10 St. Mark, Atlanta; 1911 Park Street, Bonnie Brae and Oakland, Atlanta; 1912-13 Park Street, Atlanta; 1914-16 Presiding Elder, Gainesville District; 1917-18 Athens First; 1919-24 Trinity, Atlanta; 1925-28 Grace, Atlanta. He served as trustee at Wesleyan, LaGrange and Young Harris colleges. By his own account, Rev. Belk held 215 revivals, married more than 3,000 people, buried more than 4,000, baptized 1,500 infants, received 22,000 members into the church, left

315 sermons, four lectures, and five books of prayer. He could proudly claim he never missed a session of Annual, Quarterly or District Conferences in 44 years. While serving as pastor at Grace, Atlanta, he died unexpectedly on May 25, 1928, while participating in Commencement as a trustee at Wesleyan College in Macon. He was buried in Crest Lawn Memorial Park, Atlanta.

During World War I, a large "service flag" with some fifty stars on it hung from a skylight in the Sunday School section of the building, at the rear (west end) and open to the main sanctuary. Each star represented a church member in the military. Solemn ceremonies were held marking the deaths of five members during the war. On each occasion, the flag was lowered and a gold star sewn over one of the white ones.

1918

Dean Jere M. Pound of the State Normal School at Athens became the first lay member of Athens First Methodist Church to be elected to General Conference of which we are aware. The North Georgia clergy delegation to the 1918 General Conference included former Athens First pastor Charles C. Jarrell and future pastor William P. King.

The ladies of the Parsonage Society sought permission to host a paid lecture for the purpose of raising funds to refurnish the parsonage. The Trustees expressed sympathy with the goal but declined the request under a church policy that its facilities not be used for entertainment with paid admission.

1919

At Annual Conference in December 1918, it was announced and was printed in the Conference Journal that Rev. C. O. Jones, previously of Grace and St. Mark churches in Atlanta, would be appointed to Athens First for the year 1920. In what clearly was a last-minute turn of events, Rev. Jones instead was sent to Griffin, and Rev. Elam F. Dempsey came to Athens to begin what would be a two-year term. We believe this came from a last-minute decision by Dempsey to leave the Emory faculty rather than move with the College from Oxford to Druid Hills that year. Dr. Nat Slaughter was a lay delegate for the Athens District in 1919.

Elam Franklin Dempsey, Pastor, 1919-1920

Born in Atlanta on July 6, 1878, Elam Dempsey graduated from Emory College in 1899 and earned a bachelor of divinity degree from Vanderbilt in 1906.He married Georgia Page Hunnicutt in 1906.Dempsey was admitted on trial and licensed to preach in 1899, became a deacon in full connection in 1901 and was ordained elder in 1903. His appointments were: 1900 Atlanta City Mission; 1901-02 Turin; 1903 Lincolnton and Mission; 1904-06 Student, Vanderbilt; 1907-08 Dahlonega; 1909 Broadway, Augusta; 1910

Rev. Elam Franklin Dempsey

Trinity, Atlanta; 1911-14 Milledgeville; 1915-19 Professor, Emory College, (including Dean of Theology 1917-19); 1920 Athens First and Milledge Avenue, Athens; 1921 Rome First; 1922-26 Conference Secretary of Education; 1927-30 Presiding Elder, Oxford District; 1922-30 Professor of Biblical Literature, Emory University; 1931-32 Editor, *Wesleyan Christian Advocate*; 1933-34 Madison; 1935-38 Toccoa; 1939 leave; 1940-48 Secretary, North Georgia Conference Historical Society. An effusive church historian, Dempsey was a daily columnist for the *Atlanta Constitution* during his retirement. He was a faculty member at Emory College when the decision was made to move the school from Oxford to a new campus in Druid Hills. Dempsey was among faculty who chose to return to the fulltime pastorate rather than make the campus move, and his first appointment at that time was to Athens First, and to a Methodist Church proposed for Milledge Avenue in Athens. He was elected a delegate to General Conference in 1922 and 1924 and served as a reserve in 1918 and 1926. He was a trustee of Emory College 1914-21, of Emory University 1922-30, and of LaGrange and Reinhardt Colleges. Rev. Dempsey died September 19, 1947, and is buried in Westview Cemetery, Atlanta. Dempsey authored biographies of two bishops of his era: *Life of Bishop Dickey: Bishop of the Methodist Episcopal Church, South*. Nashville: Methodist Episcopal Church South Publishing House, 1937; and *Atticus Green Haygood: he took the kingdom by violence Matthew 11:12*. Nashville, Parthenon Press, 1940; and was editor of *Who's Who in Pan-Methodism*, Nashville, Parthenon Press, 1940.

ᵍ1920 ᵎ

In February 1920, Edward Reginald Hodgson died after 30 years as a trustee. The president of Hodgson Oil Company, known to his friends as "Mr. Prince," he was an original trustee of the Georgia Institute of Technology. Elected to succeed him as a trustee at Athens Methodist was Madison G. Nicholson, Sr., an Athens native, 1888 University of Georgia graduate with a degree in engineering, and Athens merchant whose dry goods store fronted on both Clayton and Washington Streets along the west side of Jackson Street. He was on the Athens Board of Education, the YMCA board, founding president of the Athens Chamber of Commerce, and a charter member of the Athens Rotary Club. He was treasurer at the church for 31 years, treasurer of the Sunday School 45 years, and served as a church trustee for 39 years until his death in 1959.

ᵍ1921 ᵎ

Walter Anthony, Pastor, 1921-1922

Admitted on trial in 1914, Rev. Anthony's appointments included St. Mark, Atlanta before his appointment to Athens and Milledge Avenue, Athens in 1921. After two years in our pulpit, he transferred out, perhaps to the South Georgia Conference, as he is recorded as serving at Eastman in 1930. We have not been successful in locating a service record – a note some future researcher may add.

The Athens Baptist Church built a new sanctuary building at the corner of Pulaski Street and Hancock Avenue (its location today) to replace its former building downtown at College and Washington. Athens First Methodist volunteered its facilities for use by the Baptists for worship during their construction period, which offer was gratefully acknowledged. If they utilized the Methodist building, it likely was only during the actual move of church furnishings, as the Baptists still occupied their former building while the new one was under construction.

As Athens First approached the Centennial of its 1825 founding, Mrs. Marianna Frierson asked to place a marble tablet in the vestibule of the church commemorating her great-grandfather, Thomas Hancock, "who gave the grounds on which the church and parsonage stand." Placement of the tablet was approved by the Board of Trustees on the inside north wall of the church vestibule. It was moved to its current position on the east wall of the narthex during the 1963 renovation.

๑1922 ๑

Athens First applied for a $100,000 church extension grant from the Methodist Episcopal Church, South, to improve the Sunday School area of the building. The General Board refused to consider the application, as the title to the church was (and still is) held by the Trustees and not by the General church, at that time the M.E. Church, South. The Board of Stewards (today known as the Church Council) requested the Trustees transfer the title, but the Trustees declined. As no actual deed to the property ever has been discovered, it would have been necessary for the Trustees to "perfect" the deed and record such with the Clarke County Clerk of Court, and then transfer title to the M.E. Church, South, including the required "trust" clause that all individual church property is held by the larger church. [This is the trust clause that was suspended by action of the 2019 General Conference effective through December 31, 2023, allowing a significant number of local churches to disaffiliate and retain property.] From minutes of the Athens First Board of Trustees meeting of November 6, 1922: "After investigation they did not care to recommend that the Board take the responsibility of in any way interfering with the way the property was now held and thought that our notorious ownership and possession since 1824 was as good title as we could possibly get." The church Trustees further quoted from the minutes of the University of Georgia Trustees from November 1824: "On motion of Mr. Clayton, Resolved that the Board is willing to convey lot no. 36 in the town of Athens to the Methodist Society for the purpose of building a church thereon, if Mr. Thomas Hancock, the purchaser of the same, will relinquish it back to the Trustees and provided such church is built on said lot in the space of two years from this time." The church Trustees of 1922 relied in great part on the opinion of their attorney, T. S. Mell, who presumed there was a deed from Mr. Hancock to the Trustees and that it contained a reversionary clause. Mell asserted that the Trustees did not have the legal authority to change their trust and would have to do so only "upon the terms and conditions fixed in the deed from Mr. Hancock." Without an actual deed ever having been produced, the only concrete evidence of how the property was transferred is in the minutes of the UGA Board of Trustees, which note that Hancock would relinquish rights to the property back to the UGA Trustees, who would convey it to the Methodist Society.

The implication is that Mr. Hancock did not have a deed to transfer directly to the Methodists himself, as he had not made sufficient payment on the property yet to secure a deed. On review of Attorney Mell's opinion by the Church Quarterly Conference, Dr. Jere M. Pound, dean of the State Normal School, moved that Mell's opinion not be made part of the record, which motion passed. Wrote trustee John Bondurant in his 1988 history of the Athens First Trustees: "It was a crisis for Athens First, and many relationships were strained or destroyed over it."

At the 1922 General Conference of the M.E. Church, South, Athens First clergy from over the years who were delegates: William P. King, Charles C. Jarrell, and Elam F. Dempsey. These same delegates served at a special session of General Conference called in 1924.

๑1924๑

S. E. Wasson, Pastor, 1923-1926

Pastor Wasson came to the North Georgia Conference in 1911 and departed it directly from Athens, moving to Texas at the close of 1926.

Rev. S. E. Wasson

Beginning in 1911, he served Druid Hills church in Atlanta, where he oversaw construction of a new sanctuary He moved to Rome First, St. Mark's Atlanta, and Kirkwood in Atlanta before coming to Athens First. For two years he served as missionary secretary for the North Georgia Conference. He departed North Georgia to accept appointment to Asbury Methodist Church in El Paso, Texas, and reportedly was serving in the New Mexico Conference at the time of his death about 1928. But beyond that information we have not immediately been able to locate details of his ministry before and after his time in North Georgia. An index of clergy memoriams indicated his could be found in the New Mexico Conference journals, but we were unsuccessful in that.

Nearing the 100th anniversary of its founding, Athens First's membership stood at 1,238, its pastor's salary was $4,000 per year, and its total budget was $26,233.

The 1922 General Conference of the M.E. Church, South increased the number of trustees required for a church from seven to nine. The Athens First Trustees, citing the change in the Discipline, increased their number to nine and elected two new members at the same meeting on September 9, 1923: George Deadwyler and Robert C. Wilson. Deadwyler, originally from Maysville, Ga., graduated from UGA in 1890 before moving permanently to Athens, purchasing the Reeves Warehouse and establishing a cotton business in partnership with T. A. Smith. He became president of Athens Building Savings and Loan Company. He served as a church trustee until his death in 1937. Wilson, a native of Sparta, was baptized by his great-grandfather. Dr. Lovick Pierce, the first pastor appointed to the Athens Methodist Church. In 1911, Wilson married Grace Troutman, the daughter of Athens First pastor M. L. Troutman. He joined the UGA faculty in 1907 and became founding dean of the School of Pharmacy in 1914, a position he held until 1948. A daughter, Grace, married Kenneth Waters, who succeeded Wilson as pharmacy dean. Wilson served as a church trustee until stepping down in 1966 to be succeeded by his son, Troutman Wilson. Dean Wilson died in 1981 at the age of 102.

∋1924 ∈

The church installed its third organ, a Moeller three-manual with 55 stops, at a cost of $10,000. It was installed by a German organ-builder named Bender representing the Moeller organ company, who with his wife maintained and serviced it for many years. The trustees and stewards agreed to issuing bonds for $12,500 to cover the cost of the organ and remaining debt from the 1921 church renovation.

Over the years, the trustees followed a policy not to allow outside events to be held in church facilities unless they were religious in nature and free of admission charge. Rev. S. E. Wasson requested that a large Bible Conference be allowed to use the church, which request was approved under the policy. Rev. Wasson further made the request that a portion of the gallery (balcony) be set aside to allow Colored ministers of the city to attend the Bible Conference, a request the trustees also approved. Later the same year there was a request from Miss Kate Anderson to use the new church organ to take private lessons from UGA music professor Hugh Hodgson. After discussion between the Boards of Stewards and Trustees a policy was adopted that required such use of the organ be limited to members of the church who are qualified as to age and previous musical experience, and under the supervision of the official church organist. This would be limited to one person at a time to be selected by the organist, with the student, once trained, agreeing to serve as an assistant organist who would play when the main organist was absent.

The sanctuary as it appeared 1910-1962, with the chancel at the east end

FORWARD *through* THE AGES

BICENTENNIAL
ATHENS FIRST UNITED METHODIST CHURCH

Into Our Second Century

1925 ⁹ 1974

৭1925 ৩

At the church's centennial year of 1925, membership stood at 1,203 and total giving for the year was $20,863. In October 1924 the church published a 16-page pamphlet briefly outlining the history of the church over its first century, written by Dean Robert Preston Brooks of the UGA School of Commerce (forerunner of the Terry College of Business). In 1904, Brooks was one of the first recipients of a Rhodes Scholarship. Even in his 1925 history, Brooks refers to the "lost records" of the church from prior to the Civil War, some of which were not recovered until found in a downtown trash bin in 1930, then being among an even larger set of records lost again, turning up in an estate sale in northwest Georgia in 2024. The matter of these lost (and found) records is detailed at the conclusion of this book.

৭1926 ৩

The North Georgia delegation to the 1926 General Conference of the M.E. Church, South, included former Athens First pastor Charles C. Jarrell and future pastor William P. King.

Trustees chair Emmet J. Bondurant died unexpectedly while in Atlanta on March 17, 1926, and was succeeded as chair by E. D. Sledge. R. L. Patterson was elected to fill the vacant position on the board.

৭1927 ৩

William Peter King, Pastor, 1927-1928

Born February 27, 1871, in Franklin County, King graduated old Emory College at Oxford with a bachelor's and a master's, Phi Beta Kappa. He then attended Candler School of Theology at "new" Emory in Atlanta and received the Doctor of Divinity. He further attended seminary at Vanderbilt University, where he received the Founders' Medal for Oratory. In 1900, he married Mary Evans Harris, daughter of Emory professor Rev. Lundy Howard Harris, and the couple had four children. He was admitted on trial in 1896, licensed to preach in 1897, named deacon in 1899, awarded full connection in 1900, and ordained elder in 1901. He began his service in the St. Louis Conference with these appointments: 1897 Student, Vanderbilt; 1899 Marvin, St. Louis; 1900 Ferguson; 1901-02 West Plains. Transferring to the North Georgia Conference, his appointments were: 1902 Myrtle

ATHENS MINISTER ITS WAR-MAKERS SPEAKING BEFORE GEORGIA W. C. T. U.

SAVANNAH, Ga.—Intelligent public opinion of the world is turning against war as a means of settling international disputes, Dr. W. P. King, pastor of the Athens First Methodist church, declared Thursday night in an address before the Georgia W. C. T. U., in convention here.

"The intelligent Conscience of ...", declared Dr. King, speaking on "The Crusade for Peace", "... as never before the absolute stupidity and hideous crimes ...

Street, Gainesville; 1904-06 Culverton; 1907-08 Hartwell; 1909-12 Lithonia; 1913-16 Monroe; 1917-22 Griffin First; 1921-24 Editor, *Wesleyan Christian Advocate*; 1923-26 Gainesville First; 1927-28 Athens First; 1929-32 Book Editor and Editor, *Methodist Quarterly Review*; 1933-41 Editor, *Nashville Christian Advocate*; 1942 Sandy Springs and Sardis; 1943 Leave; 1944 Supply/Retired. He was delegate to General Conference eight times 1918-1940. Given Rev. King's editorship of several publications of the conference and the larger church, he has a long list of published columns and eleven published books, most notable of which was *The Practice and Principles of Jesus*, termed "an outstanding contribution to social Christianity." While pastor at Athens, he made statewide headlines with an October 1927 speech to a Savannah convention of the Women's Christian Temperance Union. Decrying "the absolute stupidity and hideous crimes of war," he praised what he called a rising number of conscientious objectors to war who "refuse to be coerced into a cruel conformity which means wholesale murder, whatever may be the dictates of blundering governmental leaders." In his speech, he went on to label as hypocrisy the United States' use of the Monroe Doctrine to object to European powers "meddling with the free states of South America" while citing that same Doctrine as authority for "our country to meddle with the internal affairs of these nations." He called for Americans to rid themselves of "the superstition that my country can do no wrong." Known as "Bill King" throughout the conference, he was noted for his intermingling of wit with wisdom and his outstanding tolerance in all situations.Rev. King died June 20, 1957, in Savannah. His funeral was held in Nashville, Tennessee. Four children survived him, including a son, George King, who still lived in Athens at the time of his father's death.

A proposal was considered to rent the parsonage garden plot to a local car rental merchant for $75 per month for ten years. This plot faced Washington Street where the back corner of today's Educational Building lies. The proceeds were to be used to rent a "more desirable" parsonage elsewhere in town for the pastor, turning the existing parsonage into additional Sunday School and office space. The plan was voted down as "not in the best interests of the church."

୨1928 ୨

Clifford Byrd Harbour, Associate Pastor, 1928-1931

Born February 22, 1892, at Piedmont, Alabama, Harbour joined the Piedmont Methodist Church in 1910. In 1917, he received his B.A. degree from Southwestern University in Georgetown, Texas, and was licensed to preach. In 1919 he married Maria Concepcion Rodriguez at Laredo, Texas, and they had four children. He began a varied career that took him to posts in Mexico and England, and to the Memphis, North Georgia, South Georgia and Alabama Conferences. He began preaching in 1919 at Cotula, Texas, 1920-21 head of the Bible Chair at Lauren's Institute, Monterey, Mexico; 1922-23 Avondale, Missouri; 1924-26 student, Yale University, where he served as a congregational minister in Killingsworth, Connecticut for three years. He earned the Bachelor of Divinity degree at Yale in 1926. Further appointments were: 1927 Donalsonville; 1928-31 Athens First as a student pastor; 1932-35 First Street, Macon; 1936-37 Dublin First; 1938-39 Thomasville District Superintendent; 1940-44 St. Luke, Memphis, Tennessee; 1945 St. John, Augusta; 1946 Grace, Atlanta; 1948 Government Street, Mobile; 1952 Enterprise; 1956 Brumhall, England; 1957 Forest Avenue, Montgomery; 1958, retired. He received the Doctor of Divinity degree from Florida Southern in 1950. He died March 31, 1972. A son, Clifford Byrd Harbour, Jr., became an elder in the Holston Conference.

W. B. Dillard, Associate Pastor, 1928-1931

These same years that Clifford Harbour was our student pastor, W. B. Dillard was superannuate (or retired) pastor.

୨1929 ୨

Lester Rumble, Pastor, 1929-1935

Rev. Rumble served seven years, the first pastor to serve Athens First more than four consecutive years after the four-year appointment limit was lifted in 1918. Born September 23, 1893, in Smarr, Ga., he entered Emory

College at Oxford in 1911, where he earned the B.A., Phi Beta Kappa. He taught mathematics at Cordele High School 1915-16 and at Emory Academy in Oxford 1916-17. He entered the U.S. Army, serving in France in World War I, rising to First Lieutenant. After the war, he returned to Emory University to earn the B.D. degree. Sixteen years later in 1935, he received the Doctor of Divinity degree from Emory. He married Mary Alice Eakes in June 1921, and they had three children. She died in December 1944, and in 1946 he married Leila Bagley, Dean of Scarritt College in Nashville, Tennessee. He was admitted on trial in 1921, made deacon in 1923 and ordained an elder in 1926. His appointments included: 1921 Adairsville; 1922-24 Trion; 1925 Student, Yale University; 1926 Oxford-North Covington; 1929 Athens First;

Rev. Lester Rumble

1935 Atlanta District Superintendent; 1936 St. Mark, Atlanta; 1946 Atlanta West District Superintendent; 1951 St. John, Augusta; 1957 Atlanta West District Superintendent; 1963 North Decatur. He was elected a clergy delegate to every General Conference 1940-1964 and was head of the delegation in 1944 and 1948. He was a member of the World Methodist Conference four times 1947-1961. Dr. Rumble died April 25, 1967. At his passing, noted North Georgia clergyman Nat G. Long wrote, "I knew him as I've known few people on this earth. He was a Christian gentleman of the first magnitude. If I had been a layman and could have selected my own pastor, there would have been none in my wide acquaintance of ministers whom I would have selected ahead of him. There has been no person outside my family with whom I would have more readily shared the deepest secrets of my life…. Lester Rumble was a man of absolute integrity. I never knew him to be anything or to do anything except that which was high, worthy, honorable, noble. I have been warmed by his friendship, inspired by his noble character, challenged by his constant attention to duty, and highly honored by his helpful companionship in all kinds of experiences in and out of the church. The imprint of his life upon mine will be imperhishable forever. God bless his memory." He was buried in the historic Methodist cemetery at Oxford. His second wife, Leila's career was prominent, as well. A high school Latin teacher early in life, she became Dean of Women at Blackstone College in Virginia and joined the faculty at Wasada University in Tokyo, Japan, teaching English. She was Dean of Students at Scarritt College in Nashville when they married, before traveling to Japan again as a missionary to women in the workforce. She then joined the General Board of Education of the Methodist Church in Nashville as Secretary for Missionary Education of Youth. Leila Rumble died in May 1970. Graveside services were held as she was laid to rest beside her husband at the Oxford cemetery.

Movement to establish a Methodist Church in "South Athens," specifically along South Milledge Avenue at a location to be determined, is referenced as early as 1899-1900, gaining impetus during the late 1910s and continuing through the 1920s. Appointment to "Milledge Avenue, Athens" was included as a part of the responsibility of several senior ministers at Athens First. More than one committee was appointed at the conference and local church levels to study the matter and develop a plan for implementation. In 1919, Athens First appointed a Board of Trustees for the new church, with Mrs. George Mell as chairman, which met over the next several years and as late as 1923 made a report of progress. Thirty years after it was first discussed, minutes of the Athens First Quarterly Conference from 1929 blamed lack of movement for the project on poor economic conditions and local bank failures, plus the death of important figures in the discussions. "A delay in this movement beyond the immediate present may result in the lapse of another thirty years before any definite action is taken," the minutes opined. Indeed, it was another 27 years. In 1956 "The Five Points Area Methodist Church" was established with 67 charter members in a service held in the sanctuary of Athens First Methodist. The church later was named St. James Methodist Church. It first met in the basement of the Henrietta Apartments at Five Points until a sanctuary building was constructed on West Lake Drive at South Lumpkin Street. The first service in the new building was held in 1961. St. James voted to disaffiliate from the United Methodist Church in 2023 and later that same year joined the new Global Methodist denomination. It now brands itself as "St. James Church, a Methodist fellowship."

Athens First gave approval for Boy Scouts to use a Sunday School classroom for weekly meetings, but only when a competent grown person was present and so long as there was no damage or complaint. Dr. E. B. Hudson agreed to vouch for the boys and to be the responsible party.

৯1930 ৯

The General Conference of the M.E. Church, South, met in Dallas, Texas. Athens First layman Dr. Nat G. Slaughter was elected as a lay delegate, the second lay member from Athens First to be elected a General Conference delegate (after Dean Jere M. Pound in 1918). He was joined in the 1930 General Conference delegation by former Athens First pastors William P. King and Charles C. Jarrell. Slaughter would go on to serve in several General Conferences over the next quarter century and was delegate from our church to the North Georgia Annual Conference for more than forty years. He would be chosen an Athens First trustee late in life, serving from 1963 until his death in 1966. Through his daughter, Nell Slaughter Dye, Dr. Slaughter was grandfather of UGA All-America football player Pat Dye, who was Auburn University's head football coach 1981-1992. Another daughter,

"Miss Julia" Slaughter

"Miss Julia" Slaughter, was a fixture at Athens First events for decades. Well-known to all the congregation, Miss Julia died in 1997 at the age of 89.

Trustee Dr. John Atkinson Hunnicutt, Sr. (whom some sources list as James Hunnicutt) died August 10, 1930. Walter B. Hodgson succeeded Hunnicutt as a church trustee but served only two years before an untimely death in 1932. An officer of the Hodgson Oil Company, Walter was a graduate of both UGA and Georgia Tech. Only 49 years of age, he had attended Sunday School and church in the morning before dying at his home the same evening. With Hodgson's passing on November 20, 1932, Judge Thomas Fitzgerald "Gerald" Green, Jr. was chosen to succeed him. Green likewise would serve only two years, dying in December 1934.

Trustee meeting minutes of October 21, 1930, express appreciation to Mr. H. V. Hood for having found and turned over to the church a minute book of the Quarterly Conference dating back to 1838. The found minute book was turned over to trustee secretary A. W. Dozier to be kept in the safe at his business with the other records of the church. These were among the same records that could not be found upon Mr. Dozier's death in 1948 and turned up in a northwest Georgia estate sale in 2024, where they were recovered and returned to the church yet again.

9 1931 9

The church building was insured for $70,000, the adjacent parsonage for $8,500, church furniture and fixtures for $4,000, and parsonage furniture and fixtures for $1,500. The organ was insured separately for $7,500.

ᵥ1932 ᵧ

Scaffolding was erected around the steeple for the purpose of painting its woodwork with aluminum paint and repairing the weathervane and arrow that topped it.

ᵥ1934 ᵧ

The 1934 General Conference of the M.E. Church, South, included former Athens First pastors William P. King and Charles C. Jarrell among the North Georgia delegation.

Trustee Thomas Fitzgerald "Gerald" Green died December 27, 1934, and was succeeded by Percy L. Huggins. Green, a Milledgeville native, 65, suffered a heart attack and died at a Kiwanis Club meeting in the Georgian Hotel. He had succeeded trustee Walter B. Hodgson, who also had died after serving only two years. Green, an Athens attorney and Judge of City Court, also taught at the UGA School of Law. He was a trustee of the University and was appointed by Governor Richard B. Russell as a member of the first Board of Regents of the University System. Huggins was an Athens native and proprietor of Huggins Auto Parts Company. He served on the city board of education, on the YMCA board, and as president of the Rotary Club. He chaired the church Board of Stewards before becoming trustee.

ᵥ1935 ᵧ

A proposal again arose to secure a rented parsonage off-site and to convert the existing parsonage to Sunday School rooms and offices. The plan was to lease a home at 219 Cloverhurst Avenue for $50 per month. In addition to giving the pastor's family a nicer home, it would provide adult Sunday School classrooms and would give church office staff better working conditions than their cramped office in the sanctuary building, heated in winter only by a non-vented gas space heater. Additionally, the full church building would not have to be heated during the week. Further, it would take the parsonage property off the city and county tax rolls. The Sunday School Department proposed to pay the entire costs, including the rent, out of its separate budget. The proposal was approved by the Board of Stewards and the Board of Trustees, albeit on a vote of 15 in favor, 4 against, and 8 "uncommitted." Four years later the church purchased a new parsonage on Dearing Street.

ʘ**1936** ʘ

George McDonald Acree, Pastor, 1936-1939

Born December 7, 1891, at Camilla, Georgia, "Brother George" Acree was one of several sons of Camilla Methodist Church to enter the ministry. His mother, Mattie Thornton Acree, died just weeks after his birth. His father, Thomas Augustus Acree, Sr., remarried Daisy Whitworth Acree, who became the beloved stepmother who raised him. Acree was licensed to preach in 1912 and graduated from Emory College in 1914, joining the South Georgia Conference that same year. His appointments were: 1914 Talbot Circuit; 1915 admitted on trial and appointed to the Americus Circuit; 1916 ordained deacon and appointed to Lee Street, Americus; 1917 transferred to the North Georgia Conference and appointed to Second Avenue, Rome; 1918 ordained elder and appointed to Lithonia;

1919 Harlem; 1920 White Plains-Siloam; 1921- 22 Young Harris, Athens; 1922 transferred to South Georgia with appointment to Eastman; 1925 Waynesboro; 1928 Cordele; 1930 St. Paul, Columbus; 1931 transferred to North Georgia and appointed to Gainesville First; 1935 Athens First; 1939 Rome First; 1942 Decatur First; 1946 West Point First; 1949 Trinity, Atlanta; 1951 Calhoun. He took sabbatical leave in 1953 and retired in 1954. While at West Point, his wife, Leah Smith of Albany, passed away. He and Leah had three daughters. A daughter and son-in-law,

Rev. George M. Acree

Mr. and Mrs. Morgan Canty, were among 103 prominent Atlanta arts patrons who died in a 1962 Air France plane crash at Orly Airport, Paris. Rev. Acree's second wife was a Rome widow and prominent churchwoman, Frances Caldwell. They lived in retirement in Rome, until she also preceded him in death. His official memoriam describes him as "an urbane man of quiet charm and natural dignity. His manner was gracious and very cordial. His grooming and dress were immaculate. He possessed a rare talent for making one feel that he was doing a good job, especially young ministers…. He is gone, but lives are richer because he passed this way." Rev. Acree died unexpectedly May 7, 1966, as he was preparing breakfast at his home in Peachtree Towers, Atlanta. His funeral was at Rome First with burial in Myrtle Hill Cemetery, Rome.

᧛1937 ᧚

William Ragsdale Cannon of Dalton, a 1937 UGA graduate, was a constituent member at Athens First while in school here. He would become dean of Emory's Candler School of Theology before being elected bishop in 1968, serving until his death in 1997. Among many notable accomplishments, he delivered the invocation and benediction at President Jimmy Carter's 1977 Inauguration, and was an official Protestant observer at the Vatican, becoming a personal friend of Pope John Paul II.

The Trustees considered and then denied a request that the vacant lot behind the former parsonage be rented to a local businessman for a used car sales lot. Determining the proposal was not in the best interest of the church, the Trustees decided to dress the lot up with a new hedge along Washington Street and a neat wire fence to replace the delapidated board one. This lot today is under the back (western) section of our Sunday School building.

Trustee George E. Deadwyler died February 20, 1937 and was succeeded by Henry Haynes West, Superior Court Judge of the Western Circuit. Haynes, an Athens native, graduated from Athens High School, entered Emory College at Oxford as a sub-freshman, and then the University of Georgia, where he earned the B.S. degree in 1915 and his law degree in 1916. West served as a U.S. Army Captain in World War I and returned to be Post Commander of the local American Legion. He practiced law in Athens and served as Solicitor General (District Attorney) before being appointed to the Superior Court bench by Governor Eugene Talmadge. He remained a church trustee until his death in 1953.

᧛1938 ᧚

U.S. President Franklin D. Roosevelt visited Athens to deliver the Commencement Address at the University of Georgia on August 11, 1938. He was driven onto the field of Sanford Stadium in his specially-equipped automobile. After the address, he received an honorary Doctor of Laws degree.

᧛1939 ᧚

Ninety-four years after the 1845 split over slavery, a uniting General Conference in St. Louis approved merger of the Methodist Episcopal Church, South, the Methodist Episcopal Church, and the Methodist

Protestant Church. The new church was known as the Methodist Church. To overcome racial concerns blocking the plan, the merger created a Central Jurisdiction into which African-American congregations were separated, a grievous concern for many which was not rectified until 1968. The merger granted the vote to laity in General Conference, something already allowed in the Methodist Protestant Church and the M.E. Church, South, but the Methodist Episcopal Church had not. Athens First and the North Georgia Conference became part of the new Methodist Church. Athens First layman Dr. Nat G. Slaughter was a delegate from North Georgia to this unification conference, as were past and future Athens First clergy Charles C. Jarrell, William P. King, Lester Rumble, and Harvey C. Holland (alternate).

A new parsonage was purchased on Dearing Street from Mrs. Callie G. Woofter for $6,300. The old parsonage next to the sanctuary had been converted into church offices and a Sunday School classroom building four years earlier when the pastor's family moved to a rented home on Cloverhurst Avenue.

ꙮ1940 ꙮ

Harvey Columbus Holland, Pastor, 1940-1946

Born in Jackson County near Commerce on January 24, 1897, Harvey Holland answered an early call to Christian ministry. He attended Young Harris College, graduating in 1918. He finished Emory University in 1920 graduating in liberal arts and in 1922 received the bachelor of divinity from Emory's Candler School of Theology. While a Candler student, he aided the pastor at Holbrook and served the summer of 1920 as one of the preachers at Holbrook Camp Meeting. There he met Mary Clifford White of Cherokee County, and they were married in the Candler Chapel the very night he received his degree from Candler. Admitted on trial in 1918, he was made deacon 1921 and ordained elder in 1922. His appointments include: 1922-23 Blue Ridge; 1924-27 Acworth; 1928-30 Woodbury; 1931-34 Hogansville; 1935-36 Manchester First; 1937-39 Rome District Superintendent; 1940-46 Athens First; 1947-51 Decatur First, 1951-55 Haygood Memorial, and 1955-57 Athens-Elberton District Superintendent. He served two quadrennia on the General Board of Missions and was for ten years a trustee of LaGrange College. Six years he was chairman of the Camp Glisson Board of Managers, and for four years Dean of the Georgia Pastors School. He was elected twice as a North Georgia delegate to General Conference, and five times as a Jurisdictional Conference delegate. Like his predecessor Lester Rumble, Rev. Holland served seven years at Athens First, a tenure unusual for North Georgia at that time. He carried on bravely as Athens-Elberton District Superintendent even in the face of serious illness, finally at Annual Conference in 1957 asking for retired status. He died the next week on June 26, 1957.

His widow, Mary White Holland, continued as a member at Athens First after her husband's death. She had taught Sunday School throughout her husband's ministry, and was a certified lab instructor, teaching training schools throughout the Conference. She accepted a position as assistant to the pastor, Rev. Bill Tyson, at Young Harris Methodist Church in Athens, a position she held for five years. She taught china painting in Athens. Active at Athens First UMC as long as she was able, she served on the Administrative

Board, and UMW Circle 7 was named the Mary Holland Circle. Mrs. Holland continued as an honorary member of the Administrative Board until her death July 5, 1997, at age 96. The last four years of her life were spent at Fair Haven Retirement Center in Birmingham, Alabama, to be near her

Mary White Holland

daughter. Harvey and Mary Holland's funerals each were held in the Athens First sanctuary, and they are buried at Westview Cemetery, Atlanta. A son, Harvey C. Holland, Jr., received a B.A. from Emory in 1945 and M.Div. from Union Theological Seminary in 1948, and served a distinguished career as an Air Force Chaplain and Colonel. Harvey Jr.'s wife, the former Miriam Haynes, became a Methodist pastor in Florida after his retirement from the Air Force. This author's grandparents were members of the churches at Woodbury and Manchester pastored by Harvey and Mary Holland when my father was a child and teen. My grandmother and father always spoke warmly of the Hollands for their compassion and support during what were hard times for our family. Mrs. Holland and I thus shared a special connection as I came to know her at Athens First through the 1980s.

☙**1943** ☙

Trustee chairman Edward Deloney Sledge died October 2, 1943, with John Parnell Bondurant II chosen to succeed him. Son of longtime trustee

chair Emmet J. Bondurant, John Bondurant was a 1924 graduate of Athens High School and received a B. S. in civil engineering from the University of Georgia in 1933. He was president of Athens Lumber Company. At the time of his selection as a trustee, Bondurant was serving with the U.S. Air Force and saw stints both stateside and in India, the board allowing him to accept

John and Mary Bondurant

the appointment in absentia. He completed his service with the rank of Lieutenant Colonel. He held several positions in local government including City Council, Zoning Appeals, Tax Equalization, Athens Housing Authority, and a Consolidation Study Commission. Mr. Bondurant was noted by several pastors for showing up at the preacher's office unannounced with an opinion to share regarding some pressing church matter. He compiled a history of the church primarily focused on the board of trustees which was published in 1988.

☙**1944** ☙

The Athens Baptist Church changed its name to the First Baptist Church of Athens.

From its founding, the University of Georgia Wesley Foundation was considered an outreach ministry of Athens First Methodist Church. For some years, the director of the Wesley Foundation was a member of the Athens First staff. The church letterhead from 1944 lists Harvey C. Holland, pastor; R. C. Singleton, Director Wesley Foundation; and Mrs. H. L. Byrd, church secretary.

Trustee Thomas F. J. Comer died November 4, 1944 and was succeeded by Carter W. Daniel. A World War I veteran, Daniel was chairman of the

Webb Crawford Company of Athens. Like many of his predecessors, he was on the board of the Southern Mutual Insurance Company. He would serve until his death in 1974.

Mr. Eustace Floyd Lampkin gave $5,000 to the church as a memorial to his recently-deceased mother, Mrs. Cobb Lampkin, a longtime church member, with the designation that it be used for building repairs and improvements. This was an unusually large gift for this period, and would be followed by a much larger gift from Mr. Lampkin a decade hence.

ᦉ1946 ᦅ

In order to give the choir a uniform look rather than the wide variety of dresses and hats worn by the ladies, it was determined to outfit the choir in vestments (robes).

Deloney Sledge and Lamar Sledge, brothers from Atlanta who grew up as members of Athens First, donated chimes and their installation cost. The chimes were a memorial to their parents, the late Mr. and Mrs. Edward Deloney Sledge. The Sledge home was on the north side of Hancock Avenue between College Avenue and Jackson Street. The elder Mr. Sledge, a prominent Athens businessman who ran a successful hardware store, had been a chairman of the church Trustees and died in 1943. Mary Newton Cobb Sledge was a daughter of Howell Cobb, Jr., an Athens attorney, and a granddaughter of Howell Cobb, an antebellum U.S. congressman and Speaker of the U.S. House who became President of the Provisional Congress of the Confederate States. Her great-uncle was T.R.R. Cobb, author of the Confederate Constitution and a founder of the UGA School of Law.

ᦉ1947 ᦅ

James William Oscar McKibben, Pastor, 1947-1951

Born July 6, 1888, in Worthville, Butts County, J. W. "Oscar" McKibben married Lena Anthony in 1915. He received a two-year degree from Young Harris College, taught school for a year, and then attended Emory College at Oxford, graduating in 1918. He graduated from Emory's Candler School of Theology in 1921. He was admitted on trial and ordained a deacon in 1916, and elder in 1918. His appointments were: 1916 Newton Circuit; 1918 East End, Atlanta; 1922 Norcross and Prospect; 1926 Haygood Memorial; 1932

Elberton; 1932 Presiding Elder, Rome District; 1936 Decatur First; 1942 District Superintendent, Augusta District; 1946 Athens First; 1951 District Superintendent, Atlanta West District; 1957 Decatur First Associate. He formally retired in 1961 but continued as Decatur First Associate until his death on November 15 that same year. Described as strong, thoughtful and helpful, he was a fine administrator. He was a faithful and loving pastor and was loved by his congregations. He was elected to General and Jurisdictional Conferences and for twenty years served on the boards of the Methodist Children's Home and of

Rev. J. W. O. McKibben

Young Harris College. He was a trustee of Paine College and of the North Georgia Conference. In McKibben's conference memoriam, Rev Henry H. Jones describes him as "a gentleman to the manner born – gentle, kind, thoughtful of others, considerate, sympathetic. He was ever polite, well-mannered, proper. His gentlemanly manner was seen in his appearance, his dress. He was so neat, clean-cut, well-groomed, just as he was in his inner life." His funeral at Decatur First Church was officiated by Bishop Arthur J. Moore, and Reverends Frank Crawley, W. S. Robison, and Henry H. Jones (this author's maternal grandfather). Rev. McKibben was buried at Decatur City Cemetery.

Annual Conference traditionally met in late November or early December, after which pastors moved to their new assignments the second week of December. This was changed to summer sessions beginning in 1947. Moving day for Methodist pastors changed to the third week of June in deference to pastors with children who faced difficulties moving midway through a school year. The conference met in July of 1947 and 1948 and has met every June since 1949. The one exception was in 2020, when Conference was held in August, and primarily online, because of the pandemic.

Nathaniel G. Slaughter and Manie Fain Slaughter gave $5,000 to the church to be used toward constructing a new educational building, on the condition that sufficient funds were raised to begin the building by January 1, 1952. The conditions were met, and the front third of today's Sunday School building and a separately funded chapel were erected in 1951-52.

Trustee David F. Miller died January 24, 1947, having served on the board since 1908. He was succeeded by Edward Scott Sell, Sr., head of the Department of Agriculture and Rural Social Science at the State Normal School. A native of Hoschton in Jackson County, Sell graduated from Hoschton High School and received the B.S.A. degree from UGA in 1910, and the M.S. degree in 1918. He taught school in Richmond County for a year before joining the State Normal School faculty and was on the UGA geography faculty for 40 years. He served on the Athens City Board of Education.

A. W. Dozier, who had served as secretary and treasurer of the Trustees since 1908, submitted his resignation from those positions in October 1947. Instead of accepting the resignation, the Trustees named Dozier "inactive treasurer" and named John Bondurant as "assistant active treasurer."

DEAN WILLIAM TATE

William Tate, legendary Dean of Men and later Dean of Students at the University of Georgia 1946 – 1971, was a longtime active member at Athens First. A Calhoun native, he came from the Tate family prominent in Georgia's marble industry. A 1924 UGA graduate, he earned a UGA master's degree in 1927 and pursued graduate work at Columbia, Harvard, and the University of Chicago. A member of UGA's track team as a student, he won the A.A.U. Cross Country Championship. A noted speaker throughout his life, he was president of UGA's Phi Kappa literary society and held its speaking key. He was an English instructor and debate coach at UGA 1924 – 1929 before joining the McCallie School in Chattanooga as head of the English department and track coach. In 1932 he married Susan Frances Barrow, a granddaughter of the university Chancellor David Barrow, also a longtime member of Athens First Methodist. Tate returned to UGA as Dean of Freshmen and assistant professor of English in 1936, becoming Dean of Students and assistant to the president, positions he held until his retirement in 1971. Tate is most noted for his role in the peaceful racial integration of UGA in 1961 and maintaining calm during anti-war protests of the Vietnam War era. He published *Strolls Around Athens* in 1975. During retirement, he maintained an active public speaking schedule across Georgia representing the UGA Alumni Society. The UGA Student Center was named for him in 1980. He died on his 77th birthday, September 21, 1980.

Dean William Tate (top three photos courtesy of UGA Libraries)

Dean William Tate taught Sunday School at Athens First for many years

Dean Tate and family in 1976, and Dean Tate in 1979, one year before his death.

ᕲ**1948** ᕲ

As Athens First approached its 125th anniversary in 1950, the membership in 1948 stood at 1,774 and total giving for the year was $32,361.

Athens First member L. H. Christian established the city's second radio station, WRFC (named using his father's initials, at 960 AM) and offered the church the opportunity to broadcast its weekly Sunday 11 a.m. worship service live. Thus began weekly broadcasts that continued for 70 years without interruption. Athens First Baptist already was on the town's only other radio station at the time, WGAU (1340 AM). For a while, the two churches alternated monthly between the two radio stations, but by the late 1950s, the Baptists settled onto WGAU and the Methodists on WRFC. The worship broadcasts were discontinued at the end of December 2018 after online streaming of both video and audio of all church services became widely adopted by the membership.

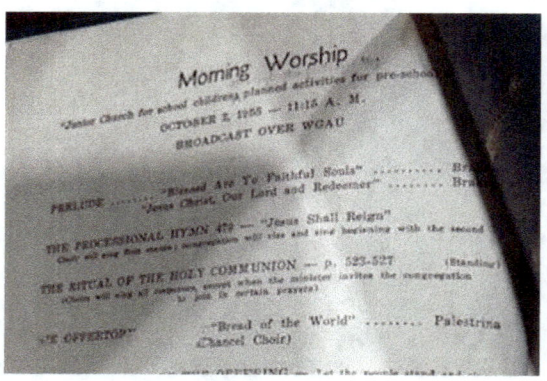

Live radio broadcast of morning worship is highlighted in a 1955 bulletin

L.H. and Sara Christian

Trustee A. W. Dozier died August 1, 1948, and was succeeded by Howard B. Higginbotham. A Madison County native and veteran of World War I, Higginbotham was an agent for Metropolitan Life Insurance Company. He would serve as a Trustee until his death in 1978. Significant church records covering the years 1838-1930 were in the possession of Mr. Dozier for safekeeping but could not be found at the time of his death. Apparently, they inadvertently had been passed on with other records of his company when it was sold to Tanner Lumber Company. The records would turn up in an estate sale of a member of the Tanner family in 2024 and were returned to Athens First.

◙1949 ◙

Robert L. Patterson, a trustee since 1926, died March 17, 1949. He was succeeded by Harold Hopkins Hinton, who had attended Athens First since age six. He was a local business leader in textiles, construction and warehouse companies, as well as a real estate developer. He built the Montgomery-Ward department store building on Broad Street, which later became J.C. Penney Co., and today is Porterhouse Grill. Among his other projects was an A&P grocery store downtown and the Wonderview Apartments, described as "modern high-class dwellings" which still stand at the corner of Milledge and Baxter. When cotton turned down because of the boll weevil, Hinton was quick to recognize the need for diversification and became Clarke County's first cattle farmer. He was chair of the church building committee for the 1951 educational building, but resigned for health reasons before construction was complete. He would continue to serve as a trustee until his death in 1956.

◙1950 ◙

Through its history to this point, the church often would raise money for buildings or repairs by selling bonds to its members and the community. The last bond issue of record was in 1938, paying six percent and yielding $14,900 to the church. These bonds were retired and burned by the Trustees in 1950.

First Methodist Church
Lumpkin Street Between Washington and Hancock

153

ᦠ**1951** ᦡ

Dow Napier Kirkpatrick, Pastor, 1951-1957

Widely known as a firebrand of a pastor, Dr. Dow N. Kirkpatrick was born January 3, 1917, raised in the Great Depression in the rural southern Illinois town of Sesser. He had an extraordinarily early start as a

Rev. Dow Kirkpatrick

Methodist minister, receiving an exhorter's license at age 13. He earned his B.A. degree from Asbury College in 1937. In 1938, he married Marjorie Savage, whose family had a long association with the development of Asbury and its theological seminary. His education continued with a divinity degree from Candler School of Theology in 1940,

and a Ph.D. in theology from Drew University in Madison, N.J. in 1945. Kirkpatrick was a vocal anti-war activist throughout his life, yet served as a Navy chaplain in the Pacific in World War II so that he could minister to U.S. military personnel forced into action by the draft. His ship was in the fleet involved in conducting the first test of the atomic bomb over water. He later pursued further coursework at Oxford, Edinburgh and Cambridge, which included studies under the legendary C.S. Lewis. In 1958 he co-organized the Oxford Institute at Lincoln College in Oxford, England, an institute held every four years since and attended by leading theologians in the world. He served several Georgia congregations during the hottest days of the Civil Rights Movement, including 1947 Sharp Memorial, where he also taught at Young Harris College; 1951 Athens First; and 1957 St. Mark, Atlanta. Under his leadership, St. Mark was the first White Methodist church to receive Black members in Atlanta and all of Georgia since the close of the Civil War. He was one of the original signers of the Atlanta Ministers' Manifesto, ultimately signed by 80 Atlanta preachers, backing integration of Georgia public schools. Through that period, he was active in a group of Black and White Atlanta ministers of all faiths, including Dr. Martin Luther King, Sr. and Jr., and future Athens pastor Bevel Jones. The group met regularly at Paschal's Restaurant and helped steer Atlanta relatively peacefully through the era when other cities were facing conflicts up to riots in the streets. For his very public stance on racial issues, he and his family received harrassment and threats. Kirkpatrick returned to Illinois in 1962, joining the Northern Illinois Conference as senior minister of First Methodist Church, Evanston, and had both Daddy King and MLK, Jr. preach from his pulpit there. In turn, he was invited to preach at Atlanta's historic Ebenezer Baptist Church. He was a social activist in stormy times. Beyond civil rights work, Dr. Kirkpatrick opposed the Vietnam War and chaired the Structure Commission which reorganized the United Methodist Church in the late 1960s and early 1970s. He was vocal in welcoming homosexuals into church membership and leadership, leading the Evanston church to vote his ouster in 1974, a move the bishop refused. Kirkpatrick nonetheless left the parish ministry later that year, serving with his wife Marjorie as a missionary in Latin America with the Board of Global Ministries, alternating their residence between Latin America and Atlanta until his retirement in 1987. He traveled worldwide, authored several books, was a delegate to the General and World Conferences, and held numerous national and international positions in the church. His sermons and papers are held by Candler School of Theology. He died in a UMC nursing home in Atlanta on March 10, 2004, at age 87 from complications of Parkinson's Disease. His memorial was held at St. Mark's UMC with officiants including Bishop Bevel Jones. "Dow's emphasis was integrity," Bishop Jones said. "He believed you had

An aerial view of downtown Athens in the early 1950s with First Methodist Church clearly seen. We can see the new educational building facing Lumpkin at Washington, which was expanded westward to today's dimensions in 1963. The rear of the sanctuary, not yet squared off, shows the same pattern of windows as have the sides, as the stained-glass windows were not added until 1963. The back of the sanctuary building marks the end of the Athens First property, with businesses occupying the remainder of the block.

The Stiles-Dimon Chapel as it appeared when new in 1952. The stained-glass window in the Chapel illustrates Mary and Joseph. Above Mary's head is the descending dove of the Holy Spirit. The left lancet depicts the Annunciation. In the right lancet, a sleeping Joseph learns from an angel that he should name Mary's son Jesus.

to be consistent between belief and action. If you believed it, you had to live it." The bishop described Kirkpatrick as following "liberation theology, a firm belief Jesus came to be identified with the poor and oppressed, and God would give the poor strength to see it through." Kirkpatrick's cremains, along with those of his wife, are buried in the Savage family plot at Asbury Cemetery, Wilmore, Kentucky.

ᕽ1952 ᕽ

The old parsonage/educational building on Lumpkin at Washington Streets was removed and approximately the front third of the current educational building was constructed, along with the Chapel. The new church school building was three stories and basically square, consisting of the easternmost part of the building as it stands today, built at a cost of $220,000. Mr. and Mrs. Lewis Chick of Chick Piano Company donated six pianos for the new building. The Chapel was built with a gift of $25,000 from Mr. and Mrs. John Stiles and named the Stiles-Dimon Chapel in honor of their parents. An organ installed in the Chapel for $4,500 was a gift from Mr. and Mrs. H. H. Hinton.

M. Reginald Smith, Director of Music and Organist 1952 – 1973

In 1952, M. Reginald "Reg" Smith began a 21-year tenure as director of music and organist for the church. Some church publications listed both Reginald and his wife, Eloise Smith, as the directors of music. A native of

M. Reginald Smith in 1955, 1963 and 1973. Reginald and Eloise Smith in 1990

New Jersey, Reginald sang in the all-male choir at St. Georges-by-the-River in Rumson, New Jersey, beginning at age eight. His father, J. Morton Smith, was baritone soloist in the same choir. It was there that J. Stanley Farrar was his choirmaster, first piano teacher, and his first organ teacher. Later he studied organ under noted teachers Dr. T. Tertius Noble, Dr. Charles M. Courboin, and Dr. Seth Bingham. He received the Bachelor of Music degree from the University of Georgia and studied further at Columbia University, the Juilliard School of Music and the Peabody Conservatory. He was choirmaster and organist at several churches in metropolitan New York and New Jersey before coming to Athens First in 1952, establishing our first multi-choir program, growing from 17 members in the one adult choir to 125 members in five choirs. He and his wife, the former Eloise Beckwith of Athens, were charter members of the National Fellowship of Methodist Musicians. He held membership in the Atlanta Chapter of the American Guild of Organists and was dean of the Athens-University Chapter. He had handbell compositions published by the H. W. Gray Co. and introduced the first handbells to Athens First, a controversial purchase at the time. The Smiths had three children born while at Athens: Regg, Laurin and Ellen. He became an influential fixture in the life of this church and continued his membership for some years after his retirement. Smith is remembered fondly by the longest-serving members of today's choir.

The University of Georgia Wesley Foundation, which for many years was an integral part of the program of Athens First, sold its house on Milledge Avenue and purchased another on Lumpkin Street across from the intersection with Carlton Street, its location today. The plan was to use the house as a meeting place and as the residence of the director, Brunson Wallace, until such time as a new student center could be built on the site. Methodist student enrollment at UGA that year was reported as 1,235, of whom 125 were active in the Wesley Foundation during the year.

The sanctuary building as it appeared following the 1952 addition of the Stiles-Dimon Chapel onto its south side.

The Athens Cooperative Nursery School, a non-profit operated by mothers who hired a trained teacher, operated for at least four years 1949-53 using the nursery rooms at the church. All children of nursery school age were eligible to attend "if their mothers are willing to do their share of the work."

158

Four dinners for church members were held each evening June 9 through June 12, 1952, for the purpose of touring the new Educational Building and making pledges to the budget for the coming year. In July, the Board of Trustees borrowed $100,000 from the Teachers Retirement System of Georgia to carry the remaining balance for constructing the new building on a 20-year note with option for earlier payment. Steward J. C. Stiles urged his fellow Stewards to increase their current pledges by 40 percent for the coming year to support a budget which was increasing from $25,565 in 1951-52 to $42,905 in 1952-53. Contributions to the church budget and building fund for the fiscal year ending June 30, 1952, totalled $85,000. The church staff at the beginning of the fiscal year on July 1, 1952 (and their salaries) comprised the pastor ($6,600), pastor's secretary ($2,600), church secretary ($2,300), hostess ($2,400), choir director ($1,000), organist ($900), janitor and cook ($2,700 total). A motion was passed at the Official Board to give each employee two weeks' vacation with pay, except for the janitor, who would get one week.

The Board of Stewards voted that expenditures not in the approved church budget not be paid unless first reviewed by the finance committee. In July, the Official Board voted to prohibit smoking in the Fellowship Hall during meetings. This was in a time when Annual Conference routinely considered motions to curtail smoking among the clergy. The Finance Commission in September purchased a lawnmower for the church so the janitor could cease borrowing the personal lawnmower of the District Superintendent to maintain church grounds. In October 1952, the Official Board heard a report from Mrs. T. W. Paschall, president of the Women's Society of Christian Service (W.S.C.S.), of plans to support a rural welfare worker in the district. Wesley Foundation Director Brunson Wallace reported on increasing student involvement in the church, and Sunday School Superintendent Bob Tuck expressed appreciation for support the church gave to the Sunday School. Smiley Wolfe urged consideration of a plan to enlarge the auditorium (sanctuary), saying in his opinion it was the greatest pressure on the church at that time. Pastor Dow Kirkpatrick introduced Eugene Dunn, a student at Candler School of Theology. Dunn would go on to serve as Athens-Elberton District Superintendent 1986-91. A December 1952 meeting of the church finance commission authorized music director Reginald Smith to spend $20 to have the turntable for the steeple chimes repaired. They further approved a motion that "all the outstanding unpaid bills now in existence be paid when funds are available."

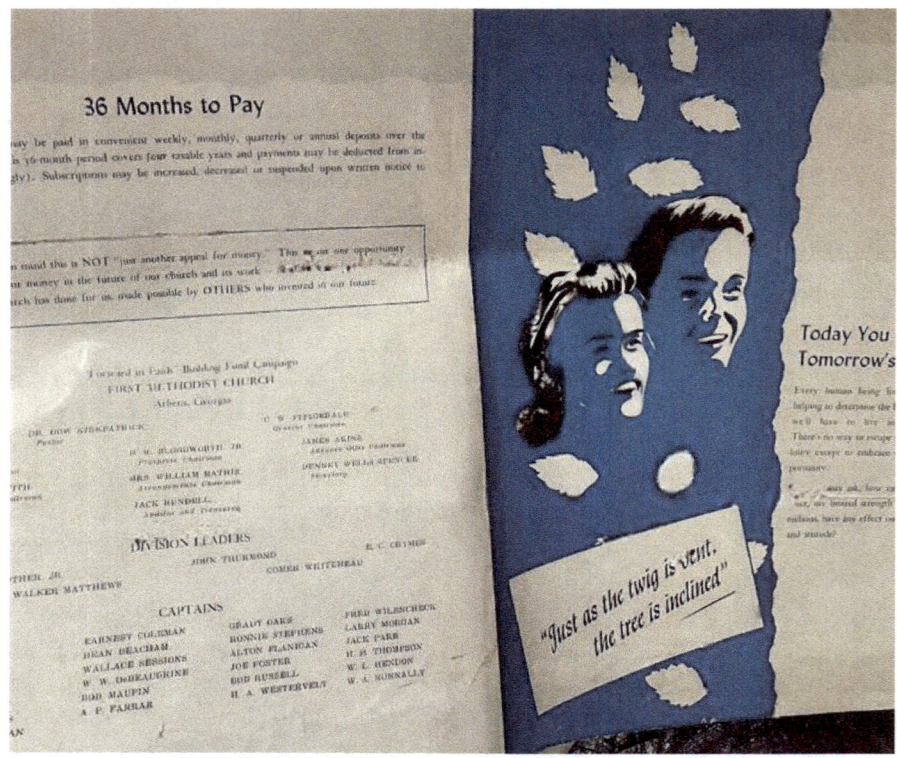

Brochure for the 1954 capital fundraising campaign

ᕷ **1953** ᕸ

The church ended the 1952-53 conference year with a $20,000 budget deficit, leading to considerable discussion among the Official Board about how to increase giving and reduce expenses. Giving for the year totalled $71,430 with an additional $6,612 given for "special offerings." Church Treasurer John Bondurant believed a contributing cause for the deficit was extra offerings being taken above those authorized by the finance committee or Official Board. He introduced a lengthy typewritten resolution to Official Board requiring all special collections be first approved by the finance committee and Official Board. Pastor Dow Kirkpatrick was grateful that the church had moved forward with the program despite the funding shortfall and opposed Bondurant's resolution. The proposal was defeated by vote of the Official Board. We note that the procedure proposed by Mr. Bondurant in 1953 is Athens First policy today. Special collections are outlined and approved in a specific calendar before the start of each budget year and others may not be added without specific board approval.

The cover of the Athens First bulletin for September 26, 1954

Trustee Henry Haynes West died December 12, 1953, having been on the board since 1937. He was succeeded by Dr. Joseph Kenneth Patrick, who came to Athens in 1908 from his native South Carolina to attend the UGA School of Pharmacy, graduating in 1910. He operated Patrick's Pharmacy in Athens from 1918 to 1943. He dispensed more than just human medicine, developing a popular compound to destroy ants – Ant-Ex. He was elected to the Georgia State Senate beginning in 1927. He was among the original owners of Athens' first radio station, WGAU, serving as its president until he sold to H. Randolph Holder and Tom Lloyd in 1956. From 1943 forward he was active in real estate. He was on the Athens City Board of Education. Patrick would serve until his death in 1963.

୨**1954** ୧

The North Georgia Conference adopted a resolution concerning the landmark U.S. Supreme Court decision in the case *Brown v. Board of Education*, authored by a committee chaired by former Athens First pastor Lester Rumble. To quote in part: "We are suggesting that in these troubled days we show a greater consideration than ever toward our Negro friends. Some cities like Atlanta, Augusta, and Gainesville have placed Negroes on the Boards of Education. This indicates that progress has already been made along educational lines between the races. Let us explore other ways of working together in community life. Christians, White and Negro, of leadership and culture, should seek to know and understand each other. All problems can be solved by Christian people working with understanding. We are in a world where no man lives to himself, and where we cannot escape the consequences of each other's living. God's ultimatum to man is respect and love for his fellow man. Our problems must be solved in this day by recognizing our interdependence, and not emphasizing independence only. Our distance apart is no longer spatial, but spiritual. Actions of human beings in any part of the world have repercussions in every part. Therefore, with mature thinking and Christian spirit, let us face the task and the future, not with fear, but with faith. God has no dead-ends for us if we follow His will. Let us therefore seek the mind of Christ."

The North Georgia delegation to the 1954 General Conference included former and future Athens First pastors Lester Rumble, Dow Kirkpatrick and Harvey Holland. Former pastor J. W. O. McKibben was a reserve delegate to Jurisdictional Conference. Athens First lay member Nat Slaughter was again in the lay delegation, and layman J. C. Stiles was elected to the Jurisdictional Conference delegation.

Athens First undertook a "program campaign," which today we would call a capital campaign, to underwrite a desired program of renovations to the physical facilities. The Guidance Service of H. P. Demand was engaged to direct the campaign, which was "to be executed by the men of Athens First Methodist Church." The goal was to raise the capital money without impacting pledges to the regular operating budget of the church. A brochure developed for the campaign is pictured on the previous page.

Over a period of many months, as early as December 1953, there was discussion by the Trustees whether the building funds raised for construction of the new Sunday School building should be turned over to the Trustees to administer. There was opposition within the church to doing so, and the Trustees determined not to press the issue. However, in July 1955 the church missed a payment on the note, causing the Trustees to renew the question of how the funds were being administered. The church caught up the tardy payment and the issue does not show up in the record again.

W. M. Barnett, Associate Pastor, 1955-1958

Retired pastor W. M. Barnett was appointed associate pastor at Athens First, serving through 1958. His responsibility was visiting shut-ins, the sick in hospitals, and new families moving into the area. He and his wife continued to live in Athens and be involved in the life of our church after he stepped down from these duties.

Rev. W. M. Barnett

Paul H. Hanna, Assistant/Associate Pastor, 1955-1958

Rev. Paul Hanna was appointed Assistant Pastor at Athens First for the year 1955-56 and Associate Pastor 1956-58, serving his first two years under Dr. Dow Kirkpatrick and his final year under Dr. Charles Boleyn.

His primary responsibility during that time was the church's programs of Christian education. Born September 5, 1927, in Atlanta, he graduated from Decatur High School and served in the U.S. Navy. He married Sylvia Roberts in 1948. He attended Oglethorpe University and received a B.C.S. degree from the University of Georgia and a bachelor

Rev. Paul Hanna

of divinity from Emory University. He was admitted on trial in 1953 and in full connection in 1955. His appointments included 1953 Fairmount,

1955 Athens First Associate, 1958 Dalton Morris Street, and 1962 Blue Ridge. He held further appointments at Tuckston, Covington First and Rome Trinity before beginning 18 years as director of the UGA Wesley Foundation, the last eight of those also serving as State Coordinator of Methodist Campus Ministries for the North and South Georgia Conferences. He retired in 1991 and enjoyed traveling and serving as chaplain on cruise ships. He and his wife Sylvia were well-known for the comedy acts they would perform at various church and community functions. In retirement, he served as interim pastor of McEver Road UMC in Gainesville and taught Sunday School at Gainesville First, where he was actively involved. Moving to Talmage Terrace in Athens in 2016, he was engaged at Athens First, including regularly assisting in serving communion. He died August 27, 2020.

Former member Mr. Eustace Floyd Lampkin, 57, of Auburn, Maine, died in October 1955 while on business in Charlottesville, Virginia, leaving a large bequest to the church, part of a complicated $3.8 million estate. Lampkin had grown up at Athens First, son of prominent parents, Mr. and Mrs. Cobb Lampkin. He graduated Athens High and UGA, and soon became very successful in the hotel industry. He had two sisters, Lucy and Lois Lampkin, and a half-brother, Clifton

Lampkin, mayor of Bowling Green, Kentucky. Owner of numerous hotels around the country, he held property in nine states and had multiple potential heirs. The church bequest carried the provision that it be used to construct a new sanctuary building in memory of his parents. It was complicated by leaving half to his wife, who was removed from the will by a codicil after the couple was divorced. Further, a death-bed memorandum dictated to a nurse and doctor potentially eliminated the church as a beneficiary. A settlement negotiated through the executor and approved by the courts clarified the church's participation at one-sixth of the net estate sharing equally with other named beneficiaries. It further freed the church from the requirement to replace its existing building, and thus made possible a major remodeling of the sanctuary in the coming decade.

Children's Choir

First row (left to right): Gretchin Lund, Patrici... ...t ...n W ...u:iod
Nancy Witcher, Gail Doney, Ralph l'tu1n•l u:or.tt Juht•r Ij.n W
row: Martha Lou Wilson, Gary 1 lmm, ii u l'a111t Su J.11 LuoJ. i,.. nm)..:cll(•r- R.,.th ttl,,.tdYrutth.
J l:, i..a I \tln ...&lll1 Hfu1 Ht 11\,l (•nttf" rn-q ..,ir •fl• ,lil1-
n i ...ui.hs Uqtlu:r

Youth Choir

front rrm· •lf"H 1n th:,hl) Jo)c·1)f1tclHYNl... J •t ;11noh.i.. I\'-tt n,\\l,•rd Rell, ylt, \tard4'
f1 lrti,111 \f Ht l;rn;dd 1111h "'Mll" ..c•.u.m. \l) m.l Ro•u H,,h'•-rhu1l. J••tit \lm:m.d.,a1.h,...nt1t• H rd,
C .mhn l'u,th •• •1 ,t "')o- lnr:lh. \.,tn1•\ Cj l1,.._.,_.. Enu,f\ Lv ulh u. Ullh· t.,holt Julm
Thur.11-•uc' Jr , , tn1- tl.lrt,, <,lhur "u ,nb- n. not 01 p, ton· C<••r Thun m\d

Wesley Singer·

Ji"ront ro,1. fh tt tu tii!t.l> \ Jb1 it ,. hKJ1t "Uh Iknnl'lt, Jt-rm \\,lllnt•c•, Jurin l' th•rsrn,, Ocmns Cl..uk.
M. H••Kini,lt{ :)rulth t'Yl°1 ui:T\1•r. C lmlrn Cl,,,Il,.. El:arnl• t•hh. \lHrt()riC' C.Omdio1. Jo 1u1 C.u-
pit,itu. Touuni,· (:ut,L. 1.Hllu· Jl1.dtnn \t't."lllmLl rrtY • M.lrluu Jort-li.Jt, Sam Coulson, Jim Frl'C'laud.
Dt•lauu Bt.lL d. £111111111 tl Vu.,,011. Hui.,dl JtteOhii, Ho) -001\J Hnntc.r, Ct-nt• Mk-hat·h, Jnn Biul,lw
Johnn)' \'n.tN, tloi,;rr I Ot. Jinl p.>omit, C.bnir rnl."mh,• not in pactur,•; N1ulim· Umwn. I.f-,thil
J>1·lit••1111,trmf\ Cc:n• l) rt:f , l. thr)n f-'r-Jd,,., Frau J lnrrh, Uhmtl' \Vfntt

The Youth Choirs of 1955

Front row (left to right): Mrs. James Coleman, Mrs. Sue Vinson, Miss Jeanette Richards, Miss Sy
Hale, Mrs. Sadie Mangleburg, M. Reginald Smith Mrs. M. Reginald Smith, Mrs. John T. Wheel
Miss Virginia Moore, Miss Betty Thomas, Mrs. ... Morrison, Mrs. Eugene Malcolm, M
June Brice. Second row: Mrs. Jos. LaRocca, Miss Elizabeth E...eridge, Miss Marian Mart
Olin S. Seabolt, R. C. Harper, Larry Morgan, George Miller, Louis Griffith, Charles S. Mangl
burg, Gordon Doran, Fred Birchmore, Dink Martin, John Bondurant, Cliff ...enson, Mrs. O.
Copeland, Mrs. John Duke, Mrs. Jack Sutton. Choir Members not in picture: Mrs. Preston Alman
Mrs. W. D. Crawford, Hank Dixon, R. C. Gilmer, Miss Louise ...arwell, Clarence Jones, Ho
Robertson, Ralph Seamon, Miss Martha Smith, Ira Teat, Mrs. W. H. Wagyoner.

The Adult Choir of 1955

The era of pipes banging in winter and fans waving through summer sermons came to an end in 1955 as air-conditioning was installed in the sanctuary and entire physical plant at a cost of $42,000. The new Sunday School building had been constructed without air conditioning just four years earlier. At the same time, the church proceeded to draw preliminary plans for a complete renovation of the sanctuary, including again reversing the configuration to return the pulpit to the west end.

The church budget grew rapidly from $25,565 in 1952, to $42,905 in 1953, and in 1955 the church budget exceeded $50,000 for the first time, but still fit on one printed page.

For two consecutive years, in 1955 and 1956, the North Georgia Annual Conference held its annual session in our sanctuary, Bishop Arthur J. Moore presiding, the seventh and eighth times Athens had hosted the conference. A "Conference News Notes" distributed daily to delegates carried such features as a brief history of Athens First, invitation to the Conference Ministers' Wives annual luncheon at the Athens Country Club, a Young Harris College alumni luncheon at the Georgian Hotel, and a flower show and program for ministers' wives staged by the Athens Garden Club at the UGA Agricultural Extension Building, followed by a tour of local private gardens.

୨**1956** ୭

With the Lampkin estate nearing settlement and the first distributions in hand, Athens First Trustees began negotiations to acquire properties making up the remainder of the block bounded by Hancock, Hull and Washington Streets. This involved three or more owners and several parcels. After some back-and-forth negotiations, the Trustees found themselves apart on an agreed-upon purchase price, with the Trustees offering $100,000 and the owner seeking $125,000. In a letter formally notifying the Official Board of the matter, the Trustees said, "Faced with the necessity of paying such an amount for this property, the Trustees feel that our intent to purchase this property must of necessity be abandoned. If the Official Board has a contrary opinion, we would appreciate your expressing it to us in order that this matter may be reconsidered."

The value of the church property in May 1956 was estimated at $472,000 for the three buildings (sanctuary, chapel, and Sunday School building) and

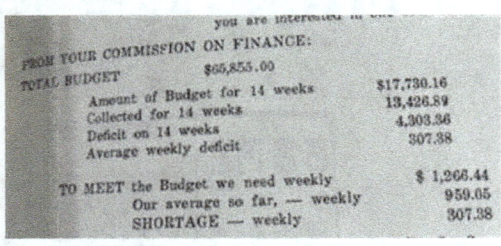

Top, this budget report from April 1956 shows that running behind on budget payments may be a bit of a tradition at Athens First.

167

Athens First Methodist as it appeared in the 1950s. Photo is dated after the
Stiles-Dimon Chapel and the first part of the Sunday School building were
added in 1952 and before the 1963 renovations.

furnishings, and $19,000 for the Dearing Street parsonage and furnishings.

Trustee Harold Hopkins Hinton, who had served on the board since 1949, died October 29, 1956. He was succeeded by James Inman "Jimmy" Akins. A native of Bulloch County, Georgia, Akins graduated from Register High School in 1933 and received a B.S. degree in agricultural engineering from the University of Georgia in 1938. He worked for Mathis Construction Company in Athens from 1938 to 1981, serving as its president the last eight years before his retirement. He also was president and owner of Akins

Concrete Company. A veteran of World War II, he served in the U.S. Navy Civil Engineer Corps (Seabees), Pacific Area. For some years, he was the single individual who knew more than anyone about the physical make-up of the church facilities and mechanical workings. He held many civic leadership positions across all areas of Athens community service. Akins left the board in the late 1980s under a new term limit policy. He died in December 2007 at the age of 91.

Victor Hugo "Hugh" McKee, associate pastor and director, Wesley Foundation 1956-1958

Born December 7, 1925, in Atlanta's West End, Hugh McKee attended Lee Street School, Joe Brown Junior High School and Boys' High School in Atlanta. He served two years in the U.S. Navy, enlisting in 1944 and becoming a World War II veteran. He graduated from Young Harris College, Emory University, and the Candler School of Theology.

McKee began 40-plus years of ministry in 1948 at a student pastor at Cumming First. His further appointments were: Maysville; Dacula First; Pierce Memorial, Augusta; Athens First associate and director, UGA Wesley Foundation; Asbury, Decatur; West Rome; Pleasant Grove, Dalton; Leland; Glen Haven; Tunnel Hill; Red Oak, Newton; and Epworth, Atlanta. Rev. McKee saw his Wesley Foundation mission as being Methodist minister to the campus, indeed, anything having to do with the Methodist church on the UGA campus. This included student involvement in

Rev. Hugh McKee

Sunday School and Sunday evening fellowship, ushering, and singing in the choirs. "The church makes a great contribution to the lives of the [college] students who allow it to do so," he wrote. The Wesley Foundation board was entirely members of Athens First, including chair Dean William Tate, vice-chair James "Jimmy" Akins, Secretary Donald Weddell, and Treasurer J. Smiley Wolfe, and eight additional First Methodist members. From 1966-68, McKee was director of Camp Glisson. In 1972, he served as an associate director for the Conference Council on Ministries. From 1973-85 he was manager of the Office of Administrative Services for the North Georgia Conference. Rev. McKee retired in 1990 and died May 1, 2022, survived by his wife of almost 73 years, Clara Gilstrap of Chickamauga.

ꝺ**1957** ꝺ

Future U.S. President John F. Kennedy, at the time a United States Senator from Massachusetts, delivered the Commencement address at the University of Georgia on June 10, 1957. He was hosted by UGA President Omer Clyde Aderhold, an Athens First Methodist lay member.

Charles Wheatley Boleyn, Senior Minister, 1957-1964

Born March 6, 1916, in Hazard, Kentucky, Charles Boleyn married Mildred Dunwoody in 1940, and they were married 58 years. He earned an A.B. degree in 1936 from Kentucky Wesleyan, where he also played basketball; the bachelor of divinity in 1940 from Candler School of Theology, Emory

Dr. Charles Boleyn in 1958
Mildred and Charles Boleyn in 1990

University; the S.T.M. degree from Union School of Theology in New York; and post-graduate study for three years at the University of Chicago. He received an honorary doctor of divinity degree from Kentucky Wesleyan College. He was admitted on trial in 1941 and in full connection in 1943. He began his ministry in 1941 in the Virginia Conference with appointment to Bellview. He moved to the North Georgia Conference in 1943 with an appointment to Allen Memorial, Oxford; 1946, student appointment at LaMoille, Illinois; 1949 Bethany; 1953 Milledgeville; 1957 Athens First; 1964 Druid Hills; 1968 Atlanta-Marietta District Superintendent; 1972 Oak Grove; 1980 Fairburn. Dr. Boleyn was an original trustee of Wesley Homes, a trustee of Asbury Seminary, and served on the board of the UGA Wesley Foundation. While pastor in Athens, he was chaplain of the UGA football team. He was president of the Christian Council of Metropolitan Atlanta, and taught courses at Emory at Oxford, the Candler School of Theology, and the Christian College of Athens. He served as delegate to General and Jurisdictional Conferences.

Shortly after the Boleyn family arrived in Athens with their four young daughters, the church determined it would be necessary to add another

An Athens First worship service inside the
Georgia Theatre in March 1962

bedroom to the Dearing Street parsonage. The Trustees obtained financing
to do this work and to pay off the remaining note for air-conditioning
the church property in 1955. Boleyn was Athens' pastor in the planning and
execution of the 1963 renovations. During that work, he led services for two
years in the Georgia Theatre on Lumpkin at Clayton Streets. He enjoyed
having his "name in lights" every weekend on the theatre marquis in
downtown Athens.

Dr. Boleyn in the 1970s became recognized as leader of a Pentecostal and
Charismatic turn among some in the conference. He and Mildred retired to
Athens in 1983 and spent their retirement years as active participants at Athens
First UMC. He started the ministry "Power for Living Today," preached scores
of revivals, had a weekly radio devotional program and contributed weekly
columns to the Athens newspaper. He suffered a fall in the stairwell of our
educational building one Sunday morning from which he did not recover. He
died December 18, 1998. His funeral was in the Athens First UMC sanctuary
followed by burial at Oak Grove UMC cemetery in Decatur.

☙ 1958 ❧

Emory R. Brackman and Charles Frazier, Associate Pastors, 1958-1960

Rev. Brackman and Rev. Frazier each were appointed to serve Athens
First in 1958 and were reappointed in 1959, serving to June 1960.

Emory Brackman was admitted to preliminary connection in 1954 and was ordained a full connection elder in 1957. His appointments were 1951 Dearing; 1952 leave; 1954 Union Point; 1955 New Hope, Marietta; 1958-60 Athens First associate; 1960 Cleveland; 1964 Collins Memorial; 1968 Woodlawn, Elberton; 1970 Morrow-Griffin; 1974 Calhoun First; 1979 Douglasville First; 1985 Berkmar; 1990 Cumming First; 1993 Toccoa First; 1996 Retired.

Charles Frazier was ordained in 1957. He spent his first year under appointment as a student at the Candler School of Theology before being appointed as Athens First associate, where he led education and youth ministries. His further service record was not immediately available in our research.

William Russell Edwards, Associate
Pastor and Wesley Foundation Director,
1958-1966

Russ Edwards served as director of the University of Georgia Wesley Foundation 1958-1966, during which time the Wesley director was a

member of the Athens First staff. Born in 1925 in Fort Valley, he was a grandson of Dr. Jere M. Pound, who served 21 years as president of the State Normal School at Athens and was active in this church until his death in 1935. Dr. Edwards attended Asbury College where he met and married Kathleen Crenshaw. He left Asbury 1943-46 for service in the U.S. Air Force during World War II, returning in 1946 to finish his degree. He was ordained into the South Georgia Conference in 1951, received his Bachelor of Divinity degree from Candler School of Theology in 1953, and began graduate work in theology when he was appointed pastor at Palmyra

Rev. William Russell
Edwards

Road Church, Albany. He was appointed 1958-1966 as director of the UGA Wesley Foundation. He retired from active ministry in 1966 and pursued a Ph.D. at UGA in counseling psychology, which he received in 1970. He worked the next 22 years in that field in UGA Health Services, continuing active involvement in the life of Athens First, often assisting in serving during communion. He served as president of the Georgia Mental Health Association, as such working closely with Georgia First Lady Rosalynn Carter. He died in 2023 with his funeral held in our sanctuary.

Trustee Percy L. Huggins, who had served on the board since 1935, died August 5, 1958. He was succeeded by J. Smiley Wolfe. A Savannah

native and graduate of Armstrong Junior College, Wolfe joined the C&S Bank which assigned him as vice-president in Athens in January 1940. He served on the Athens-Clarke Board of Education, president of the Athens Chamber of Commerce, and on the boards of Athens General Hospital, the Salvation Army, the Boy Scouts, and the Community Chest. He retired from C&S Bank in 1969. At the church, he further chaired the Board of Stewards and served as lay leader of the Athens-Elberton District.

Smiley and Elizabeth Wolfe

He would serve as a trustee until his death in 1986.

☙1959 ☙

As the church began planning for a major renovation of the sanctuary and nearly tripling the size of the Sunday School building, it was determined that another attempt should be made to obtain adjacent property before renovation plans were drawn. Therefore, a second attempt was made to purchase a portion of the block on which the church stood, land immediately to the west of the church for which Mr. Jack G. Beacham was a co-trustee. The Trustees formally offered Mr. Beacham $100,000 for the property, which offer was declined. Mr. Beacham some months later came back with an offer to sell the property for $125,000, but the Trustees decided they would not negotiate a higher amount and that failure to obtain the property would not be critical to the life of the church. Late in 1959, Mr. Beacham approached the church yet again, informing the Trustees that a long-term lease was under consideration to place a federal government facility on the property sharing the block with the church, and again informing the church that if they wanted the property, they should proceed to purchase it for $125,000. The Trustees declined the offer and proceeded with plans to renovate the church physical plant within its existing property lines.

The Trustees further discussed the opportunity to purchase a three-story brick building known as Union Hall, which stood at the corner of Washington and Hull Streets in the same city block as the church. With some repairs, the building was thought to be appropriate as extra Sunday School classroom space. With a purchase price of $16,000 and renovations estimated at some $30,000, the Trustees found a number of reasons arguing against the proposal. It was thought that improving the property that was not adjacent to existing church property might make it more difficult to purchase the intervening parcels between the church and Union Hall. Some thought the church would do better to construct additional Sunday School space on the current property. Others noted that the Lampkin Estate funds could not be used except to improve the current sanctuary building. The board voted down the proposal, with only trustee Smiley Wolfe voting in favor in absentia.

As funds from the Lampkin Estate were being received, the church found

Groundbreaking in 1959 for the new home of the UGA Wesley Foundation on Lumpkin Street at Carlton Street. Wesley Director Russell Edwards, who also was an Athens First Methodist associate pastor, wields the shovel. Dean William Tate is second from the right.

174

itself in some difficulty in its pledge campaign for the 1959 budget, as apparently members were under the impression that the Lampkin funds had eased the church's financial needs. In fact, those funds were dedicated solely to renovation or construction of a new sanctuary. The church also found itself having to refinance its note for the 1955-56 air-conditioning project because of unpaid pledges to the building fund.

Church Organization

STAFF
Bishop — Arthur J. Moore, 63 Auburn Avenue, N. E., Atlanta, Georgia
District Superintendent — Paul Turner, 225 Hampton Court / LI 6-8403
Minister — Charles Boleyn, 234 Dearing St./LI 6-6361
Minister — Emory Brockman, 163 Clover Street / LI 6-6138
Minister — Charles Frazier, 395 Glenwood Drive / LI 3-5098
Minister — Director Wesley Foundation—Russell Edwards, 397 Parkway Drive / LI 3-6937
Missionary — Olin Burkholder, Methodist Mission, APO 301, % PM, San Francisco, Calif.
Missionary — J. McRee Elrod, Methodist Mission, APO, 301, % PM, San Francisco, Calif.
Minister of Music — M. Reginald Smith, 60 Bel Air Dr. / LI 6-6905
Church Secretary — Mrs. James Townsend
Financial Secretary — Mrs. J. P. Barron
Dietitian — Mrs. R. M. Davis

OFFICIAL BOARD
Chairman — Troutman Wilson
Vice-Chairman — Comer Whitehead
Registrar — Sturges W. Lassiter
Treasurer — Arthur Darden
Chairman, Commission on Education — Anne Seawell
Chairman, Commission on Evangelism — J. L. Dickerson
Chairman, Commission on Finance — J. Smiley Wolfe
Chairman, Commission on Missions — A. B. Biscoe
Chairman, Commission on Plant Operations — Frank Hibbets
Chairman, Commission on Christian Social Relations — Richard Bloodworth, Jr.

TRUSTEES
R. C. Wilson, Chairman	Carter W. Daniel	B. S. Sell
Arthur Darden	James I. Akins	John P. Bondurant
J. Smiley Wolfe	H. B. Higginbotham	J. K. Patrick

General Superintendent, Church School — Clyde Fitzgerald
Membership Superintendent, Church School — L. Cain Smith
Superintendent, Children's Division — Mrs. Carl Doescher
Superintendent, Youth Division — Dorsey Dyer
Superintendent, Adult Division — Harold Morris
President, Woman's Society of Christian Service — Mrs. J. W. Firor
President, Men's Club — Candler Meadors

Wesley Foundation — Telephone LIberty 8-8727
Church Office — Telephone LIberty 3-5216

The church constructed a parsonage to house the new associate pastor at 110 Soule Street in the University Heights subdivision for $13,900. The house was built on a lot given to the church by member Thomas Tillman. The first family to occupy it was Rev. and Mrs. Sidney Tate.

Madison Gartrell Nicholson, a member of the Board of Trustees since 1920, died March 23, 1959. He was succeeded by Arthur F. Darden, who served until his death in 1981. An Americus native, Darden came to Athens in 1934 and served as treasurer of Athens First for 25 years. He retired from the UGA Agricultural Extension Service. A Board of Trustees resolution at his death described him as a "kind man who spoke no ill of anyone – and who was a friend to everyone."

☙1960 ❧

Athens First had three lay members as delegates to the North Georgia Annual Conference in 1960 by virtue of having for the first time a senior minister and two associate pastors. Dr. Nat G. Slaughter was joined by J. C. Stiles and Troutman Wilson.

The 1960 delegation from North Georgia to the General Conference included former pastors Lester Rumble and Dow Kirkpatrick. Future pastor Bevel Jones was a Jurisdictional Conference delegate and General Conference reserve.

Sidney S. Tate, Associate Pastor, 1960-1962

Rev. Sidney Tate was born July 22, 1935, in Athens, son of longtime North Georgia clergy member John B. Tate and his wife, Nettie. He attended LaGrange High School while his father was pastor at LaGrange First Methodist Church, then Sidney went to Emory at Oxford and on to "Big Emory," where he received his B.A. degree. He received the Master of Divinity from Drew University in Madison, New Jersey. He was admitted on trial in 1958 and in full connection 1960. Sidney married Enid Smith in 1959. She was daughter of a Methodist minister in the Troy, New York, Conference. They had two sons and two daughters. His first full clergy appointment was as Athens First associate in 1960-

Rev. Sidney Tate

62. He went to McEachern Memorial as pastor in 1962. He then went to LaGrange College as director of admissions and financial aid 1968-73. He was University of Mississippi director of financial aid 1973-83. He resumed pastoral appointments in North Georgia in 1983, serving appoinments in Tallapoosa, Newnan Springs in Rossville, Senoia, New Hope in Gainesville, Villa Rica, and Manchester. He retired to LaGrange in 2000 and was active in LaGrange FUMC and the community the rest of his life. He served on the board of directors of Camp Glisson for 14 years and planned older adult events for the Conference at Simpsonwood. Blessed with a fine singing voice like his father, Sidney was in the LaGrange First choir, the Sons of LaFayette Male Chorus, and enjoyed being songleader at camp meetings in Georgia and Mississippi. He was a volunteer chaplain with Hospice LaGrange, where he died October 16, 2015. His memorial service was at LaGrange FUMC and he is interred at Shadowlawn Mausoleum in LaGrange.

R. Gene Wiggins, Director, Christian Education 1961 – 1962

Wiggins came to Athens First in September 1961. He was an Asbury College graduate and also graduated

Gene Wiggins

ARRIVED AS A UGA STUDENT, STAYED FOR LIFE

DR. PAT MORRISON

Like many AFUMC members, Pat Morrison arrived in Athens as a UGA student. He and his wife, Dianne, are longtime members now and have served in many capacities over the years.
Dianne, daughter of former District Superintendent Bill Ruff, was Lay Leader 2006 – 2011. Here, Pat recalls how the church was when he first arrived here more than sixty years ago.

Dianne & Pat Morrison, Ben & Meg in 2000

When I entered the University of Georgia in the fall of 1961, I started attending Wesley Foundation at UGA (Wesley was supported in part by Athens First Methodist). Wesley provided bus transport to downtown Athens First on Sunday morning for 11 o'clock services.The sancuary of the church faced East toward Lumpkin Street. There was a door on that side that admitted directly into the sanctuary. It was always awkward to enter and be observed by a seated congregation.
Soon after the first fall quarter that I was in Athens, the sanctuary was closed for renovations and services were moved to the Georgia Theatre on Lumpkin. A Saturday night date at the movies was followed by Sunday services for Athens First.
During my junior year at Georgia, I lived in the home of Mrs Lucy Nicholson—she provided free lodging for two students in exchange for a few errands and having someone in the house. "Miss Lucy's" husband, Madison Nicholson, had died and she needed help in the big house. Mr. Nicholson was long-serving Athens First treasurer. Miss Lucy faithfully hosted her Circle each month in their home, the Wray-Nicholson House, 298 South Hull.

from Emory University. "Any church school worker is invited to consult him about any church school work," said the appointment announcement. His wife, Jean, also was an Asbury graduate and taught ninth grade English at Athens High School.

◎1962◎

Nat G. Slaughter, who had served as the Athens First delegate to the North Georgia Annual Conference for some forty years, was joined at the 1962 meeting at Glenn Memorial Church in Atlanta by W. A. Sutton, who soon would succeed him.

Eugene T. Bell, Associate Pastor, 1962-1963

Rev. Eugene Bell was born in Florida in 1925 and married Ruth Nadine Pixley in 1952. Graduating from Asbury College with a B.A. degree, he earned a bachelor of divinity degree from Emory. Bell was admitted on trial in 1961, was appointed Athens First associate in 1962, and was appointed to continue his education as a student at the University of Georgia in 1963.

REV. EUGENE BELL

Rev. Bell, our new associate pastor, comes originally from Century, Florida, where he was reared and where he attended school through High School. He served in the United States Marines during World War II. Following this he attended Asbury College from which he was graduated in 1950.

Following graduation from college, Rev. Bell went to work as a claims adjuster and worked in this field for 10 years before deciding to enter into the ministry. He is now in school in the Chandler School of Theology from which he will graduate this August.

Rev. Bell is married to Nadine Pixley of East St. Louis, Illinois. They have two girls, Denise, age 9, and Tonya, age 6. The Bells are living in the parsonage at 110 Soule Street.

Virginia Crowell, Director, Christian Education 1962 – 1967

North Carolina native Virginia Crowell came to Athens First from a previous position in

Virginia Crowell in 1962 and 1963

Charlotte. She graduated from Queens College in Charlotte with a major in Bible. She taught Bible in the public schools of North Carolina several years, and also taught in the public schools of Annapolis, Maryland. She did a summer of graduate work at Union Seminary in New York City, and at the time she came to Athens was pursuing a Master's in New Testament at Emory University.

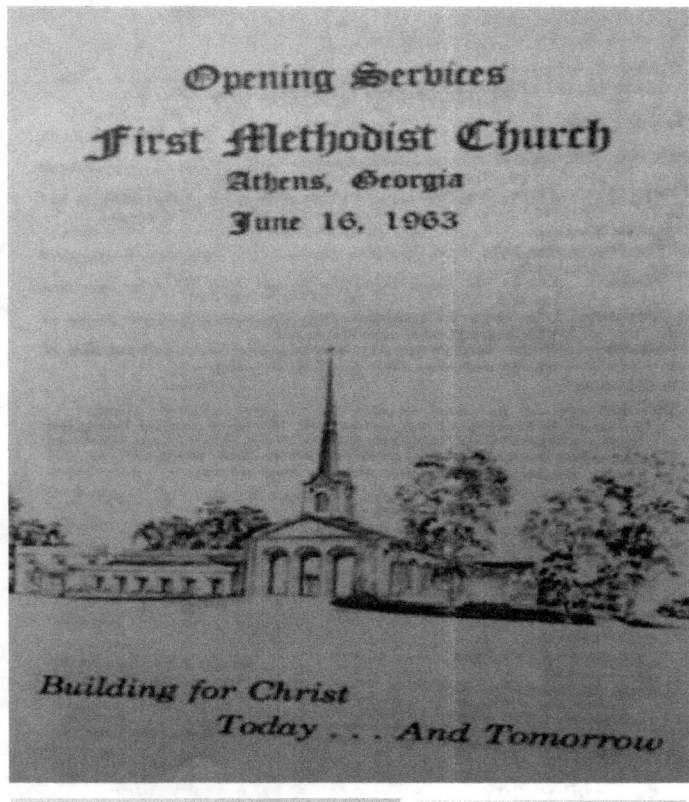

At the dedicatory service in June 1963, Bishop John Owen Smith presided and delivered the sermon.

Other participants included Senior Minister Charles Boleyn, Minister of Music Reginald Smith, Official Board Chairman W. A. Sutton, Trustees Chairman John Bondurant, and Building Committee Chairman Comer Whitehead. The service closed with the traditional hymn, "O God, Our Help in Ages Past."

CHURCH ENVELOPES

Sets of church envelopes are being mailed this week to our membership. If you have not received yours, please contact the church office, and a set will be mailed to you, and any other members of your family who may need them.

CHURCH FINANCES

This is the first Sunday of our new conference year. Could we make one suggestion for all our members. Let us pay our pledges to the church systematically and regularly using the church envelopes. Our church can only meet its obligations to others as the members meet their obligations to the church.

HELP, HELP, HELP!

The pastors of the church need your help in finding out about pastoral needs within the congregation. It will be appreciated if you will advise the church office of any need.

Some notes to the congregation in a 1962 edition of The Steeple.

CHAIRMAN OF THE OFFICIAL BOARD STRESSES THE IMPORTANCE OF OUR EVERY MEMBER CANVASS.

Comer Whitehead, the Chairman of our Official Board for the last two years, stresses the importance of our Every Member Canvass this year.

"First Methodist Church stands at a very important point in its history," says Mr. Whitehead. "We must do a better job this year than we have in the past if we are to meet the demands upon us at this time."

"We believe we can count on every member to 'Show His Faith' and 'Do His Part'," said Mr. Whitehead.

In May 1962 at the height of the Cold War and just before the Cuban Missile Crisis that October, the Board of Trustees approved designating the basement of the new Sunday School building as an official "fallout shelter."

୨1963 ୧

A major renovation that gutted, widened and lengthened the sanctuary, extended the size of the educational wing by two-thirds, and tied the three buildings together with a portico along the Lumpkin Street façade was completed in 1963, with a dedicatory service held on June 16, 1963. The total project cost $638,000, with nearly $300,000 coming from the Lampkin bequest. The amount to be financed depended on timing of the distribution of the Lampkin estate; the final distribution came in 1970. The project brought the sanctuary to its present design, with the pulpit being returned to the west end and the stained-glass windows being added. The nave was widened by 30 feet and a large chancel and organ chamber added in new construction. The steeple as originally built in 1852 and retained during the 1884 reconstruction of the sanctuary remained intact through this remodeling program, as well.

A photo of the interior of the sanctuary as it was 1910-1962. This was taken March 4, 1962, by trustee Robert C. Wilson, looking toward what is now the balcony, immediately before demolition work began for the sanctuary's renovation. The pews were distributed to various organizations as requested, including 18 going to the YMCA Camp Pine Tops.

The stained-glass windows, not part of the original renovation plan, were made possible by an $18,000 gift from Mr. and Mrs. W. A. Mathis in memory of her missionary parents, Dr. and Mrs. Ernest Samuel Lyons, and were added while the project was in progress. The Mathis family, whose construction company carried out the entire renovation project, gave the funds through gift of a house on East Rutherford Street, which the church sold for cash. The windows, created and installed by Willett Stain Glass Studios, depict stories from the Old Testament in the medallions of the left window (top to bottom), from the New Testament in the center window (bottom to top), and of the modern church since the time of Christ in the right window (top to bottom), ending with our church steeple and the UGA Arch in the lower right corner. On the opposite page is a brochure the church created in 2010 to tell the story of the windows.

The main construction contract with Mathis Construction Company came to $542,543 after change orders and credits for cost savings. Pews for the new sanctuary were constructed by Turney Wood Products, Inc. at a cost of $15,272 with $4,153 for cushions. The chancel furniture came from Ipsen Church Interiors for $14,450, and included the pulpit and lectern, altar, font, communion rail and side rails, and a Cross and four candleholders.

The major work on the physical plant in 1963 also renovated the church Fellowship Hall in the sanctuary basement, its location at least since the 1910 renovations. It completely updated the cooking and serving kitchen. In 2000, with the addition of the new Family Life Center including Hancock Hall and a new kitchen, the former Fellowship Hall was renovated into its current use as a music suite for the church's choirs and other musical ensembles.

Kempton Haynes, Jr., Associate Pastor, 1963-1964

Born August 12, 1936, Kempton Haynes was admitted in full connection in 1965. His first appointment was as associate pastor at Athens First for the year 1963-64, followed by: 1964 Vinings; 1965, new church plant in the Atlanta-Marietta District; 1966, chaplain, Georgia Mental Health Institute; 1970 chaplain, Vanderbilt University Hospital; 1976 Hinton Memorial UMC; 1977 Ellenwood; 1978 chaplain, Georgia Mental Health Institute; 1992, executive director, Ministry for Justice and Peace; 1993 consultant, Trinity UMC.

Dr. Joseph Kenneth Patrick, a trustee since 1954, died March 11, 1963,

A Guide to Our Windows

with accompanying resources for reflection and meditation

Athens First United Methodist Church
Sanctuary Stained Glass Windows

Welcome to Our Sanctuary.

This is a sanctuary—from the outside world, from your stress-filled day from the pressures of work and family. We hope you will come in from time to time to sit and be still in God's presence. It's a beautiful space that inspires worship. Worship can happen anytime, even when you are alone.

This brochure is offered as an aid to your reflections. Each panel of the stained glass windows is named and explained below. There are scriptures and hymns for meditation. Bibles, United Methodist Hymnals, and The Faith We Sing (TFWS) are found in all pews of the sanctuary.

May you find comfort in this work of art that glorifies God and all His creation. May this be a sanctuary for you.

Be still and know that I am God. Psalm 46:10

God the Father - Prevenient Grace

The Creation
Praise and Thanksgiving

In the beginning God created the heavens and the earth. And God said, "Let there be light," and there was light.

Genesis 1:1,3

In the beginning was the Word, and the Word was with God, and the Word was God.

John 1:1

Psalms 24 and 148
Hymnal 147 and 420

Abraham and Isaac
God's Providential Care

But the angel of the Lord called out to him from heaven, "Abraham!" "Here I am," he replied. "Now I know that you fear God, because you have not withheld from me your only son."

Genesis 22:11,12

Psalms 121
Hymnal 369 and 462

Moses
Following God's Call

And the Lord spoke unto Moses, "Go unto Pharaoh and say unto him, 'Thus saith the Lord, let my people go, that they may serve me.'"

Exodus 8:1

Hymnal 448

Elijah
Hearing the Voice of God

Then a great and powerful wind tore the mountains apart and shattered the rocks before the Lord, but the Lord was not in the wind. After the wind there was an earthquake, but the Lord was not in the earthquake. After the earthquake came a fire, but the Lord was not in the fire. And after the fire came a gentle whisper.

1 Kings 19:11,12

Psalms 46:10
Hymnal 534, 2128 (TFWS)

Isaiah
God's Call

Then one of the seraphs flew to me with a live coal in his hand, which he had taken with tongs from the altar. With it he touched my mouth and said, "See, this has touched your lips, your guilt is taken away and your sin atoned for." Then I heard the voice of the Lord saying, "Whom shall I send? And who will go for us?" And I said, "Here am I. Send me!"

Isaiah 6:6-8

The people walking in darkness have seen a great light.

Isaiah 9:2

Hymnal 593

God the Son - Justifying Grace

The Nativity
God's Gift

While they were in Bethlehem, the time came for the baby to be born, and she gave birth to her firstborn, a son. She wrapped him in cloths and placed him in a manger, because there was no room for them in the inn.

Luke 2:6,7

For God so loved the world that he gave his only Son, so that everyone who believes in him may not perish but may have eternal life.

John 3:16

Hymnal 239 and 246

Jesus' Baptism
Remembering Your Baptism

As soon as Jesus was baptized by John, he went up out of the water. At that moment heaven was opened, and he saw the Spirit of God descending like a dove and lighting on him. And a voice from heaven said, "This is my Son, whom I love; with him I am well pleased."

Matthew 3:16,17

Jesus in the Garden
God's Will

Going a little farther, he fell to the ground and prayed that if possible the hour might pass from him. "Abba, Father," he said, "everything is possible for you. Take this cup from me."

Mark 14:35,36

Hymnal 290 and 314

The Resurrection
Eternal Life

Why do you look for the living among the dead? He is not here, he has risen!

Luke 24:5,6

But the angel answered and said to the women, "Do not be afraid, for I know that you seek Jesus who was crucified. He is not here, for He is risen, as He said."

Matthew 28:5,6

Hymnal 302 and 321

God the Holy Spirit - Sanctifying Grace

The Holy Spirit
The Holy Spirit Within Us

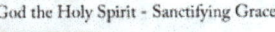

Suddenly a sound like the blowing of a violent wind came from heaven and filled the whole house where they were sitting. They saw what seemed to be tongues of fire that separated and came to rest on each of them. All of them were filled with the Holy Spirit and began to speak in other tongues as the Spirit enabled them.

Acts 2:2-4

Psalms 104: 24-34
Hymnal 393 and 542

The Apostle Paul
Missions

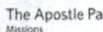

Then Paul and Barnabas answered them boldly: "...this is what the Lord has commanded us: 'I have made you a light for the Gentiles, that you may bring salvation to the ends of the earth.'"

Acts 13:46,47

Hymnal 548 and 556

Martin Luther
Saved by Faith Alone

"With all my heart I would extol the precious gift of God in the noble art of music. Music is to be praised as second only to the Word of God because by her of the emotions are swayed."

Martin Luther

Psalms 46
Hymnal 110 and 515

The Wesley Brothers
God's Grace

"Above all sing spiritually. Have an eye to God in every word you sing. Aim at pleasing Him more than yourself, or any other creature."

From John Wesley's Select Hymns, 1761

But now, apart from law, the righteousness of God has been disclosed, and is attested by the law and the prophets, the righteousness of God through faith in Jesus Christ for all who believe. For there is no distinction, since all have sinned and fall short of the glory of God; they are now justified by his grace as a gift, through the redemption that is in Christ Jesus, whom God put forward as a sacrifice of atonement by his blood, effective through faith. He did this to show his righteousness, because in his divine forbearance he had passed over the sins previously committed; it was to prove at the present time that he himself is righteous and that he justifies the one who has faith in Jesus.

Romans 3:21-26

Hymnal 378, 383, and 384

Our Church and Our Community
Making Disciples of Jesus Christ

There came a man who was sent from God. His name was John. He came as a witness to testify concerning that Light, so that through him all might believe. He himself was not the Light. The True Light that gives light to every man was coming into the world.

John 1:6-9

Go therefore and make disciples of all nations, baptizing them in the name of the Father and of the Son and of the Holy Spirit, and teaching them to obey everything that I have commanded you. And remember, I am with you always, to the end of the age.

Matthew 28:19,20

Hymnal 328, 572, and 574

The Chancel Memorial Windows were given in 1963 by the W. A. Mathis family in honor of Mrs. Mathis' missionary parents, Dr. and Mrs. Ernest Samuel Lyons. The renovation of the sanctuary and the installation of the windows were overseen by the senior minister, Dr. Charles Boleyn. The windows were designed and created by the Willet Art Studio in Philadelphia, PA. During the renovation, the congregation met for worship at the historic Georgia Theatre, complete with the weekly sermon topic appearing on the theatre marquee!

In April 2010, the Wesleyan Youth Choir, under the direction of Jana Maxwell, performed a concert of anthems that centered around these beautiful stained glass windows. "Sing to the Light" featured an anthem or hymn for each of the panels - bringing melodic and voice to the stories that are portrayed in this visual work of art. The idea for the meditation brochure grew out of the program notes used in that concert. Many thanks to Dianne Morrison and Louise Sorrells for much of the information provided here.

ATHENS FIRST UNITED METHODIST CHURCH
327 N. Lumpkin Street Athens, Georgia 30601
athensfirstumc.org | 706-543-1442

PROGRESS REPORT

Through the courtesy of the REM Studios, we have this photo of what might be called "the turning point" in the construction of our new church structure. All the destruction has been completed and construction just begun. In just the few days since this picture was taken, tremendous progress has been made on the sanctuary structure.

In addition, though not shown in the picture, all of the structural work has been completed on the additions to the Education building and now the finishing progress is under way. Regardless of what the weather does now, work can go ahead toward getting this space ready for our use in the fall of 1962.

All members of First Methodist Church who have not had the opportunity to see at first hand the tremendous changes being made in our house of worship are invited to stop by for a personal inspection of the new buildings.

The Fellowship Hall in the sanctuary basement as it appeared after the 1963 renovations. This area today is the music suite.

The sanctuary building at the height of demolition in 1962. The former chancel area is seen on the back (east) wall. The west wall has been torn away along with the former Sunday School area. The sanctuary next was widened by removing the side walls and adding 15 feet on each side, and an entirely new Chancel area and organ chamber constructed with adjacent classroom space. Finally, the new stained-glass windows were added to the new west wall, and a new corridor was built connecting the sanctuary building to the newly- expanded Sunday School building.

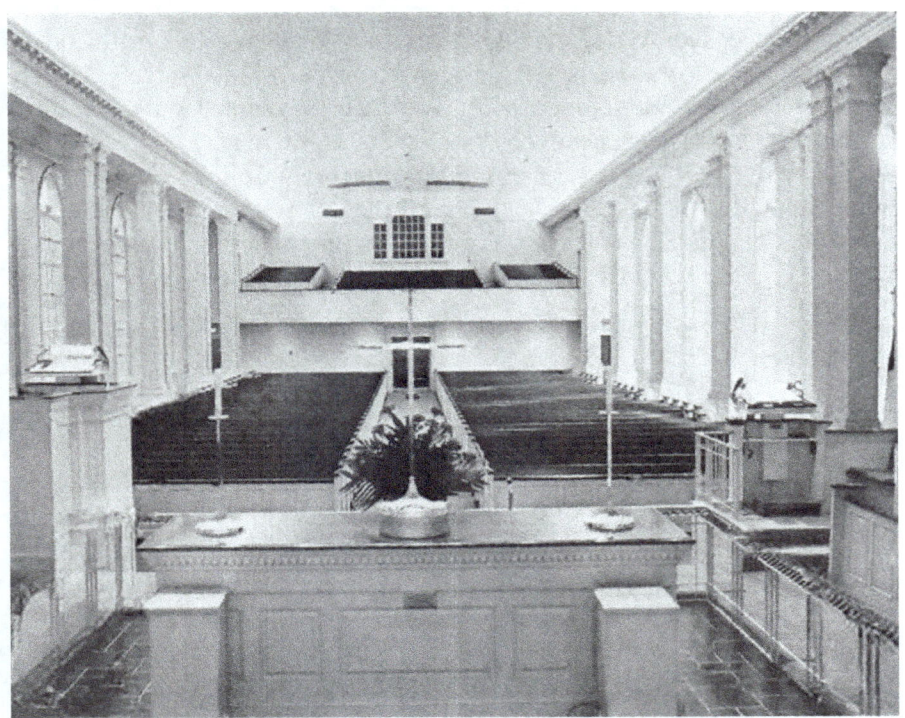

The sanctuary as it appeared looking east from the chancel at the conclusion of the extensive rebuilding of 1962-63. Columns now stand where the exterior walls previously were. The area from the pulpit and lectern westward to the stained-glass windows is entirely new construction.

The eight-sided baptismal font includes a basin and cover fabricated by master metalworker Harvey Yellin of Philadelphia. The eight sides represent the new creation – the Christian belief that Easter
occurred on Sunday, the eighth day, ushering in a new creation.

and was succeeded by Nathaniel Garnett "Nat" Slaughter, a Carroll County native who came to Athens in 1903 to open a practice in dental surgery. Already having served the church for decades as delegate to Annual Conferences and as a North Georgia delegate to the 1930 General Conference in Dallas, Texas, Slaughter also was Lay Leader of the North Georgia Conference, a director of the Methodist Board of Publications, and had represented the Athens area in the Georgia State Senate. He was a founding member of the Tuck Sunday School class. He would serve as a church trustee only three years, dying in 1966 at the age of 83.

୨1964 ୭

Frank Henry Prince, Senior Minister, 1964-1970

Born December 8, 1913, in South Carolina, Frank Prince married Madge Lowe in 1943. He received the A.B. degree from Wofford College and the B.D. from Emory University. He was admitted on trial 1944 and in full connection 1946. Appointments were: 1944 Sardis, 1948 Trion, 1952 Jonesboro, 1956 Covington, 1960 Toccoa First, 1964 Athens First, 1970 District Superintendent of the Atlanta-Decatur-Oxford District, 1976 Rome First, 1980 Bethesda-Hartwell, 1983 Retired. He lived in Dahlonega in retirement and died July 18, 1992. Unfortunately, he does not have a memoir published in the Conference Journal. Longtime member Mary Hutcherson recalls that Prince preached social justice during the difficult Civil Rights era, making one "want to take to the streets with a protest sign!" Dr. Bill Britt remembers that Rev. Hubert Flanagan spoke glowingly of Rev. Prince's time in Athens: "Hubert believed Athens First should be served by a pastor who graduated from UGA and bled Red & Black. When I was Hubert's associate, he once lamented to me, 'Athens First has not had a preacher who really loved the church since Frank Prince!'" We note that Bill Britt, not a UGA grad, indeed did come to Athens some years later and was quickly innoculated with Red & Black, loving Athens, UGA and the church to the point that Rev. Flanagan approved.

Rev. Frank H. Prince

CONGRATULATIONS TO PRINCE

Our pastor, Frank H. Prince, received a most pleasant surprise at Annual Conference this year. He was one of the ten delegates elected to the Jurisdictional Conference. In the words of our District Superintendent, W. H. Ruff, "It is indeed a high honor," and, we believe, one which was very deserving for our beloved pastor.

We congratulate Rev. Prince on this honor—mainly because we think he will tackle this new task with sincerity and integrity, but also because we love him and want the best for him. We are sure our views reflect the feelings of the entire membership of First Methodist.

The Staff

Roy Felix Major, Associate Pastor 1963 – 1966

Born June 21, 1931, in Piedmont, South Carolina, in 1961 Rev. Major married Theresa Dodson, sister of prominent North Georgia minister Malone Dodson. Major was admitted as an elder in full connection in 1960. He served churches across the North Georgia Conference for 40 years, including: 1957 Waco; 1958 Stilesboro; 1961 Elizabeth, Marietta; 1962 St. Stephen, Monroe. He was sent to Athens First as an associate in a mid-year appointment on December 1, 1963, and served until June 1966. His further appointments were: 1966 Bethesda, Hartwell; 1968 St John, Augusta; 1970 Trion; 1973 St. Luke, Augusta; 1977 Flippen; 1981 Bethany-Pine Grove; 1983 Rock Springs; 1986 Lavonia First; 1988 Francis Asbury, Elberton; 1992 Hiawassee; 1995 Chicopee-Candler, Gainesville; 1997 retired. In retirement, he was active at Watkinsville First UMC and served as chaplain at Magnolia Estates Assisted Living in Oconee County for 16 years. He died May 16, 2019, at age 87. His funeral was at Watkinsville First UMC with Reverends Malone Dodson, Steve Dodson and Emily Whiten officiating.

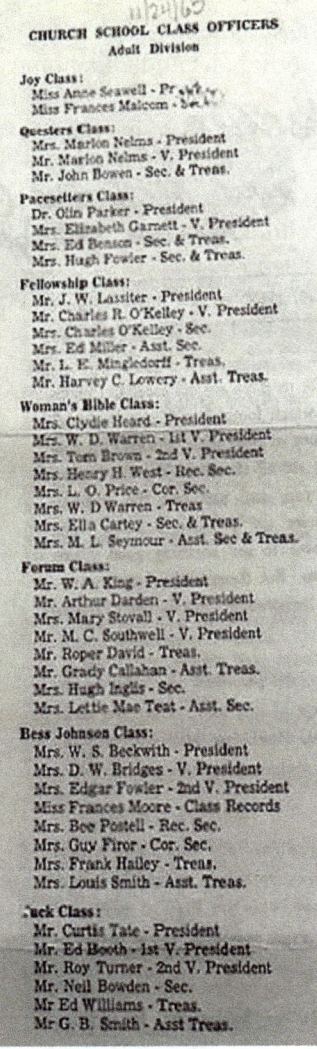

Future Athens First Pastor T. Cecil Myers was among the clergy elected as delegate from North Georgia to the 1964 General Conference of the Methodist Church. Alternates, who also served as Jurisdictional Conference delegates, included Lester Rumble, Bevel Jones, and Charles Boleyn. Judge Grady Pittard of Athens was among the lay delegates elected to Jurisdictional Conference, and Dr. Nat G. Slaughter was elected a Jurisdictional reserve.

9 1965 9

Pastor Frank Prince informed the Trustees

A MINISTRY IN SONG

SARA BRAUCHER

A fixture in our Chancel Choir more than six decades, Sara Braucher sang countless solos through those years, but her greatest joy came from leading the children's choirs.

In 1958 Charles and I moved to Athens and joined the First Methodist Church. I sang in the adult choir led by Reginald Smith. He asked me if I could teach songs to the children, and I did until we moved to Indiana and Oklahoma.

In 1966 we moved back to Athens, and I went back to the adult choir and singing songs with the children. Occasionally, we would sing songs before the regular church service began. Nancy Morgan said she would help me with the children. I continued to teach the younger children and she worked with the older children. When Mr. Reg Smith left as music director, Herb Hoffman took over, and later Martha Braswell. Nancy and I continued to work with the kids.

Dr. Cecil Meyers came and asked if we could do a Christmas program before the traditional Christmas service. I agreed and purchased music from the Baptist Publishing Company. Mary Hutcherson played the piano and made the costumes.

When Carol Reeves came as children's choir director, the children's choirs became official and supplies were funded. I taught the Joy Choir and Carol taught the Celebrate Choir. I continued to teach the children's choirs, sing in the Chancel Choir, and raise my five children with Charlie. I loved sharing my love of music with others.

I wish I continued to teach the children choir. It was so much fun, but Charlie started having health problems and needed my assistance full time.

Sara and Charley Braucher and family, at right Sara singing in Chancel Choir

that Bishop John Owen Smith planned to use the Athens First sanctuary for a May 4 meeting on the federal War on Poverty program being advanced by President Lyndon B. Johnson. The meeting at the church was to feature Congressman Phil Landrum with Bishop Smith and all his Cabinet present, as well as some 800 invited Methodist minister guests, including "a colored bishop and some colored ministers." Chairman John Bondurant called a meeting of the Board of Trustees for April 11, at which the Trustees unanimously adopted a resolution disallowing use of the sanctuary for such a meeting, under the premise that (quoting the Trustee minutes) "neither the Methodist Church nor the First Methodist Church of Athens should be the vehicle for the promotion of federal programs." Fearing it would appear the church sponsored such a program and would violate the separation of church and state, the Trustee minutes further stated, "Our church has high morale and good will among its members and intrusions into non-Church matters can only tend to divide us and to destroy the unanimity which we have worked to create."

The possibility again was raised of acquiring the Beacham property immediately west of the church in the same block. No specific plans were proposed at the time and a committee was appointed to study the matter, comprised of Trustees Whitehead, Wilson, Bondurant and Slaughter. With no action or report from that first committee having come in two years, and with trustee Slaughter having died in the interim, the committee was reappointed in 1967 with the three remaining members charged to study and bring a report.

ᵍ**1966** ᵍ

William Reese Garrard, Associate Pastor 1966 – 1968

Born September 4, 1919, on a farm in Wilkes County, William Garrard married Guinelle Cooper of Hickory, North Carolina and they had four children. He earned the B.S. degree in agriculture from the University of Georgia, where he served in the ROTC Cavalry. He further earned a Master of Divinity degree from Emory's Candler School of Theology, and a Master's in Counseling from UGA. During World War II, he retired as an officer after service in the Army Air Corps in the Philippines and Japan. He spent 30 years in pastoral appointments, including being a

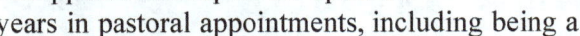

Rev. William Reese Garrard

missionary in Puerto Rico. He was best known as founder in 1969 of the Covecrest Christian Renewal Center near Clayton, Ga. Rev. Garrard died March 27, 2012, at Hickory, North Carolina at age 93. His funeral was at the Smyrna UMC in Washington, Ga., with burial in the church cemetery. A son, William R. Garrard, Jr., retired in 2010 after 14 years' service as a full elder in the Western North Carolina Conference.

Trustee Nat Slaughter died on July 3, 1966, and trustee Robert C. Wilson resigned his position on July 11, 1966. Chosen to succeed them, respectively, were Jenkins Comer Whitehead and Marcellus Troutman Wilson.

An Athens native and 1932 graduate of Athens High School, Comer Whitehead received the B.S. degree from the University of Georgia in 1936. He was faculty advisor for Chi Psi fraternity from 1936 through 1964. Employed by UGA immediately upon graduation, he rose to head the IBM Department, later the Computer Department, today known as Information Technology. He worked for UGA for 46 years, retiring from the Division of Business and Finance in 1982. He was on Athens City Council 1953 – 1975. At Athens First, he chaired the Administrative Board and served as Lay Leader. He chaired the building committee for the 1963 sanctuary renovation. He would serve on the Board of Trustees 20 years, resigning in 1986.

OUR FALL PASTOR'S CLASS

Troutman Wilson, also an Athens native, was chosen trustee to succeed his father, Dr. Robert C. Wilson, founding dean of the UGA School of Pharmacy and a longtime leader at Athens First Methodist. Both were direct descendants of the church's first appointed pastor, Rev. Lovick Pierce. Troutman graduated UGA in 1934, making Phi Beta Kappa. He served in World War II, rising to full colonel. He was a partner in Normal Hardware Company before becoming executive vice president of the National Bank of Athens, and also served as president of the Athens Chamber of Commerce. He retired from the Trust Company Bank of Northeast Georgia in 1983. He served as church trustee until 1990, when he reached a term limit under a new board policy.

◙ **1967** ◙

The associate pastor's parsonage in University Heights was not needed by the incoming associate, so it was placed for rent until such time as an associate pastor might need a parsonage.

◙ **1968** ◙

The Methodist Church and the Evangelical United Brethren merged to become the United Methodist Church. The separate Central Jurisdiction for Black churches was dissolved and its churches merged into the geographical conferences in which they lay. In Georgia, this was accomplished in 1971 when the Black Georgia Conference and the White North Georgia Conference merged, with Black churches in South Georgia becoming the Georgia Coastal District of the North Georgia Conference. Those churches became part of the South Georgia Conference in 1972.

Oscar David Crosby, Jr., Associate Pastor 1968 – 1969

Rev. Crosby was born September 26, 1924, in Birmingham, Alabama. In 1948 he married Frances Timberlake, and they were married 54 years. They had one daughter. Oscar served in World War II with the 11th Armored Division in Europe, holding regular reunions with the soldiers in his unit over the next 50 years. Rev. Crosby then attended Auburn University, graduating with a degree in agriculture. He worked several years with the Alabama Extension Service before answering a call into ministry. He entered Candler School of Theology at Emory University in 1963. While in seminary, he was pastor of the Hoschton Circuit, including Hoschton, New Liberty, Center and Bethlehem churches. Upon graduation, he was ordained elder and appointed as an associate minister at Athens First. His further appointments were Comer, Princeton, Clarkesville, Buford and Clayton First, from which he retired in 1987. In retirement, he served Mount Zion UMC in Alto for 11 years. He volunteered with Georgia Mental Health while serving churches. He helped establish the Habersham Soup Kitchen and Habersham Sharing and Caring. Oscar faced a long battle with cancer and died January 2, 2002. His funeral was at Whitfield Funeral Home Chapel in Demorest, with interment in Yonah Memorial Gardens.

᧐1969 ᧐

The church had several changes to program and staff in 1969. Ernestine Adams began as Director of Christian Education. Max Mayo, who had directed a recreation program for several years, ended his time and was succeeded by Archie Buie, a Candler Theology student who was charged with being a part-time minister to youth, working only on weekends. The Florida Southern College graduate had served in the U.S. Army. The church also in 1969 started a kindergarten program in Parkview Apartments at the request of the Athens Housing Authority. The program was operated by one paid staff member and volunteers from the church.

᧐1970 ᧐

Thomas Cecil Myers, Senior Minister, 1970-1976

Born October 25, 1919, in Trenton, Dade County, Cecil Myers moved with his family to Chickamauga after his father died when Cecil was quite young. His mother married Judson A. Bowen, who had a great influence on Cecil's life. As a member of Elizabeth Lee Methodist Church, Cecil was called to ministry under the guidance of the Reverend William H. Gardner. After graduating from Chickamauga High School, Cecil attended Young Harris College and was forever grateful to Dr. Jack Lance for making it possible for him to do so. Attending a student conference at Wesleyan College, he met a student from Brenau College,

Dr. T. Cecil Myers

Elizabeth McCurry of Hartwell. They married at Hartwell First Methodist in 1943. Cecil received the A.B. degree from the University of Tennessee at Chattanooga in 1942 and taught at the McCallie School in Chattanooga that year. He earned the Bachelor of Divinity degree from the Candler School of Theology at Emory University in 1946. During this time, he was Youth Director for the North Georgia Conference, so he and Elizabeth visited youth groups in many churches and worked at Camp Glisson and youth assemblies.

He was admitted on trial in 1944 and received a student appointment that year to Brookhaven Methodist Church, a post he held until 1951 where he oversaw construction of a new church building. He was admitted in full connection in 1946. He received an honorary Doctor of Divinity degree from LaGrange College in 1959. Further appointments were: 1951 Trinity, Atlanta, 1957 Sam Jones, Cartersville, 1960 Grace, Atlanta, 1970 Athens First, 1976 Peachtree Road, Atlanta. He and Elizabeth retired in 1984 and made their

He was considered one of the great pulpiteers of his generation and likely would have been a bishop had he not declined the nomination of the North Georgia Conference.

home in Hartwell. He was a delegate to General and Jurisdictional Conference six times. Being elected first in the clergy delegation, Dr. Myers declined North Georgia nomination as a candidate for Bishop, citing health reasons and a preference to remain in the pastorate. Noted for the live broadcasts of his sermons on Atlanta television during his pastorate at Grace Church, he also was author of six popular books: *"Faith for a time of storm,"* New York: Abingdon Press, 1963; *"Thunder on the Mountain,"* New York: Abingdon Press, 1965; *"When Crisis Comes,"* Nashville: Abingdon Press, 1967; *"Happiness is Still Homemade,"* Waco: Word Books, 1969; *"Living on tiptoe: the healing power of love,"* Waco: Word Books, 1972; *"You can be more than you are,"* Waco: Word Books, 1976. He served as a trustee of LaGrange, Reinhardt, and Young Harris colleges and the Methodist Children's Home. After a long battle with cancer, Dr. Myers died June 16, 1995, in an Anderson, S.C. hospital. His funeral was at Hartwell First with Bishop J. Lloyd Knox officiating. He was buried at Northview Cemetery, Hartwell.

Malcolm Lang "Mac" Paterson III, Associate Pastor 1970 – 1971

Born in Mobile, Alabama, Mac Paterson grew up in Shubuta, Mississippi. He obtained the BA degree from Millsaps College and the Master of Divinity from Emory University. He served churches throughout the Mississippi and North Georgia Conferences during his 37-year ministry.

Rev. Malcolm L. "Mac" Paterson III

Rev. Paterson came to Athens First in 1970 after two years at Marvin UMC in Augusta. His obituary described Mac Paterson as "a character, who offered his unconventional personality in service and friendship with others in his calling as a United Methodist minister." He had a strength in connecting with people of whatever station and reveled in family and friendships. "He never met a stranger. He could, and did, strike up a conversation with anyone he met." He died February 10, 2011, following a three-year battle with cancer. His funeral was at McDonough First UMC.

A newly constructed home at 190 Highland Drive in the Kingswood subdivison off Timothy Road was purchased for $40,625 as a new parsonage. The Dearing Street parsonage was sold for $27,500.

◙**1971** ◙

Henrietta Baucom, Director of Youth Activities 1971 – 1972

Henrietta Baucom became Youth Director Novembr 1, 1971, but stayed on staff only seven months. A native of British Columbia, Canada, she held a Certificate in Bible and Christian Education from Briercrest Bible Institute in Canada. She studied at L'Ecole de Commerce in Neuchatel, Switzerland. She worked three years as counselor for the Intervarsity Christian Fellowship at the Women's Branch of Virginia Polytechnic Institute in Radford, Virginia, and was Director of Youth Activities for Christ Methodist Church in Hartford, Connecticut. She worked four years for the Methodist Board of Missions in South Africa, working with her husband in adult literacy programs. She and husband Dr. Kenneth Baucom had three children. Wrote

Henrietta Baucom

Pastor Cecil Myers in announcing the appointment, "All parents, please give wholehearted cooperation in our youth program. Without your active assistance and goodwill, the entire program is limited. I call on all young people in First Church to get involved in the planning, the carrying out of the plans, in making ours a Christ-centered youth program, concerned with people, with issues. I dare you to give Christ and your church your very best." Unfortunately, the Baucoms departed in June 1972 for another mission appointment in Africa.

The Athens First Lay Leader for 1971 was Billy Hudson. Annual Conference delegates were J. Smiley Wolfe and Sam Heys.

◙**1972** ◙

Clarence L. "C.L." Harris, Associate Pastor, 1972 – 1976

Rev. Clarence L. Harris (who went by "C.L.") was born January 21, 1910, in Fayette County. He attended the Forsyth County schools. At age 17 he moved to Carrollton where he worked for a textile company. He married Nellie Ruth Hardegree in 1929 and they had two sons. During World War II he worked a ship construction job in Brunswick, building "Liberty Ships"

DR. CHARLIE SHEDD TO SPEAK
WEDNESDAY NIGHT, NOVEMBER 17

Dr. Charlie Shedd is recognized as one of the nation's most authorities on youth problems. He is author of The Stork Is Dead, Promises to Peter, Letters to Philip, Letters to Karen and many other books.

On Wednesday night he will speak to parents and other adults, and later to young people. Thursday morning at breakfast he will speak to teachers and other workers with youth.

Here is the schedule:

Wednesday   6:00 P.M.   Dinner
  6:45 P.M.   Parents & Adults meet with Dr. Shedd
  7:30 P.M.   Youth meet with Dr. Shedd
Thursday   7:00 A.M.   Breakfast at Davis House with Dr. Shedd for teachers of youth or other workers

Nationally noted authority on youth issues, Dr. Charlie Shedd, came to Athens First to conduct a seminar in November 1971. He would return to Athens First as Minister of Stewardship in 1986 following his retirement. One of his best-known publications was *"Promises to Peter,"* referring to his son, Peter Shedd, of our congregation.

for the U.S. Navy. Returning to Carrollton, he worked for a department store. While undergoing training to become a store manager, he felt called to the ministry and began summer classes at West Georgia College to complete

C. L. Harris

his bachelor's degree, followed by theological study at LaGrange College and Emory University. Ordained an elder in 1945, he served appointments at Buchanan; Bowdon Circuit; Carrollton Circuit; Unity,LaGrange; Menlo-Bethel; Boynton; Tillman Memorial; Palmetto; Chatsworth;

Oconee Street, Athens; and Athens First, associate, from which he retired. At Athens First, his responsibilities were pastoral visitation, evangelism, and social concerns. After retirement in 1976, he returned to the pulpit at Prospect Church, Athens. He retired a second time in 1982 and moved to Peachtree City. Even then, he filled pulpits at Philadelphia and New Hope Churches, McDonough, continuing to serve until shortly before his death on May 11, 1996, at Emory University Hospital. He is buried in Westminster Gardens in Peachtree City.

Charles Johnson, Associate Pastor, 1972 – 1983

A Mississippi native, Charles Johnson came to Athens First in 1972, first as Minister of Program. He attended public schools in New Albany, Mississippi, earned a B.A. degree from Millsaps College, and the M.Div. degree from Candler School of Theology at Emory University. He and his wife, the former Gwen Harwell, arrived in Athens with three children under the age of seven: Beth, Lynn and Charles Jr. Ordained in the North Mississippi

Charles Johnson

Conference, he served appointments as Minister of Christian Education at the First United Methodist churches at Clarksdale and Starkville before coming to Athens. His responsibilities here included the full Christian education program, from Sunday School classes to teacher recruitment and training, to leadership training and youth activities. He also was coordinator for the Council on Ministries. His position broadened over the years to that of Pastor of Church Administration. After eleven years on our staff, Johnson returned to the North Mississippi Conference to a position as administrator at Trinity Place in Columbus, a United Methodist senior living facility. Pastor Bill Floyd wrote, "Charles' contribution to the life and faith of this church is immeasurable. He will be sorely missed, but we wish him Godspeed in this new ministry."

Robert C. "Bob" Barnes, Director of Youth Ministries 1972 –1974

Following the brief tenure of Henrietta Baucom as youth director and her departure in June 1972, Robert Barnes took that position effective September 1972. A Michigan native, Barnes was a Detroit Conference MYF officer during high school. He earned the B.S. degree from Florida Southern College, the M.E. degree from Hardin-Simmons University, and pursued graduate work at the University of Mississippi, Southern Methodist University and Abilene Christian College before coming to the University of Georgia in the Ph.D. program in counseling psychology. He previously

was Director of Youth at Leggett Memorial Methodist Church in Biloxi, Mississippi; Director of Christian Education at First Methodist Church of Gulfport, Mississippi; at Tyler Street UMC in Dallas, Texas, and at St. Paul UMC in Abilene, Texas. His wife, the former Dorothy Kraft, taught Health Education at UGA and previously was a Methodist missionary at Kinnaird Christian College in Pakistan. She also was a prospective candidate for a doctoral degree at UGA.

In welcoming Barnes to the position at our church, Pastor Cecil Myers wrote: "It is not enough to bring a man like this to our staff. With all of his experience and qualifications he cannot do the job without the cooperation of parents, youth, the

198

LANIER GARDENS NEARING COMPLETION

Sometime in January, Lanier Gardens will be consecrated, and the first resident will move in. What an asset this facility is going to be to the Athens area! It is a thing of beauty, of convenience, and priced within reach of those with moderate retirement income. There are few frills, but ample comfort and efficiency have been built into it.

Help is still needed to provide furnishings and equipment for the public areas. Any amount of money will be welcomed, or you may equip any one of several public rooms completely. All of us ought to be so proud to have this facility that we'd want to have a part in making it the finest and best of its kind anywhere. There are memorials available, and gifts may be given in honor of loved ones. For complete information call either the Reverend Jay Irby, (546-1480), the Administrator, or Mr. Jimmy Akins, (548-4494) Chairman of the Advisory Board.

Administrative Board, and all the members of the church. *We make a mistake if we think our problems can be solved by hiring a new staff member!* (Dr. Myers wrote the previous sentence in all-Caps.) Not so. He simply gives guidance, love, hope, encouragement. He brings ideas and possibilities. But without the enthusistic support of the membership it will all come to nothing. For a long time, we have talked about the kind of youth program at First Church that will inspire and challenge and involve the very fine young people in our church. We have the best chance to make these dreams come true we have ever had. We have talked long enough. How about pitching in now, parents, youth, officials of the church, and all the rest of us, and with prayer, commitment, work, time, energy and making that dream come true. Bob will give the guidance. Let's give the support!"

❧1973 ❧

Herbert P. Hoffman, Director of Music 1973 – 1977

A native of Youngstown, Ohio, Herb Hoffman came to Athens First in February 1973.
He became interested in choral conducting while in high school where he was student conductor for two years and directed the boys' octette. After one year at Youngstown College, he transferred to Westminster Choir College in Princeton, New Jersey, where he studied for two years with Dr. John

Herb Hoffman

Finley Williamson and Dr. George Lynn. He subsequently attended summer master classes at Westminster for five years. While at Westminster, he was in choral groups that sang with the New York Philharmonic Orchestra and the Philadelphia Symphony Orchestra. Upon the sudden death of his father, Herb left Westminster to return to Youngstown and help support his family through church work and a job at the Republic Rubber Works. The church asked him to take a fulltime position as Director of Christian Education and Music, which led one year later to his being called to a church in Pontiac,

CHAPEL CHOIR TO SING

There is an advertisement on television that says, "You've come a long way .." That can be said of the youth choir of First United Methodist Church. This group, with 38 enrolled, will present the entire Sunday evening service this week, singing the program they will later present on tour. I want to urge every member of this church to come and give them support and encouragement. This is something we have wanted and for which we have worked. So instead of criticizing our youth, encourage them.

Twenty eight of the members of the choir will go on tour, beginning Friday, June 7. In order to go, attendance was required at a certain number of rehearsals. Thirty two of the total number met that requirement. They have worked hard in preparation for this event.

The group will sing in such places as Central Presbyterian Church, Anderson, S. C. First United Methodist Church, Waycross, First United Methodist Church, Jesup, Epworth y-the-Sea, etc. They will return, Tuesday, June 21.

Sunday night they will sing the full concert of sacred music. It also includes handbell d a skit, "Taxicab" by Champion. Herb Hoffman is the director, and Andy Andela e accompanist.

Others going with the young people on tour are The Reverend and Mrs. Jay Irby a s. Herb Hoffman. The group will travel by Southeastern Greyhound. They have earr ch of the money for the trip.

Enrollment for the youth choir for next year will begin June 15. Any young person des 7 through 12 is eligible. Call Mr. Hoffman at 543-5216 for information. A m er trip is planed for next summer.

See you in church Sunday night for a thrilling worship experience!

Herb Hoffman and Andy Andela with the Youth Choir

Michigan, allowing him to resume his education, part-time, at the Wayne State University Detroit Institute for the Musical Arts. There he eventually completed his degree. He further served churches in Ferndale, Michigan; Cuyahoga Falls, Ohio; Phoenix, Arizona; and Fort Mitchell, Kentucky, developing at each a full program of graded choirs. He was a certified lay worker in the United Methodist Church and had held conference-level positions in the Detroit Conference and the Western Jurisdiction. With his wife, Doris, he worked with religious and secular drama and interpretive dance. Doris worked in the UGA College of Veterinary Medicine as information specialist in the dean's office.

Palm Sunday 1973 marked the dedication of a new organ, made possible by a $60,000 gift from Louis T. and M. Smith "Smitty" Griffith. Built by

Louis T. Griffith

W. Zimmer and Sons of Charlotte, it boasted 44 ranks, 2,341 pipes, and chimes. It would serve the church for the next 48 years. A concert on Palm Sunday evening featured the UGA Men's Glee Club and the Wesleyan College Choir. Louis, an active church leader and longtime member of the Chancel Choir, would be named a church Trustee in 1992. This author fondly notes that Louis Griffith was a mentor and close friend. It was Louis who initially invited me to Athens First and to join the choir. He was soloist in our wedding, and I was quoted in the *Athens Banner-Herald* as part of his news obituary, where I termed him "the consummate Southern gentleman."

Andrew Andela, Organist 1973 - 1975

With the acquisition of a significantly larger Zimmer organ in early 1973, Andrew "Andy" Andela joined our church staff as organist and music assistant in September 1973. A graduate of the Guilmont Organ School in New York City, he was Associate of the American Guild of Organists and held a Bachelor of Sacred Music from Westminster Choir College with a major in organ. He played recitals throughout the New York/New Jersey area and was organist for two years at First UMC of Westfield, New Jersey, before coming to Athens. After two years here, Andela accepted a position as organist and choirmaster at Wesley Monumental UMC in Savannah.

୨**1974** ୧

A note-burning service was held as the congregation celebrated being debt-free, having retired the debt from the 1963-64 remodeling project 46 months early.

Michael T. Egan, Director of Youth Ministries 1974 – 1977

Mike Egan joined the staff at Athens First as Director of Youth Ministries in September 1974. A native of Burlington, Iowa, his wife was the

former Naomi Craig. He attended the University of Iowa, Long Beach State University, and Georgia State College. He brought experience in directing children's, youth and adult choirs, a director of drama, and as actor in productions of "Oklahoma," "H.M.S. Pinafore," and "See How They Run." His resume

Mike Egan

included performance with the San Diego Light Opera Company and director of a full production of "Oklahoma."This, coupled with his experience in directing camps, retreats, leading arts and crafts, Bible studies, and recreational sports, recommended him to our church selection committee. Pastor Cecil Myers wrote, "…to have successful youth activities, parents and other adults must cooperate. Encourage your young people to be a vital part of what is going on in the church, see that they are on time, pray for those who teach and counsel them, and give your money generously to support the program. And when you are asked to teach or counsel, agree quickly and gladly. Encourage – don't knock! We have wanted a full time Director of Youth Activities for a long time. He is here. Where are you?" Egan led a very successful youth and choir program for three years before his 1977 resignation.

All churches in Athens were invited to a community celebration in our Athens First sanctuary to mark the 150th anniversary of the founding of the Athens Methodist Church. The joint choirs of the several downtown churches provided the music and the sermon was by Dr. Charles Hasty, pastor of the First Presbyterian Church. The service and a reception following in our Fellowship Hall also was a farewell to longtime Athens First Baptist pastor Dr. Julian Cave and his family, who were moving to Charlotte, N.C. Mrs. Lenora Cave was a popular radio host on WGAU while she was in Athens.

The annual report of Athens First United Methodist Church for the Conference year ending June 30, 1974, showed 147 additions to the membership rolls during the year, and 107 lost by death or transfer, a net gain of 40 members to a total of 2,327. Sunday School reported 977 enrolled with average attendance of 479. Short term courses enrolled 718. United Methodist Women membership was 341. Total giving for all purposes was just more than $260,000. Pastor Cecil Myers expressed sadness, however, that for the first time in his ministry a church he led did not pay all its conference apportionments. "We lacked completing what we were asked to do as our fair share of the total support of the church. I hope this will never happen again." This author is not aware of this having happened any other year in my 50+ years in this congregation. The closest we came was one year during Pastor Larry Bauman's time here when the Administrative Board heard a motion to line-item the apportionments, striking certain lines members deemed objectionable. Rev. Bauman told the board that he would seek appointment elsewhere if they chose to pass that motion, and it failed.

BICENTENNIAL
ATHENS FIRST UNITED METHODIST CHURCH

Completing Our Second Century

1975 - 2024

First United Methodist Church a 'Landmark'

In 1825, Thomas Hancock deeded the lot that lies between Washington Street and Hancock Avenue and faces on Lumpkin Street to the trustees of the Methodist Church. It was given with the stipulation that a building be built within two years.

There had been two previous Methodist meeting houses, one built in 1804 and the other in 1810. Hope Hull was the moving force among Methodists in the area, and after his death in 1818, Methodist nearly

disappeared from Athens.

The building erected in 1825 gave new life.

It was a frame building 40-feet square with a balcony on three sides, and a pulpit so high that a man six feet tall could stand under its floor.

The Rev. Thomas Stanley, a teacher in the Athens Female Academy, served as preacher for the first year.

The first preacher assigned by the conference to

serve the Methodist Church in Athens was Dr. Lovick Pierce. Dr. Robert C. Wilson, now 96 years of age, is a great-great-grandson of Dr. Pierce and was baptized by him. Dr. Pierce's son, the Rev. George F. Pierce, later became a bishop in the Methodist Church.

The church grew, and in 1835 it was enlarged by adding 20 feet at the west end.

See CHURCH on Page 6

From Page 1

Church History

In 1852, the old building was given to a Negro congregation and was moved to the foot of Hancock AVenue. A new church, costing $6,500 was built, and the outer walls of that building form part of the outer walls of the present structure.

The present steeple remains unchanged since it was built in 1852.

In 1870 a pipe organ was installed. In that same year, Oconee Street Methodist Church was organized with members from First Methodist Church. A Ferdinand Phinizy reportedly disliked music in the church and promised a large sum of money to Oconee Street as long as it didn't have an organ.

In 1884, the church was remodeled to provide Sunday School space.

In 1906, a parsonage was built at the corner of Lumpkin and Washington streets which was used until 1939.

In 1910, the church was again remodeled and the pulpit was moved from its original location to the Lumpkin Street end, making it necessary for all who came to church to face the congregation. That same year, the Tuck Bible Class was organized.

The year 1924 saw the installation of a new Moeller organ, while 1938 saw the purchase of a new parsonage on Dearing Street at a cost of $6,300 which served as the home of the church's ministers until 1970.

The new education building was erected on the corner of Lumpkin and the new education building was erected on the corner of Lumpkin and Washingtin during 1950-52 where the old parsonage had stood. It cost $220,000, and the chapel was built at the same time.

In 1960-63, the sanctuary was remodeled, and the pulpit moved to its original location. The steeple remained intact, while the memorial lancet windows were installed.

The new parsonage at 190 Highland Drive in Kingswood was purchased in 1970, while the new Zimmer organ was installed during 1972-73, a gift from the Louis T. Griffith family.

The year 1974 saw the final payment made on remodeling the Sanctuary, some 46 months ahead of schedule.

In commenting upon the church and its history, Dr. Cecil Myers, pastor, noted:

"The church has grown to a membership of 2,321. The first recorded financial report showed a total of $9.01, while last year First United Methodist members gave $310,577.

"First United Methodist Church is one of the most strategically located churches in the country. Thousands of students and faculty have been a part of the church and have gone over the world to influence other people for good. The steeple has been a landmark for well over a century, but even more important in every way, involved in the loves of people, setting the spiritual and moral tone of the area, mkaing its influence felt in the social concerns of the day, bringing children, youth, adults to Christ, and then giving them nurture in the process of Christian growth.

"We celebrate 150 years of service. We celebrate the greatness of God in guiding our forefathers and us to this point. We give thanks for the great salvation brought to us by our Lord Jesus Christ. We celebrate the guidance of the Holy Spirt as we face our future."

Dr. Myers added: "Our aim for the coming years, adopted by the Council on Ministries and the Administrative Board as a result of our year-long study is: 'A deep and renewed commitment to Christ and to our responsibility for nurture and training in Christian living and community involvement.'"

Methodist Church Plans Anniversary Celebration

The First United Methodist Church of Athens will celebrate its 150th anniversary starting in January, and the pastor, Dr. Cecil Myers, has declared, "This will be a great period in the life of our church."

Myers has told the church membership: "January marks the beginning of our anniversary celebration. I sincerely hope this is going to be a great year of renewal and revival for our church. Your prayers, your labors, your enthusiasm will help make it so.

Dr. Myers said highlights of events to come include:
• Jan. 5 — at both morning services, Holy Communion,

using John Wesley's Covenant Service.
• Jan. 5 — 7 p. m., a special service honoring the people from First Methodist who have entered the ministry. They include John Brackett, David W. Burnett, James J. McCrab III, Randell R. Mackoe, Jr., Holland L. Morgan, K. Richard Johnson and Wiley Stephens.
• Jan. 7 — 11 a.m. (no early service), Bishop William R. Cannon will dedicate the church sanctuary, the payment on the renovation work has been completed.
• Jan. 12 — 7 p.m., Rev. Frank Prince, former pastor of First Methodist now serving as district superintendent of the Decatur-Oxford District of the Georgia Methodist

Church, will preach. A reception will follow.
• Jan. 19 — 11 a.m., Installation of the Church's Administrative Board.
• Jan. 19 — 7 p.m., Dr. Charles Sineath, former pastor now serving Oak Grove Methodist in Atlanta, will preach. A reception will follow.
• Jan. 26 — 7 p.m., Joint service with all Athens churches. Dr. Charles Hasty will preach. An the choir will be made up of all choirs in Athens.
• Feb. 2 — 8:40 and 11 a.m. sessions, Dr. Eugene T. Drinkard, Athens-Elbert District Sex-intendent, will preach, offering a challenge for the fire

• Feb. 2 — 7 p.m., Drama depicting the history of First Church, written by Youth Director Mike Egan.
• Feb. 3 — Youth rally for all youth of Athens, featuring "Truth," a Christian rock group.
• Feb. 3 — 7 p.m., Community Night, featuring a nationally-known speaker and involving civic clubs, the Chamber of Commerce and industry, the public service.

Rev. Myers announced that members of First Methodist are urged to "invite friends to join us for this birthday event...and invite those with no church home in Athens to become a part of our church.

Newspaper articles from the Athens Banner-Herald tell the story of how Athens First celebrated its 150th anniversary in 1975.

∽**1975**∽

As Athens First celebrated the 150th anniversary of its founding, "The Steeple" for August 13, 1975 listed 104 members who had been on the rolls 50 years or longer. The longest-time member was Miss Kate Holliday at 76 years, followed by Mrs. C. Joseph Brockman at 75 years.

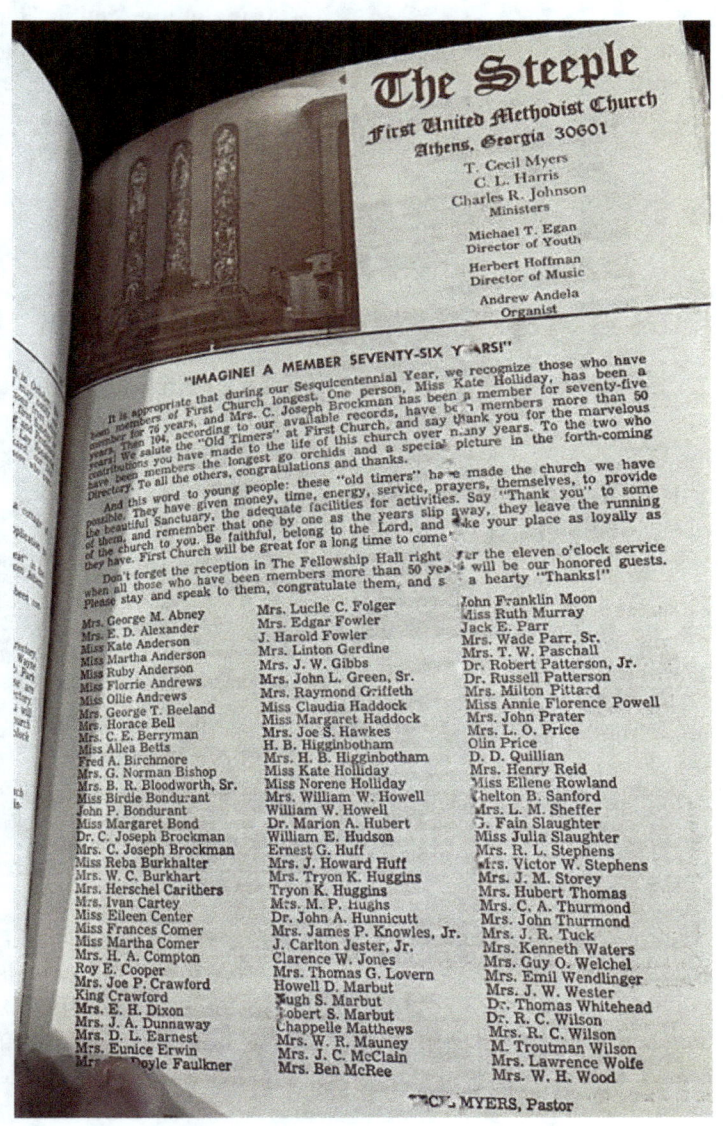

The Steeple
First United Methodist Church
Athens, Georgia 30601

T. Cecil Myers
C. L. Harris
Charles R. Johnson
Ministers

Michael T. Egan
Director of Youth

Herbert Hoffman
Director of Music

Andrew Andela
Organist

"IMAGINE! A MEMBER SEVENTY-SIX YEARS!"

It is appropriate that during our Sesquicentennial Year, we recognize those who have been members of First Church longest. One person, Miss Kate Holliday, has been a member for 76 years, and Mrs. C. Joseph Brockman has been a member for seventy-five years. Then 104, according to our available records, have been members more than 50 years. We salute the "Old Timers" at First Church, and say thank you for the marvelous contributions you have made to the life of this church over many years. To the two who have been members the longest go orchids and a special picture in the forth-coming Directory. To all the others, congratulations and thanks.

And this word to young people: these "old timers" have made the church we have possible. They have given money, time, energy, service, prayers, themselves, to provide the beautiful Sanctuary, the adequate facilities for activities. Say "Thank you" to some of them, and remember that one by one as the years slip away, they leave the running of the church to you. Be faithful, belong to the Lord, and take your place as loyally as they have. First Church will be great for a long time to come"

Don't forget the reception in The Fellowship Hall right after the eleven o'clock service when all those who have been members more than 50 years will be our honored guests. Please stay and speak to them, congratulate them, and say a hearty "Thanks!"

Mrs. George M. Abney
Mrs. E. D. Alexander
Miss Kate Anderson
Miss Martha Anderson
Miss Ruby Anderson
Miss Florrie Andrews
Miss Ollie Andrews
Mrs. George T. Beeland
Mrs. Horace Bell
Mrs. C. E. Berryman
Miss Allea Betts
Fred A. Birchmore
Mrs. G. Norman Bishop
Mrs. B. R. Bloodworth, Sr.
Miss Birdie Bondurant
John P. Bondurant
Miss Margaret Bond
Dr. C. Joseph Brockman
Mrs. C. Joseph Brockman
Miss Reba Burkhalter
Mrs. W. C. Burkhart
Mrs. Herschel Carithers
Mrs. Ivan Cartey
Miss Eileen Center
Miss Frances Comer
Miss Martha Comer
Mrs. H. A. Compton
Roy E. Cooper
Mrs. Joe P. Crawford
King Crawford
Mrs. E. H. Dixon
Mrs. J. A. Dunnaway
Mrs. D. L. Earnest
Mrs. Eunice Erwin
Mrs. Doyle Faulkner

Mrs. Lucile C. Folger
Mrs. Edgar Fowler
J. Harold Fowler
Mrs. Linton Gerdine
Mrs. J. W. Gibbs
Mrs. John L. Green, Sr.
Mrs. Raymond Griffeth
Miss Claudia Haddock
Miss Margaret Haddock
Mrs. Joe S. Hawkes
H. B. Higginbotham
Mrs. H. B. Higginbotham
Miss Kate Holliday
Miss Norene Holliday
Mrs. William W. Howell
William W. Howell
Dr. Marion A. Hubert
William E. Hudson
Ernest G. Huff
Mrs. J. Howard Huff
Mrs. Tryon K. Huggins
Tryon K. Huggins
Mrs. M. P. Hughs
Dr. John A. Hunnicutt
Mrs. James P. Knowles, Jr.
J. Carlton Jester, Jr.
Clarence W. Jones
Mrs. Thomas G. Lovern
Howell D. Marbut
Hugh S. Marbut
Robert S. Marbut
Chappelle Matthews
Mrs. W. R. Mauney
Mrs. J. C. McClain
Mrs. Ben McRee

John Franklin Moon
Miss Ruth Murray
Jack E. Parr
Mrs. Wade Parr, Sr.
Mrs. T. W. Paschall
Dr. Robert Patterson, Jr.
Dr. Russell Patterson
Mrs. Milton Pittard
Miss Annie Florence Powell
Mrs. John Prater
Mrs. L. O. Price
Olin Price
D. D. Quillian
Mrs. Henry Reid
Miss Ellene Rowland
Chelton B. Sanford
Mrs. L. M. Sheffer
G. Fain Slaughter
Miss Julia Slaughter
Mrs. R. L. Stephens
Mrs. Victor W. Stephens
Mrs. J. M. Storey
Mrs. Hubert Thomas
Mrs. C. A. Thurmond
Mrs. John Thurmond
Mrs. J. R. Tuck
Mrs. Kenneth Waters
Mrs. Guy O. Welchel
Mrs. Emil Wendlinger
Mrs. J. W. Wester
Dr. Thomas Whitehead
Dr. R. C. Wilson
Mrs. R. C. Wilson
M. Troutman Wilson
Mrs. Lawrence Wolfe
Mrs. W. H. Wood

T. C. MYERS, Pastor

SON OF A PREACHER MAN KNOWS THE IMPORTANCE OF SUNDAY SCHOOL

Charley Whittemore grew up in a Methodist parsonage, a son of Rev. Max Whittemore, who served pastorates across North Georgia 1932-

Charley & Debbie Whittemore, Rev. Max Whittemore

73, including Young Harris of Athens 1943-47. Charlie has taught the Outreach Sunday School Class since 1991. He reflects on the experience:

"I was not an original member of the Outreach Class. Debbie and I were attending the Disciples Class when a group of friends came to me in 1991 to ask me to teach the Outreach Class. I have always felt I was a facilitator, more than a teacher. This invitation was a life preserver since I had not been retained as a football coach at the end of that season. This gave me new focus and purpose.

My faith has grown stronger, and I have gotten more out of Sunday School than those who attend. Digging deeper into the Bible has helped me grow personally. I would encourage anyone who is seeking a strong relationship with God to volunteer to facilitate a Bible study and step out with a group of people in their faith walk.

In a large church like Athens First Methodist, I think it is important for church members to get plugged into a more defined group with similar life experiences. Sunday School provides congregants this opportunity. This becomes your "faith-family." They can relate to your joys, trials, and family experiences. They can become a resource in studying and praying."

YOUNG ADULT CLASS SELECTS NAME

Our Young Adult Class has selected a name and will now be known as the Outreach Class. This class is for those adults in their twenties or early thirties who are beginning their careers or who are in graduate school. It meets in room 109 on the ground level of the education building.

The group is now studying Bruce Larsen's "Living on a Growing Edge." Next quarter the study book will be "The Kink and I" by James Mallory, M.D.

Those interested in more information about the class are invited to call the officers, Mr. and Mrs. John Massey, 549-3197, or Mr. and Mrs. Danny Shive, 543-8778.

Grover C. McNeill, Organist 1975 – 1976

Grover McNeill succeeded Andy Andela as organist and assistant director of music. The native of Houston, Texas, held a degree in public school music from Baylor University, with concentration in vocal music. He studied at Southern Methodist University majoring in music education with an organ concentration. He taught music and band in a public high school, was organist for Manor Baptist Church and Alamo Heights Baptist Church, both in San Antonio, Texas. He had experience in directing instrumental and handbell groups and playing the organ. He held membership in the American Guild of Organists, the Fellowship of Methodist Musicians, the Hymn Society of America, and the Phi Mu Alpha

Grover McNeill

Sinfonia music fraternity. After Andy Andela's two years here followed the many years of stability under Reginald Smith, Grover McNeill would serve less than a year, when the opportunity arose to return to a fulltime position at Alamo Heights Baptist in San Antonio, where he had been parttime before. McNeill's time here was followed by a series of one-year tenures until the arrival of John Hebblethwaite in 1978 for four years in the position, and then Martha Braswell, who served 17 years.

A confirmation class in the mid-1970s

FROM "FAMILY FRIEND" TO THE ALTAR

THE JACKSONS

Through the 1970s, Athens First had a practice of assigning a "family friend" to each new member to help them become acclimated to life in their new church. Usually this was a person who had a role in bringing the new member in, or who lived in their neighborhood, or was a work colleague. On at least one occasion, family friends might wind up in a 50+-year marriage!

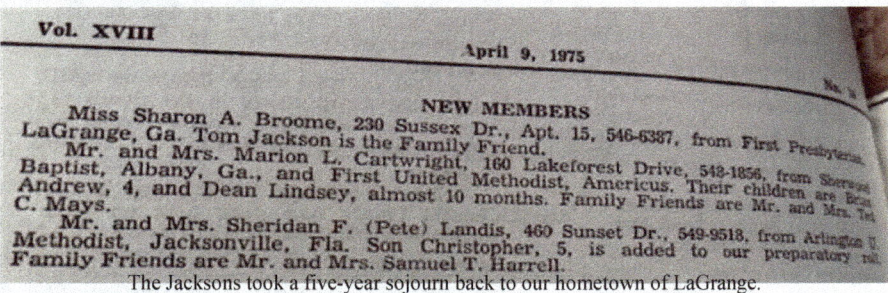

Vol. XVIII   **April 9, 1975**   No. 1

NEW MEMBERS

Miss Sharon A. Broome, 230 Sussex Dr., Apt. 15, 546-6387, from First Presbyterian, LaGrange, Ga. Tom Jackson is the Family Friend.

Mr. and Mrs. Marion L. Cartwright, 160 Lakeforest Drive, 543-1856, from Sherwood Baptist, Albany, Ga., and First United Methodist, Americus. Their children are Brian, Andrew, 4, and Dean Lindsey, almost 10 months. Family Friends are Mr. and Mrs. Ted C. Mays.

Mr. and Mrs. Sheridan F. (Pete) Landis, 460 Sunset Dr., 549-9518, from Arlington U. Methodist, Jacksonville, Fla. Son Christopher, 5, is added to our preparatory roll. Family Friends are Mr. and Mrs. Samuel T. Harrell.

The Jacksons took a five-year sojourn back to our hometown of LaGrange.

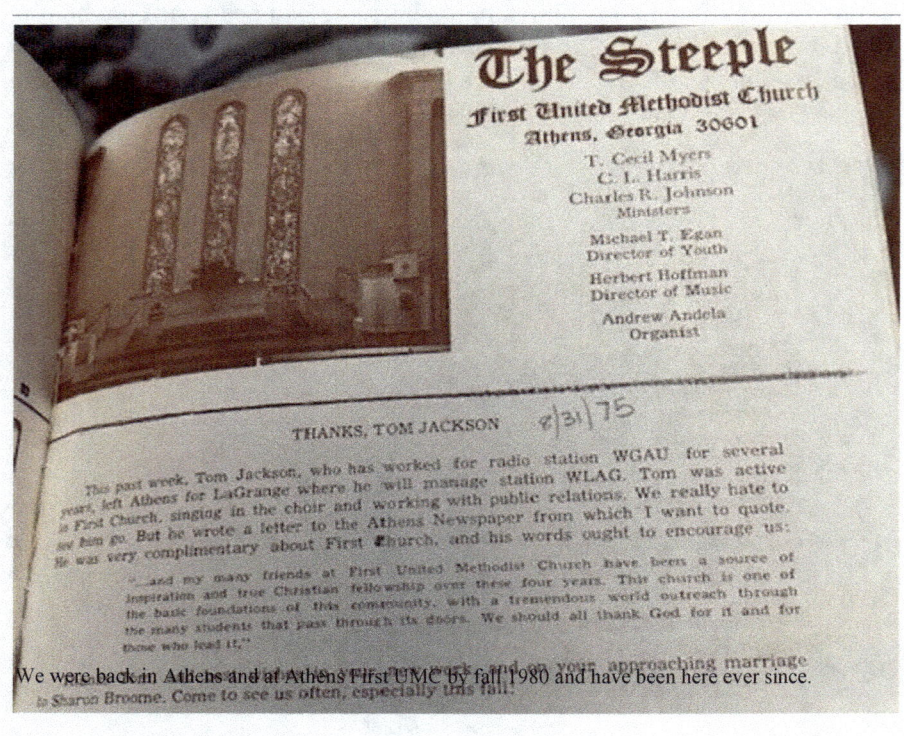

The Steeple

First United Methodist Church
Athens, Georgia 30601

T. Cecil Myers
C. L. Harris
Charles R. Johnson
Ministers

Michael T. Egan
Director of Youth

Herbert Hoffman
Director of Music

Andrew Andela
Organist

THANKS, TOM JACKSON   8/31/75

This past week, Tom Jackson, who has worked for radio station WGAU for several years, left Athens for LaGrange where he will manage station WLAG. Tom was active in First Church, singing in the choir and working with public relations. We really hate to see him go. But he wrote a letter to the Athens Newspaper from which I want to quote. He was very complimentary about First Church, and his words ought to encourage us:

"...and my many friends at First United Methodist Church have been a source of inspiration and true Christian fellowship over these four years. This church is one of the basic foundations of this community, with a tremendous world outreach through the many students that pass through its doors. We should all thank God for it and for those who lead it."

We were back in Athens and at Athens First UMC by fall 1980 and have been here ever since.

9 **1976** 9

Lewis Bevel "Bev" Jones III, Senior Minister, 1976-1982

Born July 22, 1926, in Gracewood, Ga., Bev Jones spent a significant part of his childhood in Athens when his father was pastor at Young Harris

Methodist Church, 1928-35. Of those years, Bev wrote, "The front yard at 694 Boulevard was as big as a football field, the little frame church on the corner was a veritable cathedral, Chase Street School looked like the Smithsonian Institution, and the Southern Mutual Building was the tallest building in the world." Bev Jones received the bachelor's degree from Emory in 1946 and his divinity degree from the Candler School of Theology in 1949. He married Mildred "Tuck" Hawkins in 1948. Admitted on trial in 1949, he was founding pastor of Audubon Forest Methodist Church in Atlanta's Cascade Heights that same

L. Bevel "Bev" Jones

year and remained there for ten years. He was admitted to full connection and ordained as an elder in 1951. He was an author of the 1957 Atlanta ministers' statement for racial reconciliation known as the Ministers' Manifesto, which he called one of the most significant achievements of his ministry. He went on to serve: 1959 LaGrange First; 1963 St. Mark, Atlanta; 1967 Decatur First; 1976-82 Athens First; 1982-84 Northside. In 1984 Dr. Jones was elected Bishop, serving twelve years in the Western North Carolina Conference before his retirement. Thus, he became the third who had served Athens First as pastor, after Pierce and Key, to be elected Bishop. Bev Jones was described by Emory historian Gary Hauk as "Georgian by birth, Christian by faith, Methodist by conviction, proud Emory alumnus, seeker of justice, advocate for peace and unity among peoples, engaging teacher, eloquent preacher, and pastor to the despairing and

Future Bishop Bevel Jones during his time as senior minister at Athens First UMC.

dispossessed as well as to the powerful and the privileged." In retirement, he served as bishop-in-residence at Candler School of Theology. He was a long-time trustee of Emory and seven other UMC institutions and was on the board of the Carter Center. He held honorary doctoral degrees from Emory, LaGrange College, High Point University and Pfeiffer University. For years he was honorary chaplain of the Atlanta Braves. At Bishop Jones' death in 2018, Emory President James Laney said Bev had "an infectious twinkle in his eye that gave him unparalleled access to people's hearts. His humor, velvet voice, and passion for the church made him one of the best- loved preachers of his generation." Jones authored *"One step beyond caution; reflections on life and faith,"* Decatur, Ga.: Looking Glass Books, 2001. A son, David Bevel Jones, served appointments in North Georgia as an elder 1977- 2017, including Morrow First, East Point First, Varnell, Avondale Pattillo, St. John, Trinity-on-the-Hill Augusta, Snellville, Glenn Memorial, and Decatur First.

Wesley Daniel Stephens, Associate Pastor, 1976-1991 (continued as retiree to 1998)

At the same time Bevel Jones was appointed senior pastor, Wesley Stephens was appointed associate pastor. A native of Athens, it was noted

in "The Steeple" upon his arrival that "Wesley will not have to learn to love the Dogs, as Bev will." (Bev always was a Tech fan but kept it under wraps while in Athens). Wesley served beyond his official

Wesley and Annette Stephens

retirement in 1991,

extending his 15 years of appointment to a full 22 years of service, finally fully retiring in 1998. Born in Athens in 1927, he married Annette Aiken in 1952. He received the A.B. degree from the University of Georgia and the Bachelor of Divinity from Emory. He was admitted on trial in 1951 and full connection in 1953. His appointments were: 1951 Powder Springs First, Assistant; 1952 Cave Spring; 1956 Palmetto First; 1957 Colonial Hills; 1959 North Rome; 1961 Mansfield; 1965 Chickamauga; 1969 Dallas First;

1973 Tillman Memorial, Smyrna; 1976 Athens First Associate. Wesley was known for his acerbic wit and the chance that he would say the unexpected at any moment, yet all undergirded with a rich heart filled with compassion and care for each member. An untold number sought him out and were able to confide in him, receiving valuable counsel over his 22 years at Athens First. At the time Rev. Stephens died in 2024, he stood second on the chronological role of conference elders in full connection.

Michael Shawgo, Organist, 1976 – 1977

Originally from central Illinois, Mike Shawgo received a Bachelor of Music degree in organ performance from Illinois Wesleyan University in Bloomington. He gained additional study under J. Marcus Ritchie at the Cathedral of St. Philip in Atlanta and with Dexter Bailey in Chicago. He is a member of the American Guild of Organists, the Organ Historical Society, the American Theatre Organ Society, and Phi Mu Alpha. At this writing, he is organist and directs the Quartet Choir at Second Presbyterian Church, Chicago.

Michael Shawgo in 2024

The Chancel Choir in 1976

ᴐ**1977** ᴐ

The associate pastor's parsonage on Soule Street was sold for $29,000 as it was not needed by the incoming associate Wesley Stephens – "Family too large, parsonage too small," he said. That same year, the bookkeeping function for the church was moved from a member's home to the church office to be carried out by professional staff, with plans made to hire both a business manager and an advanced-skill bookkeeper.

Pierce Arant, Interim Director of Music and Jane Palmer, Interim Organist 1977

Sylvia and Pierce Arant and family in 1979

With the departure of Herb Hoffman as music director and Michael Shawgo as organist, the church engaged longtime member Pierce Arant, an assistant professor of choral music at the University of Georgia, to direct the church choirs beginning in January 1977. Hoffman accepted a position at Munsey Memorial UMC in Johnson City, Tennessee. He submitted his resignation here in November 1976 effective the following January.

A native of Orangeburg, South Carolina, Dr. Arant graduated Wofford College with a degree in English, and Converse College with a degree in music. He held the master's degree in voice from Yale University and an Ed.D. in music education from UGA. At the time, Arant was director of the University Chorus and the UGA Men's Glee Club. He taught choral conducting and private voice. Pierce and Sylvia, and their daughters Meli and Sylvia, had been active members of AFUMC since coming to Athens in 1966. Meli sadly lost her battle with an extended illness in 1987 at age 23. Sylvia remains actively involved here today. Pierce served as chair of the Worship Commission, as a member of the Administrative Board, and often was soloist with the Chancel Choir. His funeral service in our sanctuary in

March 1997 was one of the largest in attendance in recent memory, as UGA choral alumni were invited to sing for him once again. The front half of the church was filled with choristers, who made magnificent music in loving tribute to their mentor.

Interim organist Jane Palmer was from Anderson, South Carolina, holding a bachelor's degree from Mars Hill College and a master's from UGA. She previously had been organist and children's choir director at Central Presbyterian Church of Athens (now Alps Road Presbyterian Church).

As part of the transition, youth director Mike Egan took on the additional responsibility of directing the youth choirs.

Beth Luton, Youth Director 1977-1982

Elizabeth "Beth" Luton joined the church staff as a program assistant in charge of youth in December 1977. She had been a volunteer worker  with the youth since September of that year while a wide search was conducted and the committee "finally came right back home in making its selection" as Beth had become "well-known and well-acquainted with our needs and resources." Born in Colorado Springs, she grew up in Clarksville, Tennessee and its UMC. Her mother was a General Conference delegate for their home church and conference. Beth attended the Peabody Demonstration School (now the University School of Nashville) and had a B.A. in health and physical education from Baldwin Wallace College in Berea, Ohio. She earned a master's degree in education

Beth Luton

from the University of Georgia. She had been assistant to the director of UMC Camps for the Tennessee Conference. While at Athens FUMC, she married Thomas B. Cook, a local attorney active in the church who later would serve as chancellor (attorney) for the North Georgia Conference. They had three sons. Beth would resign as youth director in 1982 and was endorsed by the church in candidacy for ordination as a deacon. She served as a minister of youth at Commerce, Briarcliff, Atlanta First and Snellville from 1986-1997. She received the Master of Divinity degree from Emory University's Candler School of Theology in 2000 and was ordained as an Elder in the North Georgia Conference in 2002. She worked at the Candler

School of Theology from 2000-2008 directing various non-degree programs, including the Course of Study for local pastors. She moved back to Tennessee in 2008 to accept a position as Assistant General Secretary at the United Methodist General Board on Higher Education in Nashville. In April 2009, she married fellow Peabody School alumnus Doug Andrews. Beth battled breast cancer during her latter years, succumbing to a final recurrence July 27, 2009. Memorial services were held at both West End UMC in Nashville and Druid Hills UMC in Atlanta.

John Hebblethwaite, Director of Music and Organist 1977 – 1982

John Hebblethwaite and family

The vacant director of music and organist positions drew some twenty applicants, with John Hebblethwaite being chosen to fill both positions effective in September 1977. A native of Evanston, Illinois, he received the B.A. degree in Organ and Vocal Music Education from Lawrence University in Appleton, Wisconsin. His Masters in Church Music was from Northwestern University. He came to Athens having served the previous eight years as choir director and organist at

John Hebblethwaite directs choir rehearsal prior to a Sunday service in 1979

216

The choir during a 1979 worship service. Note the design of the organ pipe chamber as it had been since 1963. A new organ purchased in 2020 required additional pipes and their incorporation into the sanctuary's design.

First Presbyterian Church of Gastonia, North Carolina. His wife, Mary Hebblethwaite, likewise held a Master's in Organ Performance from Northwestern University and was a vocal soloist.

ǝ1978 ǝ

A $350,000 remodeling program of the full church facility was accomplished during 1977-78. Pastor Jones called for greater vision, imagination and motivation among both the staff and the membership citing, in particular, the need to develop more innovative programming in youth ministries and leisure ministries. He lamented the associate pastor, Charles Johnson, being "bogged down" in administrative and facilities matters, and the church approved adding a fulltime building superintendent to the staff. The previous part-time music director, Pierce Arant, and organist, Jane Palmer, resigned in favor of creating fulltime positions. The new staff members in music and youth were having a "shake-down" period, Jones said, as the newly-hired combination music director/organist John Hebblethwaite transitioned from his previous position in a Presbyterian church, and Beth Cook had completed her work at UGA and could devote more time to her duties as a program assistant with children and youth. The church approved the employment of a dietician and cook to run the kitchen and serve the many meals incorporated into the church program.

A Sunday worship service in the late 1970s.

᧙1979᧙

The church purchased for $55,000 the Professional Building across Hancock Avenue from the main church campus, a 55-foot-wide property fronting on both Hancock Avenue and Dougherty Street [site of today's Synovus bank parking lot]. Property behind the church previously owned by the Beacham family, with whom negotiations to purchase had been unsuccessful, by then was owned by the Athens-Clarke County Unified Government. The newly-purchased property across Hancock was exchanged with Athens-Clarke for an equivalent 55-foot-wide strip adjacent to and across the back of the existing church property stretching from Hancock to Washington Streets. It was the first addition to the church's property footprint since the original land grant in 1825.

The church received gift of a bus used to transport members and youth to various off-campus group functions. This would evolve over the years into our program of maintaining several 15-passenger church vans.

An early church van - 1979

⊝**1980-1981**⊝

The Athens First budget in 1980 was $348,729 and increased to $383,862 for 1981.The senior minister's salary in 1980 was $27,257 plus travel and housing expenses. The Athens First Lay Leader in 1981 was J. Smiley Wolfe. Delegates to Annual Conference that year were Louis Griffith, Helen Taylor, and Tom Nash, who had been an Academic All-America football player at UGA, and would go on to a long career as a Savannah attorney.

⊝**1982** ⊝

Gwyn Spell, Interim Director of Music Debbie Henson and Woody Entrekin, Interim Organists

Gwyn Spell

In February, John Hebblethwaite resigned from his dual position as director of music and organist, with interims appointed during a search period. Also that year, Beth Luton Cook resigned as a program assistant in the youth program. In November, Mrs. Cook was recommended by the church in her candidacy as a diaconal minister.

William Richard "Bill" Floyd, Senior Minister, 1982-1984

Rev. William R. "Bill" Floyd

Born September 17, 1930, in Atlanta, Bill Floyd was a product of Atlanta Public Schools and the leading basketball scorer in the city's high schools in 1948. Floyd graduated Emory University with a bachelor's degree in 1954 and a Master of Divinity from Candler School of Theology in 1957. He was made a probationary member in 1955 and admitted as an elder in full connection in 1957. He received the Doctor of Divinity degree from LaGrange College in 1989. Bill married his childhood sweetheart, Joyce Hancock, who was his partner in ministry and in life until her death in 2009. His call to the ministry was under the guidance of his father-in-law, Rev. B. W. Hancock. His appointments were: 1955 Eastland Road, 1961 Blue Ridge, 1962 Skyland, 1966 Roswell, 1973 Northside, 1977 Dalton First, 1982 Athens First, 1984 Northside, 1991 Retired. He continued to serve at Roswell and Dalton First in retirement. In 1982, the Conference sent Bevel Jones from Athens First

Christmas Eve in the early 1980s

to Northside, Atlanta. Former Northside pastor Bill Floyd, then serving at Dalton First, came to Athens First. Floyd encouraged Athens First to hire his director of music at Dalton, Mike Moffitt, which the church did. When Bev Jones was elected bishop in 1984, Floyd was returned for a second tour at Northside after only two years in Athens, much to the consternation of the Athens congregation. Moffitt followed him to Northside shortly thereafter. Preaching was the heart of Bill Floyd's ministry, believing his primary call as pastor was to deliver God's word. His pulpit style was conversational laced with humor, emphasizing that God's good grace is available to all. He had a storytelling gift, in both oral and written form. Dr. Floyd died November 4, 2015, at his home in Roswell. His memorial service was at Roswell UMC, with burial beside his wife at Green Lawn Cemetery, Roswell.

Phillip Barrineau, Minister of Education and Youth 1982 – 1986

Phillip Barrineau worked as AFUMC's Minister of Education and Youth while he pursued his doctorate in Counseling and Student Development at UGA. He obtained the Ph.D. in 1989. A graduate of Tift County High School, he attended Abraham Baldwin College, obtained the AB in Christian Education from Asbury College, and the Master of Divinity from Asbury Seminary. He came to Athens from a position as Minister of Youth Education at Waycross First UMC since 1980. His wife, Nancy, was an English teacher and daughter of a United Methodist minister in New York. After his time in Athens, Barrineau worked

Phillip Barrineau

as a counselor at Pembroke State University in North Carolina before opening his own practice as a licensed clinical mental health counselor in Greensboro, North Carolina in 2016.

Michael Moffitt, Director of Music, and Martha Braswell, Organist 1982 – 1986

Mike Moffitt was a graduate of Dalton High School, Middle Tennessee State University with a B.S., and a Master of Music from Louisiana State University. He was director of choral music at Dalton High School before becoming Director of Music Ministries at Dalton First UMC. There he oversaw four children's choirs, a 90-member youth choir, and a 48-member

Mike Moffitt

Chancel Choir. Mike was an accomplished soloist, and taught voice, choral ensembles, vocal pedagogy, opera workshop, class voice, opera and song literature, guitar, class brass, marching and concert band, class guitar and music theory. Adding to his effectiveness was his wife, Nancy, also an accomplished musician and soloist. Upon Mike's arrival, Woody Entrekin served a brief period as organist through mid-1982 pending the search

that resulted in Martha Braswell being hired as organist. Moffitt departed in 1986 to rejoin former pastor Bill Floyd at Northside UMC in Atlanta. Braswell was named both Director of Music and Organist, holding the joint positions until 1999.

Martha Braswell

The Chancel Choir sings in a 1983 worship service

☙1984 ☙

William Albert "Bill" McKoy, Senior Minister, 1984-1987

Bill McKoy was a native of Barnesville, Ga., born in 1938. He was made a probationary member in 1961 and elder in full connection in 1963. His appointments were: 1961 Student; 1962 Marietta First; 1963-67 Director of Conference Youth and Camp Glisson; 1967 College Park First; 1970 Cleveland; 1972 Decatur First; 1977 Winder First; 1980 Gainesville District Superintendent; 1984 Athens First; 1987 Withdrawn; 1990 Sugar Hill; 1991 Director of Development, International Nursing Services Association at Emory; 1993 Cokesbury, Atlanta; 1998 Stone Mountain; 2003 Retired. Upon the election of Bevel Jones as Bishop and the unexpected return of Bill Floyd to the pulpit at Northside to succeed him, McKoy was called mid-year from his position as Gainesville District Superintendent to fill the Athens First pulpit. After a successful three-year pastorate here, McKoy resigned from Athens First and withdrew from the Conference for personal reasons in August 1987. He was readmitted to the conference and resumed appointments in 1990, retiring in 2003. He was author of *"Facing death from a Christian perspective; decisions which death demands,"* Nashville: Discipleship

Dr. Bill McKoy

Resources, 1976. His dissertation was: *"Developing churchmanship among youth,"* 1971.

Ronald Emaile Preuss, Associate Pastor, 1984-1985

Born November 14, 1944, Ron Preuss was admitted as a probationary member in 1967 and as elder in full connection in 1970. His appointments

Rev. Ronald Preuss in 1970 and 2024

were: 1967 student; 1969 St. Matthew, East Point; a mid-year appointment on January 1, 1984, as Athens First associate; 1985 three months' leave June through August before assuming an appointment September 1, 1985, as Director of Children's Ministries for the Florida Conference; 1989 Jones Memorial; 1997 Chicopee Candler; 1998 Cumming First; 2011 Retired. At this writing he is a resident at Wesley Woods retirement home in Newnan.

୨**1985** ୧

Diane Neely (Shedd), Associate Pastor, 1985 – 1991

Rev. Diane Shepherd Neely had been an associate pastor at Statesboro United Methodist Church in South Georgia before coming to Athens First UMC in 1985. While in Athens, she married widower Charlie Shedd, who was retired and serving our church as a Minister of Stewardship. Neely returned to South Georgia as an associate pastor at Valdosta First UMC 1997-2019. She retired in 2019 but

Rev. Diane Neely

continued as an associate at Valdosta First through the 2021 church year when she entered full retirement.

Two U.S. Presidents visited Athens and the UGA campus in 1985. Vice President George H. W. Bush, who would be elected President in 1988, was featured speaker in the UGA Coliseum at a ceremony marking the Bicentennial of the adoption of the UGA Charter. Former U.S. President Gerald Ford, who served 1974-77, visited Athens to speak at a seminar at the UGA School of Law, hosted by Athens first member J. Ralph Beaird, Dean of the Law School.

୨**1986** ୧

Micheal Lee Selleck, Associate Pastor, 1986-1995

Born in 1951, Mike Selleck married Christine, whom most know

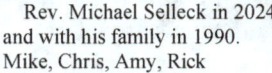

Rev. Michael Selleck in 2024 and with his family in 1990. Mike, Chris, Amy, Rick

as "Chris," in 1970. The West Michigan Conference admitted him as a probationary member in 1976 and an elder in full connection in 1980. He was appointed by West Michigan beyond the bounds of the conference as a student in 1976 and in 1986 was appointed to Athens First as associate pastor and minister to youth. He transferred membership to the North Georgia Conference in 1994 and in 1995 was appointed director of the North Georgia Conference Council on Ministries. In 1999 he was appointed to North Springs UMC and in 2004 as executive director of Connectional Ministries. He officially retired in 2016 but took further appointments in retirement in 2017 at Johns Creek and 2020 at Dacula. Mike Selleck was a dynamic youth minister under whose leadership our youth program flourished. He was a friend and confidant to many who now are adults in our congregation. In retirement, he and Chris have maintained a summer home in Michigan and live the remainder of the year in Athens, where both continue to be active in the life of Athens First.

A LIFETIME (THUS FAR) IN AFUMC CHOIRS

Thomas Jones grew up in Athens First UMC, and has been in the choirs of Athens First literally all his life. He was in children's and youth programs and choirs, and as of 2025 is a student at the University of Georgia and sings in the Chancel Choir. Thomas reflects on what being a youth at Athens First has meant to him.

I have been a part of the Athens First children's music program for most of my life. I grew up singing in the Sonshine and Joy choirs and also sang in Route 56, so it was no surprise that I would sing in the Wesleyan Youth Choir when I reached seventh grade. However, I doubt that I could have anticipated just how much I would enjoy being in that choir.

I participated in the Wesleyan Youth Choir from seventh grade all the way until I graduated from high school. There was a great sense of community in the choir since everybody in the choir knew each other, deepening not only our bonds but also our love for singing. Encouraging this love for singing was none other than Janis Maxwell, the Wesleyan Youth Choir director. Janis helped me realize my passion for singing music as well as which vocal part I should sing when my voice started changing (thanks, puberty). All of the adult volunteers were incredibly nice and would take care of us in case anything went wrong. It really felt like we were a family in that choir.

The Wesleyan Youth Choir isn't just about singing; it's also about fun and games. Every summer we would go on a choir tour, travelling to different places and singing while also enjoying ourselves with fun attractions. In my tenure we travelled to Baltimore, Chicago, and even New York City. There are also other fun opportunities for singing in the youth choir, such as the annual Variety Show where we would perform musical numbers and skits.

Overall, the Wesleyan Youth Choir was a big part of my teenage experience growing up in the church. It helped me develop my singing skills, love for music, and community. It is an experience that I cannot recommend enough. I will never forget my time in it.

Thomas Jones and 2016

na and S n Jones in 2008 nt in 20

Jones in 2008

Our Vibrant Athens First Youth

Charlie Shedd, Minister of Stewardship, 1986 – 1987

An Iowa native, Charlie Shedd retired to Athens to be near his son, Peter Shedd, and family. He had been senior minister at small country churches

and big-city cathedrals in Colorado, Nebraska, Oklahoma, Texas and Georgia, and as founding minister built Memorial Drive Presbyterian Church in Houston into one of the country's largest Presbyterian congregations. Described as "a master communicator of homespun wisdom," Charlie's books on marriage and parenting, coupled with a nationally syndicated radio broadcast, gained widespread note: some 40 titles included *Letters to Karen, Letters to Philip, Promises to Peter,* and *Brush of an Angel's Wing*. His first wife, Martha, died

Dr. Charlie Shedd

after the couple retired to Athens. He remarried to Dianne Neely, then an associate pastor at Athens First. A third marriage was to Anna Ruth Hulme, who survived him at his death at age 88 in Ardmore, Oklahoma in 2004.

Martha Braswell, Director of Music and Organist 1986 – 1999

Having already served as organist since 1982 when Mike Moffitt was director of music, Martha Braswell assumed the dual role of director

of music and organist when Moffitt departed to rejoin former pastor Bill Floyd at Northside UMC in Atlanta. For several years in the late 1990s, she was joined by Beverly Brown as choir accompanist and organist when Martha needed to direct the choir without being at the organ board. In late 1999, Mary Ann

Martha Braswell   Mary Ann Fitzgerald

Fitzgerald joined the staff to assist with the organist and pianist positions.

TRUSTEES REORGANIZATION

By its 1828 state charter, the Athens First Trustees were a self-perpetuating board of lifetime appointees for more than 160 years. After considerable discussion among church leadership for some years about the advisability of rotating Trustee membership to better represent what has become a very large and diverse church membership, the board appointed a committee to study and make a recommendation. The committee of Ed Benson and Lee Pierson reported with some alternatives, and the board ultimately adopted a new procedure by unanimous vote on October 12, 1986.

Under the plan adopted, the board put an end to appointments for life, requiring future members to retire at the end of the six-year term in which their 72nd birthday occurs. The board in office at the time of adoption exempted itself from the age limit. The board still was to be composed of nine members as called for in the United Methodist Discipline, but they are assigned six-year terms rather than the three-year terms provided in the Discipline. Trustees are limited to two consecutive six-year terms, or 12 years total.

The new policy continued a goal to maintain balanced representation across a variety of vocational fields for the benefit of the church, including legal, banking, construction and maintenance, insurance, social services and business management. To initiate the rotation plan, the board in office at that time assigned two-year terms (class of 1988) to Jimmy Akins, Gene Epting and Troutman Wilson, four-year terms (class of 1990) to Billy Hudson, Carlton James and Lee Pierson, and a six-year term (class of 1992) to the newest member,

Martha & Jimmy Akins

Mary & Billy

Mary Jean & Lee Pierson

Robin & Ed Benson

Carlton & Claire James

Ed Benson. Akins moved in favor of the plan, James seconded the motion, and it passed unanimously.

The board s u b s e q u e n t l y elected Allen Green to the position recently vacated by the resignation of Comer Whitehead, and Louis Griffith to the position vacated by the death of Smiley Wolfe, each in the class of 1992 and under the new limitations.

The plan differs from United Methodist Discipline in providing two six-year terms with an age limit of 72, rather than two three- year terms, and in not making the trustees subject to nomination by the Church Council.

Children launch balloons as part of vacation Bible school in the summer of 1989. At left in the photo Rev. Dianne Neely leads the activity. This photo is in the driveway behind the sanctuary where the children's playground stands today. The Professional Building across Hancock Avenue stands where the Synovus Bank is today. The door at right (behind the pink balloon) led into the Tuck classroom and was sealed off in the 2000 renovations.

David & Gail Walton with Chris in 2000

David Walton, Church Treasurer 1986 – 2000, Business Administrator 2001 – 2021, Accountant & Bookkeeper 2022-present

In 1986, church member David Walton began 38 years of service to the financial realm of Athens First, the first 14 of those years as the lay member who was church treasurer, then moving onto the staff as business administrator in 2001. Along with Nancy Wortham, his predecessor as bookkeeper, David moved the accounting function from paper records to a computer database and has during his time has helped manage a growing membership and budget.

Athens First's lay delegates to Annual Conference in 1986 were Louis Griffith, Tom Cook, Helen Taylor, and Betty Whitten.

⊜**1987**⊜

Bishop (retired) Joel C. McDavid, Interim Pastor, August - December 1987

Bishop Joel C. McDavid
1916-2003

Following the consecutive, relatively short pastoral terms of Rev. Bill Floyd and Dr. Bill McKoy, retired Bishop Joel McDavid brought a steadying hand to the congregation. He served four months in the Athens First pulpit, August-December 1987. An Alabama native ordained elder in the Alabama-West Florida Conference in 1946, McDavid served appointments in Auburn, Montgomery and Mobile before being elected bishop in 1972. He served first as bishop in Florida and then in North Georgia, from which he retired to teach at Candler School of Theology. In 1992 he moved to Mobile as Bishop-in-Residence at Dauphin Way UMC. He died in Mobile in 2003.

Athens First's lay delegates to Annual Conference in 1987 were Louis Griffith, Tom Jackson, Helen Taylor, and Betty Whitten.

Jere W. Morehead

Throughout its history, Athens First has benefitted from being the home church of numerous faculty, administrators, staff and students from the University of Georgia. Over the past century, these include UGA presidents Walter B. Hill, David C. Barrow, Omer C. Aderhold, Henry King Stanford, and Jere W. Morehead. The youthful faculty member pictured here in 1987 is Jere Morehead, who was chair of staff-parish at the time Bill Britt came to Athens First in 1997, and has been UGA President since 2013.

Minnie Dean, Willie Geter and Terry Stephens were longtime staff members at Athens First known and loved by all. Minnie served in the kitchen and greeted each person by name on Wednesday nights as she served the delicious church fellowship dinner. Willie and Terry were custodians, but more than that, they were friends to all and particularly the young people.

Minnie Dean

Willie Geter

Terry Stephens

1988

Larry A. Bauman, Senior Minister, January 1988 – June 1992

Born April 11, 1931, in Nashville, Tennessee, Larry Bauman graduated the Baylor School, took his A.B. degree at Duke University, the Bachelor of Divinity at Emory, and the Master's and Doctor of Sacred Theology degrees at Candler School of Theology. He married Martha Davis in 1953, and they had three children. He was admitted on trial in 1953 and in full connection in 1955. His appointments were 1953 Apison in the Holston Conference, and in North Georgia beginning in 1954 Buchanan, 1955 Celanese, 1959 Eatonton First, 1964 St. Paul, Gainesville; 1968 Carrollton First; 1973 Glenn Memorial, Atlanta; 1984 Atlanta-Decatur-Oxford District Superintendent; 1988 Athens First; 1992 Dalton District Superintendent; 1994 retired. He came to Athens First in a mid-year appointment beginning January 1988 and held the pulpit here for four-and-a-half years. Dr.

Dr. Larry A. Bauman

Bauman is remembered for his kindness and gentility. Few remember him ever expressing anger or frustration. A leader among North Georgia clergy, he was a delegate to General Conference in 1988. After retirement, he was named a pastor emeritus at Glenn Memorial UMC. He died in 2021 at the age of 90.

Tom Jackson in 2015

Tom, Sharon (Sherry), Stan and Hal in 1987

Athens First member Dr. Tom Jackson, who compiled this church history, became the third lay member of this church ever elected to the General Conference, following Dean Jere Pound and Dr. Nat Slaughter. Jackson went on to a total of four terms, representing North Georgia at General Conferences in St. Louis (1988), Louisville (1992), Cleveland (2000), Fort Worth (2008), and was an official observer at Charlotte (2024). At the time of his first election, Jackson was Athens Bureau Chief for Atlanta TV station WXIA and filed stories from the St. Louis conference on the adoption of a new United Methodist hymnal, among other issues. Later that year, he began work as University of Georgia public relations director, a position he held 27 years, retiring as UGA's vice president for public affairs. He also served at the

Southeastern Jurisdictional Conferences of 1992, 2008, and 2024. He was an Athens First delegate to the North Georgia Conference many years from the 1980s through the time of this writing in 2025. He delivered the Laity Address to Annual Conference in 2019 and was named Lay Co-Leader of the new South East District in 2024. Among his many church committee involvements was the Building Committee that oversaw construction of the new Family Life Center 1998-2000. Tom came to Athens and Athens First UMC as a University of Georgia student in 1971. He and his wife, Sharon (Sherry), were married in our sanctuary in 1975, and after moving to their hometown of LaGrange for five years, returned to Athens and have been members of the congregation continuously since 1980.

The Athens First Lay Leader in 1988 was Helen Taylor. Lay Delegates to Annual Conference were Louis Griffith, Tom Jackson, Helen Taylor and Betty Whitten.

᧑**1990**ᧉ

The Athens First delegates to Annual Conference in 1990 were Tom Jackson and Betty Whitten. The Lay Leader was Louis Griffith.

᧑**1991**ᧉ

Grady Wigley, Associate Pastor, 1991-1993 (continued as retiree to 2008)

Grady Wigley quickly became a beloved minister of congregational care after being appointed to Athens First in 1991, serving many years beyond his formal retirement in 1993. He was as active in congregational ministry

after retirement as he had been before, carrying the title Minister of Congregational Care from 1994-2008. His 17 years' service is third in length all-time among our pastors after Wesley Stephens (22 years) and Martha Aenchbacher (18). Born August 31, 1925, in Atlanta, he

Rev. Grady Wigley

married Doris Camp in 1947. They had three children. He was a U.S. Army World War II veteran. Grady earned the A.B. degree from the University of Georgia and was a graduate of the Candler School of Theology. Admitted on trial in 1962, he served: 1957 Maysville; 1961 Prospect, Lawrenceville; 1964 Colbert; 1968 Rockmart First; 1972 Mount Zion, Marietta; 1977 St. James, Athens; 1984 Aldersgate, Augusta; 1991 Athens First associate; 1993 retired. He and Doris remained actively involved in the life and care of Athens First through 2008, where we knew Grady for his quiet, caring demeanor and his diligent program of visitation to the sick and shut-in members of the congregation. He died May 20, 2021, with services held at Aldersgate, Augusta.

Carol Russell Scroggs, Associate Pastor 1991-1993

Born in 1950, Carol Scroggs was admitted as a probationary member in 1981 and was ordained elder in 1986. She and her husband, Herbert, were a clergy couple sharing an appointment, until his untimely death July 7, 1986, at the age of 33, left her with two young sons to raise. Herb, who was born in 1953, grew up in Grace Methodist Church in Atlanta, was ordained deacon in 1982 and elder in 1984. Herb served New Hope, 1982-84 Palmetto and 1984-85 Owl Rock, Atlanta. Carol served 1981 Pleasant Hill, Summerville; 1982 Colonial Hills; 1983 Jones Memorial. In 1985, they were appointed jointly to the Warren County Circuit, otherwise known as the Norwood Charge. Herb struggled with malignant melanoma through that time until his death, after which Carol

Rev. Carol Scroggs

remained as pastor in Norwood until 1989. His funeral was at Grace UMC and he was buried at Arlington Memorial Park in Sandy Springs. From that moment, Carol has felt that his ministry continued through hers. Carol's further appointments were 1989 Hardwick; 1991 Athens First associate; 1993 Princeton, Athens; 1995 Summerville First; 1996 Jefferson First; 1999 Pine Mountain; 2001 Atlanta First associate; 2006 Buchanan; 2008 Zebulon-Concord. She retired in 2014 but continued in her appointment at Zebulon-Concord for that year. At this writing (2024) she serves as one of two chaplains at Lanier Gardens and Talmage Terrace, the United Methodist senior living facilities in Athens and is active in the life of Athens First UMC.

The Athens First Lay Leader in 1991 was Helen Taylor. Dr. Taylor also was a lay delegate to Annual Conference that year, along with Tom Jackson.

๑1992 ๑

Garnett Marion Wilder, Senior Minister, 1992-1997

A noted leader among clergy of the North Georgia Conference, Dr. Wilder was an erudite preacher, scholar and author. Born March 22, 1930, in Carrollton, Garnett's family returned to their home in Royston when he was age 2, and he spent his childhood through high school there. He was brought into the faith by evangelist Harry Denman at age 9. Wilder felt called to preach at a revival at Poplar Springs Campground in Franklin County at age 14. He met his future wife, Marian Pinson, at a district youth camp in Hartwell in 1947. They were married in the Oconee Street Methodist Church in Athens

Dr. Garnett Wilder

in 1950. He graduated Reinhardt College in 1949, received his B.A. from the University of Georgia in 1951, and graduated cum laude from Candler School of Theology in 1954. He was admitted on trial in 1951 and in full connection in 1953. He studied in the Ph.D. program of Drew University and received a doctorate in systematic theology from Emory University in 1959. He taught theology at Candler for 20 years. His appointments over a 48-year career in the pulpit were: Center Charge, 1951 Buchanan, 1953 Celanese, 1955 Woodstock, NY, while a student at Drew; 1959 Bowden, 1963 Woodlawn, Augusta; 1968 Rome

First, 1976 Decatur First, 1981 District Superintendent, Atlanta-Decatur-Oxford District; 1987 Snellville First and 1992 Athens First. He held many positions of leadership in the North Georgia Conference and served on the General Board of Higher Education Ministry. He was elected by North Georgia five times as a clergy delegate to the General Conference, and six times to the Jurisdictional Conference. Dr. Wilder was a noted leader across the conference through his time at Athens. The Georgia Council on Civic and Moral Concerns selected him to debate on statewide television with Georgia Governor Zell Miller regarding a proposed statewide lottery. Over Wilder's strong opposition, the lottery was passed by a narrow margin of Georgia voters, giving birth to the state's HOPE Scholarship program which was impetus

The Athens First United Methodist Women in 1991 lovingly and expertly created needlepoint kneeling cushions to adorn the sanctuary altar. The medallions variously symbolize Christian sacraments, discipleship, and Biblical history. 54 total medallions were planned, designed and stitched by 18 women of the UMW.

for tremendous growth and academic improvement at UGA. Wilder brought distinguished guest speakers to the Athens First pulpit, most notably Anglican Archbishop Desmond Tutu of South Africa. (We regret being unable to find a photo of Archbishop Tutu in our pulpit.) At the conclusion of his time at Athens First, Dr. Wilder retired in 1997. He served as a retiree in residence at Decatur First UMC, where he died in the pulpit while preaching a sermon November 29, 1998. His last words were, "Trust God." His funeral was at Decatur First United Methodist Church, where Decatur layman and eulogist Roger Quillen captured him perfectly: "He never flinched from telling the truth that God inspired him to tell, no matter what the consequences.... Garnett showed us that Christians need not check their brains at the door on their way into the church; that the Christian faith can hold its own against any competing thought system; and that the good news of Jesus is no less relevant and the Christian faith no less defensible just because the world changes its philosophical fads." His publications include: *The evangelical theology of Edwin Lewis, Promises to Keep; Between the Times;* and *Using Your Emotions Creatively.* Following his death, his widow and family donated a sterling silver cross for the sanctuary altar in his memory to replace the one that had been in use since the 1963 renovation.

SOARING

OVER ATHENS SINCE 1852

The O'Neil Steeplejacks family preferred rappelling over
scaffolding to accomplish the 1992 renovation.

The landmark steeple that has stood as part of three different sanctuary structures more than 173 years has received two substantial renovations. As part of a 1910 sanctuary renovation, church trustee Emmet J. Bondurant fashioned a six-foot-long arrow and weathervane which was mounted on a bicycle hub to rotate atop the steeple. At the time, crosses generally were limited to Roman Catholic steeples and Protestant churches used other symbols.

When Dr. Bill McKoy arrived as senior minister in 1984, he proposed our church join others then trending toward adding crosses to Protestant churches. The proposal was not met with unanimous acceptance, particularly from trustee John Bondurant, whose father had fashioned the existing weathervane. Those church members who agreed with Dr. McKoy that the church should "follow the Cross and not the way the wind blows" prevailed.

The original church bell from 1852 remains in the steeple, although it has not operated for years. The O'Neils pose in front of their completed handiwork.

Through a generous bequest from the will of church member and Athens newspaper publisher Robert W. "Bob" Chambers, Jr., the steeple renovation proceeded in 1992. The O'Neil family of St. Augustine, Florida – believed to be the only steeplejack family in the country – spent four months dangling above downtown Athens, fixing every piece of missing slate, replacing every termite-damaged board, painting every exposed service. Before completing the job, they fashioned the new gilded Cross and presented it in a Sunday worship service to pastor Dr. Garnett Wilder and the congregation, placing it the following week atop the spire.

The weathervane was returned to the Bondurant family, and most recently was owned by Lee Epting of Athens. The congregation was greatly saddened to learn that a member of the O'Neil family died in a fall from another steeple not longer after our job was completed.

AFUMC's Mark Maxwell stands with the large arrow fabricated by trustee Emmet Bondurant.

The 1992 General Conference took action regarding the minimum size of conferences allowed to have their own bishop rather than sharing one. It allowed the South Georgia Conference to be removed from the Atlanta Area by vote of General Conference, meaning that North Georgia and South Georgia would have separate bishops. This arrangement lasted only 28 years, as the two conferences were combined under one bishop again in 2024 following loss of members and churches during disaffiliation. Discussion continues as to whether the two conferences should merge back into one Georgia Conference, as was the case prior to 1866.

THE SHOULDERS WE STAND ON IN THE CHURCH

Margie Shedd was lay leader at Athens First 2012 – 2023. She and husband Peter are constant presences at the church serving in myriad ways. In this essay, Margie recalls other laity in our church who were leaders in generosity of service.

When we look back through the ages to the beginning of our church, we see many names that also are part history of Athens. Famous names. Names we know. And we are grateful to each one of them. But there are so many people who came before us who each just did their part. Week after week. Day after day. There was Richard Morgan and Gene Weekley who repaired everything in the church. These men were ever-present checking the plumbing, fixing equipment in the kitchen, painting chips on the walls and everything else you can think of, giving generously of their time without compensation and still

Margie and Peter

in their place in the sanctuary every Sunday. And Leonard Cobb. He went door to door during the Sunday School hour and counted the attendance and picked up the Sunday School offering. (Did you even know we used to always collect Sunday School offerings?)

And then there were the women. So much of our history just records the men. A church, our church, wouldn't even be here without women. They held the church together. They nurtured our young, provided food for our gatherings, and made sure the sanctuary was always cared for and beautiful. And they were leaders. Ann Seawell, Louise McBee, Helen Taylor and Betty Whitten are just a few of the women who served our church wearing so many hats. Their service included heading building committees, serving on and leading the Trustees (once women were allowed), serving the greater church by chairing North Georgia committees and creating beautiful places in our church like the Hope Garden. We stand on the shoulders of so many members, who help make this church what it is today through their lifetime of selfless service and their generosity of time, talent and tithes. What are we doing for the generations to come?

Richard and Nancy Morgan

Louise McBee

Helen Taylor

Betty Whitten

Elizabeth "Beth" Camak LaRocca-Pitts, Associate Pastor, 1993-1996

Beth LaRocca is an Athens native whose father, Joe LaRocca, was a member of St. Joseph's Catholic Church and whose mother, Blair LaRocca, had been a member of Athens First since the family moved to Athens in 1949 as Joe joined the UGA faculty. Beth felt a deep commitment to going into the ministry from an early age but would be unable to answer that calling as a woman in the Roman

Beth LaRocca as a Duke University student in 1979 and Rev. Beth LaRocca-Pitts, Senior Minister at Oak Grove UMC in 2024

Catholic faith. She transferred membership from her father's church to her mother's when she was in high school in 1974, before going off to Duke University where she prepared to enter seminary. Athens First provided some financial support for her in 1980 as she went to work in Calcutta, India, with Mother Teresa. She wrote to the church, "…my desire to become a minister has always been supported and encouraged by the members of First Church and for this I am eternally grateful. You are in part responsible for giving Jesus another servant in the ministry and for this you should be proud of yourselves and the witness that you give to others."Beth was recommended by the Athens First Administrative Board in 1981 as a candidate for ordination and entered the conference as a probationary member in 1983. She was ordained elder in 1986. She married Mark Pitts in 1991. Her appointments to date include: 1983 Student; 1984 Bishop Circuit; 1987 Student; 1993 Athens First associate; 1996 Duke Divinity School; 2002 Snellville; 2004 Watkinsville First; 2010 St. Mark, Atlanta; 2020 Oak Grove, Decatur.

Rev. Rick Price

Ricky Kevin "Rick" Price, Associate Pastor, 1993-1998

Born August 19, 1950, Rick married Susie in 1991. He was admitted as a probationary member in 1984 and on full connection as elder in 1986. His appointments were: 1984 Rock Chapel; 1989 Blue Ridge; 1992 Hopewell, Murrayville; 1993 Athens First associate; 1998 Pleasant Grove, Cumming; 2003 Clarkesville; 2011 Cornerstone; 2016 retired.

∽1994 ∽

The church purchased the former Classic movie theater building across Washington Street, land today part of the Washington Street parking deck. The purchase was made under the general goal of expanding the church property as nearby opportunities presented themselves to increase options for future growth and expansion.

SERVANT LEADERSHIP - A SERVANT WHO LEADS

Robert Miles today is chair of our Church Council. His involvement at Athens First goes back many years. It has helped carry Robert and the Miles family through the growth of three sons into fine men, through the devastating illness and death of their beloved wife and mother, Felecia, and through the joy of having son Joshua answer a call to ministry and to become ordained in the North Georgia Conference. And ask Robert to show you pictures of his grandchild! Here, Robert shares the beginning of that story:

My participation in Athens First UMC began with the birth of our second and third children. The commute to Jonesboro, Ga. – Andrews Chapel UMC with Felecia and three boys was just not working for our family. There were several members of Athens First that we had come to know and fellowship with outside of the church. Pat and Gale Allen, Hoke and Linda Howard, as well as Rev. Garnett

Robert Miles teaching Sunday School in 2000

Miles in 2016, Joshua, Robert, Caleb and Nathan

and Marian Wilder. It was just a natural transition to then get involved in the Sunday School with our three boys Joshua, Caleb and Nathan. While being attentive to my own sons, I grew more into my mentoring of other children of the church. So, what began in the late 1990s as a parenting with a purpose role turned into a wonderful opportunity to assist with other children of AFUMC. Robin Stewart continued to ask, and I continued to say yes. Sunday School involvement transitioned into Route 56. My other roles within the church have come about with me attempting to be the hands and feet of Jesus through the Welcome Ministry and other roles in church leadership.

❥1995❧

The Athens First Lay Leader in 1995 was Louis Griffith. Our delegates to Annual Conference were Tom Jackson and Betty Whitten.

❥1996❧

The youth of the church through this period produced and performed annual large-scale drama productions, including *Jesus Christ, Superstar* and *Joseph and the Amazing Technicolor Dreamcoat* under the direction of Melanie Rowell. As the church had no auditorium or stage facilities other than the sanctuary itself, that is where the productions were staged, complete with lighting and a house orchestra. The program was a major impetus for including a stage in the new Hancock Hall, which at that time was just in the planning stage.

This scene is from *Joseph and the Dreamcoat* featuring Christopher Felton as Joseph.

George Earl "Chip" Wilson, Jr., Associate Pastor, 1996-1997

Rev. Chip Wilson

Born in 1957, Chip married Pam in 1981. He was admitted to probationary membership in 1982 and full connection as elder in 1985. His appointments were: 1981 Buford First, 1983 Grace, Atlanta, 1987 Inman Park, Atlanta, 1991 Dalton First, 1996 Athens First, 1998 Washington First, 2005 Lewis Memorial, 2008 Jasper UMC, 2015 Bethany, Smyrna, 2020 retired, 2021 a retired clergy appointment to Hickory Flat, Canton.

⚙1997⚙

William Oslin "Bill" Britt IV, Senior Minister, 1997-2008

The appointment of 39-year-old Bill Britt to Athens First in 1997 was a marked departure from the traditional appointment to Athens of a senior member of the North Georgia Conference as a capstone on their career, or a step on the path to being a candidate for bishop. Born in 1958, the Thomaston, Ga. native graduated Stetson University, received the Master of Divinity from Candler School of Theology and the Doctor of Ministry from United Theological Seminary. He married Wendie Ham in 1983. He entered probationary membership in 1982 and was ordained elder in 1985.

The Chancel Choir in 1997

Construction of the new Family Life Center on the newly-acquired land, including Hancock Hall, a gymnasium, youth meeting spaces and new church offices, commenced in 2000, with the building occupied in 2002.

PAVING THE WAY
for a Landmark Exchange

Athens First has an interesting history of involvement with Athens movie theaters – first, meeting for two years 1962-64 in the Georgia Theater while the sanctuary and church complex underwent reconstruction, and then in 1994 finding itself owning the Classic Triple Theater.

The Classic movie theater, which stood across Washington Street from the church since 1969, opened as a state-of-the-art 1,200-seat rocking-chair theater with a 70mm screen. But the auditorium proved to be too large for the demand and soon was divided into three smaller theaters, labeled the "Classic Triple." Even so, with challenges of the economy and a lack of downtown parking for a movie theater, after only 25 years of operation it closed in 1994 and was offered for sale.

Athens First UMC purchased the property with a short-term view for overflow space, but under the general goal of expanding property holdings for future expansion. The theater proved impractical for church use, however, as the floor in the large auditorium sloped sharply from one end to the other and would require major renovation. But the property, which extends through the block from Washington to Clayton Streets, was more than desirable for the local government to use for part of another downtown parking deck. In 1997, discussions began in earnest.

With the city's desire to avoid having to demolish the theater and to receive a usable parking lot in the deal, the church proceeded with demolition and paved a parking lot on the site. The new parking lot was swapped for the city parking lot behind the church in March 1999. In special Wednesday evening and Sunday worship services in May 1999, church members celebrated finally owning the entire city block on which the sanctuary stands.

The landmark sign for the Classic Triple was preserved, and is displayed today on the Georgia Theater at the corner of Clayton and Lumpkin Streets.

His appointments have been: 1981 Ebenezer, Forsyth; 1984 associate at Trinity-on-the-Hill, Augusta; 1988 Trinity, Cartersville; 1997 Athens First. After his eleven years in the Athens First pulpit, which to that date was the longest tenure served by a senior minister here, Dr. Britt was appointed in 2008 as senior minister at Peachtree Road UMC in Atlanta, where he still serves as of this writing (2025).

Shortly after his arrival, Dr. Britt and church leaders met with Athens city officials in hope of swapping the former Classic Theater building, which the church purchased in 1994, for the city-owned parking lot which occupied the remainder of the block on which the church stands, including a former service station which stood at the corner of Hancock and Hull. The city expressed a preference to swap parking for parking, so the church proceeded to demolish the theater and pave a parking lot in its place.

Athens First was pleased to welcome Dr. Britt back to our pulpit in March 2025 as part of the Bicentennial Celebration. Here, he looks back on his time in Athens.

Bill and Wendie Britt with Sara and Will in 2000

When I was appointed to Athens First United Methodist Church in 1997, Bishop Bevel Jones pulled me aside at Annual Conference and told me that I was being appointed to the most influential pulpit in the state of Georgia. If you knew Bev, you knew he often engaged in hyperbole, and I sort of dismissed his words. However, after about a year, I came to understand what he meant. In many ways, in the state of Georgia, all roads seem to lead through Athens.

Through its two centuries, this flagship church has helped

provide the spiritual formation and values for countless leaders in our state – politicians who came here as students (some stayed and others moved on to another part of the state); professors who teach at the University of Georgia and worship at this great church; business leaders who have gathered here to worship, pray, and serve in the name of Christ; and even young adults who have heard God's call to ordained ministry through Athens First UMC – Bishop William R. Cannon, Wiley Stephens, Beth LaRocca Pitts, Betsy Butler, and Josh Miles quickly come to my mind. This realization is both inspiring and humbling. You never wanted to show up to lead worship or a Bible study without having prepared to bring your best.

Athens First UMC is a teaching church. That is a part of the church's DNA and will continue to shape its ministry as it prepares for a third century of ministry in Athens.

Margaret Davis Freeman, Associate Pastor, 1995-2006

Margaret Freeman came to Athens First as youth minister in 1995 and completed requirements for ordination as deacon in 1997. Her first appointment was in 1997 to continue as associate pastor and minister to youth at Athens First, a position she held for eleven years altogether.

Rev. Margaret Davis Freeman

Born in 1959, she married James Freeman in 1988. She became a leader in conference youth activities for many years. Like Mike Selleck before her, Margaret Freeman has a large contingent of youth during her time here who are now adult leaders in this and other churches, and who remember her with great affection. In 2006, Rev. Freeman took leave to move with her husband, a veterinary research scientist, to Franklin, N.C. In 1997, in an appointment beyond the bounds of the local conference, she became associate pastor at Franklin First UMC in the Western North Carolina Conference.

᧗1998 ᧖

Carolyn Capers Moore, Associate Pastor, 1998-1999

Rev. Carolyn Moore

Born in 1963, Carolyn Capers married Steven Moore in 1986. Having felt called to preach at 13, she did not at first follow that call, but it renewed when she was 30. She earned a B.A. in religion from the University of Georgia, a master of divinity (1998) and a doctor of divinity (2018), both from Asbury Theological Seminary. She was admitted on probationary membership in 1998 and became elder in full connection in 2001. Her duties during five years as associate at Athens First included responsibility for starting and maintaining a contemporary worship service in the historic Morton Theater, across Washington Street from our sanctuary. In 2003, she was appointed to Evans, Georgia, to begin a new congregation. As founding pastor of Mosaic UMC in Evans, she became increasingly activist in the Wesleyan Covenant Association and in the formation of the Global Methodist Church. After leading Mosaic in 2023 to disaffiliate from the United Methodist Church and join Global, she continues as pastor there.

Janis Maxwell

Janis Maxwell, Youth Choir Director 1998 – 1999 Interim Co-Director of Music December 1999 – July 2001 Co-Organist and Accompanist July 2001 – Fall 2005 Director of Youth Music Ministry Fall 2005 – 2007 Organist 2007 – 2021 Director of Children's and Youth Music Ministry 2021 – present Interim Director of Music February – August 2022

Janis Maxwell became part of the church staff in August 1998 and has ably served the music ministry of our church in a variety of ways over the 27 years since. The list of titles outlined above shows the many ways in which Janis has utilized her talents in the service of the church through music and worship. She served as primary organist 14 of those years and remains a ready fill-in on the organ when one is needed. At present she leads the Wesleyan Youth Choir and oversees the full program of children's choirs.

Following a trend across the conference, in 1998 Athens First determined it to be in the pastor's best interest to purchase and own their own homes, which Dr. Britt proceeded to do. The Highland Drive parsonage was sold.

On April 18, 1998, a crowd estimated at more than 100,000 surrounded Athens First as the world-famous Athens-based rock band Widespread Panic staged an album release party in the streets. With the performance stage set at the intersection of Washington and Pulaski Streets, the crowd filled the roads for blocks around. A festival of tents and displays covered the property behind the church where the new Family Life Center would be constructed two years hence.Tense negotiations occurred between the church, the city and the band's agents over the fact that a wedding was scheduled in the sanctuary at the same hour as the concert. With an agreement to move the wedding one hour earlier and the start of the concert one hour later, accommodation was reached, and the newlywed couple exited the front doors of the sanctuary onto Lumpkin Street into a throng cheering them.

A crowd estimated at 100-thousand packs Washington Street beside the church for a Widespread Panic concert on April 18, 1998.

THE IMPORTANCE OF SMALL GROUP INVOLVEMENT

Dianne Wall tells how important it is to get involved in the church beyond participation in Sunday morning worship.

After moving to Athens, I visited several churches in the Athens area but did not feel any were right for me. On my first visit to Athens First, I felt welcomed. I knew at that time this would be my church. This became my great gift from God.

Dianne Wall

On April 5, 1998, I joined Athens First United Methodist Church. The Reverend Doctor William Britt was the senior minister.The doors were opened for me to become active in many areas of the church life. This church brought many people into my life who will be friends forever.

The United Methodist Women became important for me. I served as the secretary for the UMW executive board for fifteen years. When there was an opportunity to begin a new circle, I opened my home for the new circle to meet each month. It grew and today there are over twenty-five women who attend this circle every month

I had the privilege to serve on the Altar Guild for many years. The Intercessory Prayer Group began in 2006, and I continue in this ministry today.

I was invited to attend the Outreach Sunday School Class, and the members opened their arms and welcomed me. It has been a blessing in my life to be with the loving people in this class.

There are so many opportunities to serve in this wonderful church. One must be willing to be available and willing to serve as asked. If not asked, one can volunteer. There are so many needs in the church to be met. It has been my honor to be a small part of this loving and growing church. It is a joy to be a member of Athens First United Methodist Church and its ministries in the Athens community.

The Athens First lay delegates to 1998 Annual Conference were Tom Jackson, Dianne Morrison, Margaret Timm, Betty Whitten, and Dan Blitch. The Athens First Lay Leader for several years was Ken Mauldin.

э**1999** э

Finally – we own the entire block

Exchange of the parking lot built on the former Classic Theater property was completed with the Athens-Clarke County government in March 1999. The church obtained the remaining property on the block bounded by Lumpkin, Hancock, Hull and Washington Streets. The congregation concluded worship on Sunday, May 9, 1999, by marching single file out of the sanctuary and around the entire block to ceremonially claim it for the Lord's work.

For three consecutive years, 1999-2001, Athens hosted the North Georgia Annual Conference at its new Classic Center, with Athens First serving as the host church. Bishop G. Lindsey Davis presided. It represented the ninth, tenth and eleventh times Athens had hosted Annual Conference.

The congregation files out of the sanctuary following 11 a.m. worship on Sunday, May 9, 1999, and walks around the entire newly acquired block, ceremonially claiming it for the Lord's work. After 174 years, Athens First finally had achieved the goal of owning the full city block bounded by Lumpkin, Hancock, Hull and Washington. This photo is along Hull Street.

Susan Carse-McLocklin, Associate Pastor, 1999-2004

Rev. Carse-McLocklin was born December 7, 1959. She earned the B.A. degree at Bethany College in 1982, and the Master of Divinity at the

Candler School of Theology, Emory University, in 1986. Ordained in the West Virginia Conference, in 1986 she was appointed campus pastor at Marshall University, and took a student appointment to attend the University of Georgia 1989-92. She took leave from the West Virginia Conference in 1992, and in 1995 transferred to the North Georgia Conference where she was appointed Winder First Associate. She was appointed Minister of Program Development at Athens First for the years 1999-2004. At the conclusion of her Athens appointment she took family leave and returned to West Virginia, where she took Honorable Location in 2008 with a position outside the church.

Above, Rev. Susan Carse-McLocklin. Right, a children's time during a 2000 worship service

Longtime organist and director of music Martha Braswell departed for a position in Texas. For an interim period, December 1999 – July 2001 during the search for a permanent director of music, the various duties of directing children, youth and adult choirs and playing organ and piano were shared by Janis Maxwell, Beverly Brown and Carol Reeves.

The Athens First Lay Leader in 1999 was Ken Mauldin, and lay delegates to Annual Conference were Tom Jackson, Claire Swann, Helen Taylor, Dan Blitch, Margaret Timm, and Roy O'Donnell. Normally a charge has one lay delegate for every clergy appointment it receives. However, Athens First some years has more lay delegates than this allocation, as members receive appointments to Conference by the District Superintendent to represent the district-at-large.

੭**2000** ੭

From 2000 to 2002, Athens First constructed a $5 million, 43,000-square-foot addition on the newly acquired property, containing a gymnasium with indoor track, a new Fellowship Hall to replace the one previously located in the sanctuary basement, a youth center and new offices. The project was steered to completion by a building committee chaired by trustee Lee Pierson. After 177 years, Athens First facilities finally occupied the entire city block.

Old-Style Worship

First United Methodist Church members, from left, Jeanne Lagrone, behind the horse, Mary Hutcherson, Beth Belle, Janis Maxwell and Sarah Sleppey admire the horse ridden by First UMC Senior Minister the Rev. Bill Britt on Sunday. As part of First UMC's 175th anniversary, Britt rode to church on a horse and members of the congregation wore clothing reminiscent of the early 1800s.

Jeff Blake/Photo Staff

One Of Athens' Oldest, Largest Churches Celebrates 175th Anniversary

BY LEE SHEARER
Staff Writer

Athens First United Methodist Church

Children at First United Methodist Church watch from the church's balcony as the Rev. Bill

Athens First celebrated the 175th anniversary of its founding. An Athens Banner-Herald feature published October 2, 2000 pictures senior minister Bill Britt riding to the observance on horseback, greeted by church members dressed in period costume.

Betty and Bill Simpson

Bill and Betty Simpson gave the beautiful garden and fountain on the north side of the sanctuary building in memory of Bill's parents, Ed and Elise Simpson. It originally was to have been in the inner courtyard of the church, but when the decision was made to utilize that space for the new Hope Garden, the Simpson garden was designated for its current location. It was completed and dedicated in 2000.

9**2001** 9

The Athens First lay delegates to Annual Conference in 2001 were Tom Jackson, Helen Taylor, Betty Whitten and Mike Derrick (a district- at-large appointment from Covington). The church lay leader that year was Ken Mauldin.

A terrorist attack on our nation on September 11, 2001, killed almost three thousand Americans at the World Trade Center in New York City, the Pentagon in Arlington, Virginia and in a field near Shanks Ville, Pennsylvania

where a third hijacked plane believed bound for the U.S. Capitol or the White House was forced down by heroic passengers. The tragedy, killing more Americans than lost their lives in the Pearl Harbor attack 60 years earlier, caused people to reach out to the church for strength, solace and comfort in unprecedented numbers. At Athens First, the Sundays immediately following September 11th were filled beyond capacity, with every seat occupied, chairs in the aisles and worshippers standing along the walls. It was a time of crisis in which people turned to God. Numbers such as those in worship attendance for those weeks have not been seen since.

Stephen Mitchell, Director of Music 2001 – 2022

Stephen Mitchell was born and raised in Pensacola, Florida. He attended Birmingham-Southern College where he received a Bachelor of Arts with a concentration in choral conducting and church music. Upon

Stephen Mitchell

graduation, Stephen spent four years as a Choral Scholar at Wells Cathedral in Wells, England, where he sang daily choral evensong in the choir of men and boys. Stephen then became Director of Music at Trinity UMC in Birmingham, Alabama. In July 2001, he came to Athens First as Director of Music, a position he held until January 2022. Over his 21 years directing the program, the choir grew in both size and accomplishment. With Stephen's arrival as director of music, the duties of organist and pianist for worship and all choirs were shared by Mary Ann Fitzgerald and Janis Maxwell. In fall 2005, Janis returned to fulltime director of children and youth choirs and Mary Ann became the fulltime organist.

⑨**2002** ⑤

The church purchased two office buildings, known as the Saye property, fronting the block of Lumpkin Street from Hancock to Dougherty Streets. For some years, the space was used for Scout meeting rooms, Sunday School classes and some was leased to the University of Georgia and other businesses.

The Saye Building is visible at the right of this photo from Easter Sunday 2024.

Mark Maxwell – Director of Media Ministries

An accomplished classical guitarist, Mark has been associated with AFUMC in a variety of capacities since being invited by music director Martha Braswell to play for a service in 1982. Today he coordinates all

Mark Maxwell

media production, including online streaming and audiovisual support for many church events. He grew up in Embry Hills UMC in Tucker. On football scholarships, he attended the Air Force Academy and Georgia Tech (where he played under Coach Bill Curry) before ultimately earning a degree in classical guitar from UGA in 1985. In addition to his work with the church, Mark operates a production business which has produced and recorded projects for the Smithsonian Institution, the Weather Channel, Kenny Rogers, REM, the College Football Hall of Fame, and serves as film archivist for UGA athletics. He has been married since 1991 to Janis Maxwell, longtime AFUMC organist who now serves as Director of Children's and Youth Music Ministry.

∽2003 ∽

Having met in Athens from 1999-2001, the North Georgia Conference moved its 2002 meeting to Augusta and thus determined there was no hall in Georgia to compare with the Classic Center, which opened in Athens in 1995. In 2003, the Conference returned to Athens for the 12th time, beginning a stretch that at this writing is 22 years and counting of consecutive annual meetings in the Athens Classic Center, with Athens First as the host church. Presiding Bishops through this period are G. Lindsey Davis, B. Michael Watson, Sue Haupert-Johnson and Robin Dease. Athens First's lay delegates to the 2003 session were Betty Whitten, Roger Roemmich and Helen Taylor. Athens First members serving as district-at-large delegates were Hank Huckaby and Alison Griner. During the Covid-19 pandemic, the 2020 and 2021 sessions of Annual Conference were held online, originating from Athens, but without a full assembly. Through 2024 the Conference had met in Athens 33 times, with the first eight of those in the Athens First sanctuary and since 1999 25 of 26 years have been at the Classic Center. At this writing, the Conference is under contract to continue its annual meetings at the Classic Center through 2026. It is not clear what impact the proposed merger of the North and South Georgia Conferences might have on the longtime partnership with the Classic Center beyond 2026.

At the 2003 Annual Conference: John Simmons, host district superintendent; Athens-Clarke Mayor Heidi Davison; Athens First delegate Hank Huckaby; host committee member Johnny Fowler; Athens First senior minister Bill Britt.

Rev. David Moore

David Francis Moore, Associate Pastor, 2003-2007

Born in 1958, David Moore married Katherine in 1985. Admitted to probationary membership in 1983, he was ordained elder in 1987. His appointments include: 1983 student; 1985 Starrsville; 1992 Crossroads; 2000 leave; 2003 Athens First; 2007 Midway, Auburn; 2016 Covenant, Smyrna. In 2023, Covenant disaffiliated from the UMC, and Moore continues to pastor it as a Global church. He is Global's "connectional elder" for Cobb and Paulding counties.

୨2004 ୭

Rev. Martha Aenchbacher

Martha Lee Aenchbacher, Associate Pastor, 2004-2022

Martha Aenchbacher was an associate pastor at Athens First for 18 years, placing her second among our clergy all-time in length of service after Wesley Stephens' 22 years. Born in 1964, she married Dr. Lonnie T. Harvel in 1998. He was a faculty member at Georgia Tech who became vice president for educational technology at Georgia Gwinnett College. Admitted as a probationary member in 1998, Martha was appointed to Midway UMC in Alpharetta. She was ordained elder in 2001 and was appointed associate pastor at Athens First in 2004. Lonnie became the original web designer for the North Georgia Conference, was active in the Athens First choir and was pursuing ordination as a deacon when he unexpectedly died in 2010 at age 47. His funeral was among the largest we have seen in our sanctuary. Martha, a widowed young mother with two small children, remained at Athens First for nearly two decades as the daughters grew to adulthood. Martha became a mainstay of congregational care, visiting the ill and shut-in and caring for the many needs of a large congregation in a warm and effective way. In July 2022 she took leave to pursue education in grief counseling in London and in December 2022 secured appointment beyond the bounds of the conference as a chaplain at Royal London Hospital, where she serves at this writing.

☙2006❧

Former U.S. President George H. W. Bush visited Athens and the UGA campus for a second time, giving the dedicatory address April 7, 2006 for UGA's Coverdell Building. In the above photo, at left on the dais is Athens First layman Henry M. "Hank" Huckaby, who at the time was UGA's Senior Vice President for Finance and Administration. Huckaby later would serve in the Georgia General Assembly, would become Chancellor of the University System of Georgia, and would be elected twice as a North Georgia lay delegate to the United Methodist General Conference.

Rev. Will Zant in 2008 and 2024

William Carter Zant, Associate Pastor, 2006-2009

Born in 1979, Will Zant married Blair Boyd in 2008. He became a probationary member in 2006 and was ordained an elder in full connection in 2009. His appointment to Athens First was his first and has been followed by: 2009 North Springs, 2013 Cannon and 2018 Haygood Memorial, where he serves as of 2024. His wife also is an ordained elder in North Georgia, currently serving as Director of the Conference

Children's Choir, 2005

Center for Congregational Excellence. She and Will were appointed as co-pastors of Cannon UMC 2013-18 before moving into the current separate appointments.

2007

Jimmy Carter visited the UGA campus numerous times over at least 45 years, from his election to the Georgia General Assembly in 1962, through his years as Governor 1971- 75, as President of the United States 1977- 81, and during his distinguished years as a former President. In 2007, Carter chose the

University of Georgia to host a reunion of his administration on the 30th anniversary of his inauguration. Most of his top leadership were in attendance to discuss "The Carter Presidency: Lessons for the 21st Century." Many Athens First UMC laypersons were involved in the staging and hosting of the momentous three-day event.

Amihan "Amy" Robin Valdez-Barker, 2007-2011

Amy Valdez-Barker was appointed associate pastor at Athens First in 2007, first with duties as minister to families with youth. Born in 1975, Amy Valdez married Richard Barker in 1992. Originally admitted in the Wisconsin Conference where she served as Conference Youth Coordinator, she transferred to North Georgia in 2008 and was ordained deacon in 2011. She holds a master's degree and Ph.D., both from Garrett Evangelical

Rev. Amy Valdez-Barker in 2008 and 2024

Theological Seminary. Following Athens, in 2011 she was appointed director of Vital Ministries for the conference. In 2013 she became chief connectional ministries officer of the Connectional Table, the chief ministries arm of the General UMC. In 2017 she was named executive director of Global Mission Connections for the General Board of Global Ministries, succeeding Rev. Dr. Mande Muyombo of the Congo, who was elected Bishop. In March 2021 she was appointed to the WeARE Connection and in September 2021 to Candler School of Theology as adjunct faculty. In 2022 she was appointed to Mountain Park UMC and in 2023 to the Ministry Collaborative as the Congregational and Pastoral Formation Curator.

Mary Ann Fitzgerald departed as organist in May 2007 and was succeeded by Janis Maxwell as fulltime organist and Director of Youth Music Ministry. As such, a substitute organist often was required, a position filled regularly by longtime church member Beth Rector. Janis Maxwell would serve as organist until 2021.

❺2008 ❺

Charles Edward "Chuck" Hodges, Senior Minister, 2008-2022

Born in Atlanta in 1954, Chuck Hodges grew up in Warrenton, Ga. following his father's career in the postal service. Rev. Hodges attended

Rev. Chuck Hodges

the Citadel and graduated from Valdosta State College. He married Penny Bolkcom in 1978. Obtaining a master's in divinity from Oral Roberts University, he was admitted to probationary membership in 1984 and was ordained an elder in North Georgia in 1986. His appointments were: 1982 Grovetown; 1985 Chamblee First; 1988 Waleska (and Reinhardt College chaplain); 1993 Dallas First; 1996 Peachtree City; 2008 Athens First; 2022 Retired. At this writing, Hodges' 14-year tenure is the longest of all senior pastors in our 200+-year history. His very successful time at Athens First likewise was marked by two significant crises: the Covid-19 pandemic and Rev. Hodges' personal battle with cancer. He lives at Lake Oconee in retirement.

Chuck Hodges served as Athens First UMC Senior Minister 14 years - longer than any other in our first two centuries. He offers a personal reflection on those years:

I was appointed to serve as the senior minister of Athens First UMC in the summer of 2008. I arrived here in a season of personal grief struggling with the recent death of my mother. To be in a transition during this time of sadness was a great challenge, but little did I know that I had been sent to serve a church family that was more than willing to walk with me through this valley.

I would come to learn over and over again that this is the defining character of Athens First. To be here was to be a witness to the power of God's love offered through a people who were committed to being a beloved community. Again and again I saw it in the way all were welcomed. It was evident in the pursuit of excellence in all areas of church life. There was a generous spirit reflected in the love offered, the faith exercised, the hope that was steadfast and the resources given. Every challenge was met with an attitude of what could be and a willingness to embrace the future unafraid.

I was so encouraged during these years. That is a gift I continue to cherish. One of the primary reasons I believe this church has such a rich history is that it has always been grounded in a deep desire to be a source of light and a beacon of hope to the community. There is a commitment that sustains this congregation to keep the main thing the main thing. Jesus said, "This is my commandment that you love one another the way

I have loved you." Evidence of such love permeates the life of this family and I feel sure that will continue to be true for years to come. That baton will be passed to successive generations, who I feel sure will love in new and creative ways that define Athens First as it moves forward.

Athens First member Henry M. "Hank" Huckaby became the fourth layperson in the church's history to be elected to the General Conference, serving in 2008 at Fort Worth and in 2012 at Tampa. Huckaby also was chair of the North Georgia Conference Council on Finance and Administration, was the state budget director under Governors Zell Miller and Sonny Perdue, was senior vice president for finance and administration at the University of Georgia, represented Clarke and Oconee counties in the Georgia General Assembly and was chancellor of the University System of Georgia from 2011-2017. He served as finance committee chair at Athens First for two three-year terms and was an Athens First delegate to the North Georgia

Henry M. "Hank" Huckaby, 1941 – 2021

Annual Conference. He died in 2021. His widow, Amy Huckaby, remains an active member at Athens First.

Trustee Betty Whitten was a driving force behind creation of the beautiful Hope Garden constructed in 2008-09 in the inner courtyard of the church. Rather than create a columbarium, which is a structure with drawers for cremains, the church decided to have ashes buried throughout the space with plaques on the memorial wall. Dr. Whitten in her will established a fund at Athens First UMC to be used to maintain the Garden.

☙2009❧

Rev. John A. Page

John Anthony Page, Associate Pastor, 2009-2013

Born in 1969, John Page married Stacey in 1997. He was ordained elder in 2008. His appointments were 1999 Sugar Hill; 2006 Graysville; 2009 Athens First; 2013 Cave Spring; 2021 Faith, Cartersville; 2022 Leave, 2023 Retired.

☙2010❧

Margaret "Meg" Morrison

Margaret Grace "Meg" Morrison, who grew up in Athens First, answered a call to the ministry and was entered on probationary membership in 2010. She was ordained elder in full connection in 2016. Her appointments to date include: 2006 Watkinsville First; 2007 Macedonia-Redwine Circuit; 2009 Comer; 2010 Connectional Ministries; 2012 Trinity-on-the-Hill, LaGrange; 2015 Lawrenceville Road; 2021 Stone Mountain First; 2023 Jodeco Road, 2024 North Decatur. She is the granddaughter of Methodist minister Bill Ruff, who spent his retirement years as an active part of our congregation. Meg's parents are Pat and Diane Morrison, active members at Athens First.

STEWARDSHIP AS A COMMUNION STEWARD

JANE HARVEY

For approximately 15 years I have taken responsibility for Communion preparation as well as maintaining volunteers to assist with that preparation and clean up every time it is scheduled at AFUMC. Carlyn Haley actually recruited me those many years ago to help in securing volunteers to prep for the 8:30 service every week and then for the 9:30 and 11 am service typically once a month.

During the new Quimby organ installation, church services were held in Hancock Hall. Preparation for Communion was totally moved out of the Sacristy due to the huge hole that was to accommodate the new pipe system for the organ. Preparation of the elements was done in the office workroom and rolled into Hancock Hall when we had Communion. It was a challenging time but with volunteers helping we were able to meet that need.

As a person who still irons her pillowcases and top sheets at home, being responsible for the laundering and ironing of the Communion linens at home is a practice that I actually enjoy! I find myself remembering friends and family members from over the years who taught me about Communion and the importance of the significance as the Lord's Supper!

I am truly blessed and thankful for all the AFUMC friends and volunteers who willingly continue to prepare

Jane Ha...
Raegan Harvey in 2009

Communion with me year after year. It is my prayer that I can continue to serve our Lord in this capacity for years to come.

◉2012◉

The silver Wilder memorial cross in use of the sanctuary altar since 1989 was replaced by the large marble cross in use today, given as a memorial to the late church trustee Carlton M. James, Jr.

◉2013◉

Elizabeth "Beth" Lockerbie Dickinson, Associate Pastor, 2013-2017

Born in 1976, Beth Dickinson grew up in Lilburn as a member at Harmony Grove UMC. A 1994 graduate of Parkview High School and a 1998 graduate of the University of Georgia with a degree in chemistry, she began her career as a chemist. She married Keith Dickinson in 1999 before receiving a call to ministry while volunteering with youth in her home church. She graduated from the Candler School of Theology and was commissioned as a deacon in 2003. She switched orders and was ordained elder in 2008. Her appointments have been: 2003 McKendree; 2006 Vinings; 2013 Athens First associate.

Rev. Beth Dickinson

Beginning in 2017, she took three years medical leave to address debilitating pain from Thoracic Outlet Syndrome, a condition that involved six surgeries over two years. After the last of those surgeries in 2019 in Boston, she re-entered the active clergy and was appointed in 2020 to Barrow Community Church before moving to her current appointment as associate pastor of Bethlehem UMC in 2021. Another surgery in 2024 required another period of leave extending into the spring of 2025.

Elizabeth Marie "Betsy" Butler, Associate Pastor, 2013-2024

Born in 1967, Betsy married Rhett Butler in 1994. She was a lay member of Athens First with her family, heavily involved in its outreach mission to the local community when she answered a call to ministry. After completing her probationary

Rev. Elizabeth M. "Betsy" Butler

period and educational requirements, Betsy was ordained a deacon in full connection in 2016. Through a fortuitous opportunity she was appointed to our church, where she served for 11 years. In August 2024, she took leave to pursue work in hospice ministries. She maintains her ordination and her active involvement in the congregation at Athens First.

୨2016 ୧

Robert "Bob" Wayne Winstead, Executive Pastor, 2016-2021

Rev. Dr. Bob Winstead, who recently had retired from full-time ministry, was hired as executive pastor at Athens First UMC in 2016.

Born in 1951, Bob grew up in many states and several countries as his father was career Navy. At the young age of 16 Bob became a professional drummer in Jacksonville, Florida playing with many bands and notably The Second Coming, a band which later became The Allman Brothers. After serving in the Navy as a SeaBee builder, Bob began a career in general contracting building several major projects including supervising construction of the transportation tunnel under Hartsfield Jackson Airport in Atlanta. In 1980 Bob answered a call to the ministry, went back to college and seminary while serving as a student

Robert "Bob" Wayne Winstead

pastor until he was admitted as a Probationary Member of the North Georgia Conference in 1986, becoming an elder in full connection in 1989. In 1995 Bob received his Doctorate in Ministry degree from the University of Chicago. His appointments were: 1981 Yorkville Circuit, 1983 Mizpah, 1987 St. Luke, Mableton, 1990 Mt. Bethel, Marietta, 1993 North Springs, 1999 Ebenezer, Conyers, 2004 Haygood Memorial, 2008 Candler School of Theology faculty, where his work focused on congregational organization and supervision and personality type in religious leadership. He retired in 2014 but continued to teach part-time at Candler. In 2016 he accepted an appointment in retirement to New Hope, Lawrenceville. In September 2016 he came to Athens First, where he served as Executive Pastor through 2021 before fully retiring. Here he not only organized and modernized the church administrative functions but was able to fill the pulpit during the serious illness of senior minister Chuck Hodges, oversaw the renovation of the sanctuary and the installation of a magnificent new church organ and helped guide the congregation through the Covid pandemic of 2020. In retirement, Bob continues to teach for the General Council on Finance and Administration (GCFA) and the General Board of Higher Education and Ministry (GBHEM). He and his wife, the former Evelyn Wyck Bain, a member of our congregation whom he met while serving here, remain active in the life of Athens First. The Winsteads make their home in Athens First UMC following full retirement and in doing so extend a long tradition of distinguished retired clergy (photos, following page) who have joined our congregation and greatly enriched its life by their presence and participation.

∋2017 ∋

Susan Martin Taylor, Associate Pastor, 2017-2019

Susan Taylor was appointed associate pastor at Athens First in 2017. Born in 1956, she grew up as a Southern Baptist. She married Larry Taylor in 1988. She received her bachelor's degree from Emory, did graduate work at West Florida and the University of Hawaii and earned her doctorate from the University of Georgia where she worked in teaching and administration. After raising five children and stepchildren, she answered a call to ministry in her 40s. Taylor was admitted as a probationary member in 2003 and ordained elder in 2006. Her appointments were: 2001 Demorest,

Rev. Susan Martin Taylor

2003 Duluth First, 2006 Hopewell, Murrayville, 2008 Simpsonwood, 2012 Starrsville, 2017 Athens First associate. She retired from fulltime ministry in 2019 at the conclusion of her service with our church and split time between her home in Flowery Branch and her daughter's home in Amsterdam.

Allison Lee Griner Collins, a lifelong member of Athens First, was ordained a deacon in full connection after answering a call to ministry. Born in 1982, she married Jason Collins in 2018. Her appointments to date include: 2012 Milledgeville First associate; 2016 Cumming First associate; 2019 Leave. Her parents are active Athens First members Kathy and Don Griner.

Allison Griner Collins

OUR LONGEST-LIVED MEMBER

STAN SINGLETON

The longest-living member of Athens First to our knowledge was Dr. Stanton James "Stan" Singleton, who died December 27, 2017, at the age of 106 years and two months. He lived his last years in our Methodist retirement center at Talmage Terrace and was active in the congregation well into his hundreds. Each year he was recognized on his birthday and would stand during a worship service to be acknowledged by the congregation. Born in 1910 in Cobb County, Stan grew up in Forsyth County. He attended Young Harris College before obtaining his bachelor's and master's degrees from the University of Georgia. After service in the Navy in

Stan Singleton

World War II, he completed his Ph.D. at Ohio State University. His wife of 58 years, Marget, predeceased him in 1998. Teaching was Stan's passion. He taught in one-room schools in Middle and South Georgia before becoming principal first at LaGrange High School and then at the UGA College of Education Demonstration School which was located in Baldwin Hall. After World War II, he joined the UGA Education faculty serving 41 years before retiring in 1978. A passionate and dedicated member of our church, Stan asked that memorial gifts in his memory go to the fund to purchase a new organ.

ᓂ2018ᓂ

Operation and maintenance of the increasingly delapidated Saye Building, which fronts Lumpkin Street from Hancock to Dougherty, became prohibitively expensive. The church determined to demolish it for parking. The Athens-Clarke government blocked the demolition by expanding the downtown historic district to include the church's property. The matter was under dispute for more than six years, with the church finally resorting to filing a lawsuit against the city.

Some of the many Methodist clergy and spouses who have been active in the Athens First congregation during their retirement.

Bill & Grace Ruff

Wesley & Annette Stephens

Paul Hanna

Lynette & Dan Maxey

Carolyn Morris & Herbert Owen

Mildred & Charles Boleyn

Doris & Grady Wigley

Russell & Kathy Edwards

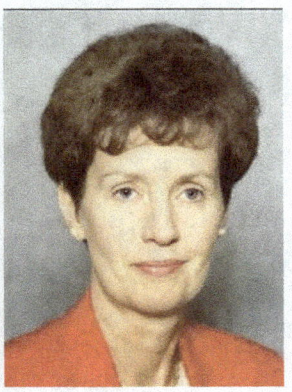

Pat McKoy

ꃍ2019 ꃎ

Joshua David Miles, Minister to Youth and Associate Pastor, 2019-2021

Rev. Josh Miles

Born in 1989, Josh Miles was three years old when his family transferred into Athens First from his mother's home church, Andrews Chapel UMC in Jonesboro. He grew up here as a child and youth member. He was hired as youth minister at Athens First as he pursued a call to ministry. His mother, Felecia Miles, passed away while Josh was just 19. At this writing his father, Robert Miles, is chair of the Church Council at Athens First. Josh married Emily Rivers in 2021. He was admitted as a provisional deacon in 2019 and was appointed to Athens First as associate pastor and minister to families with youth, a position he already had held as a layperson. He was appointed associate pastor at Peachtree Road

United Methodist Church in Atlanta in 2021, switched orders and was ordained a full elder in 2024. At the 2024 annual conference, the clergy executive session at which Josh was approved for ordination was held in our sanctuary, the very sanctuary in which he had grown up. Each new elder was to carry a Bible important to them; Josh brought the third grade Bible he had been given as a child at the same altar by Bill Britt, the senior minister under whom he now serves. His ordination was held three blocks down the street at the Classic Center.

ᥐ2020 ᥐ

In 2020, a nationwide Covid-19 pandemic closed the church along with much of the nation as public assemblies were prohibited for months. The church initiated online live transmission of worship conducted by Rev. Hodges alone in the sanctuary, speaking into a camera, so that the membership could worship while watching from their homes until the church could reopen safely. The live broadcasts continue today and have become a robust ministry component, as for the first time some members join from distant locations through their online connection. No services were held in the sanctuary from March 15 to August 2020. When services resumed, for some months attendance was limited and advance registration required to control capacity. There were no hymns or congregational liturgies in the services to avoid spreading the disease.

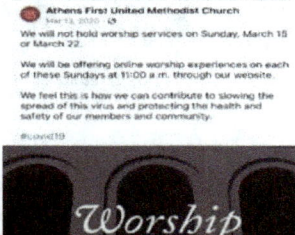

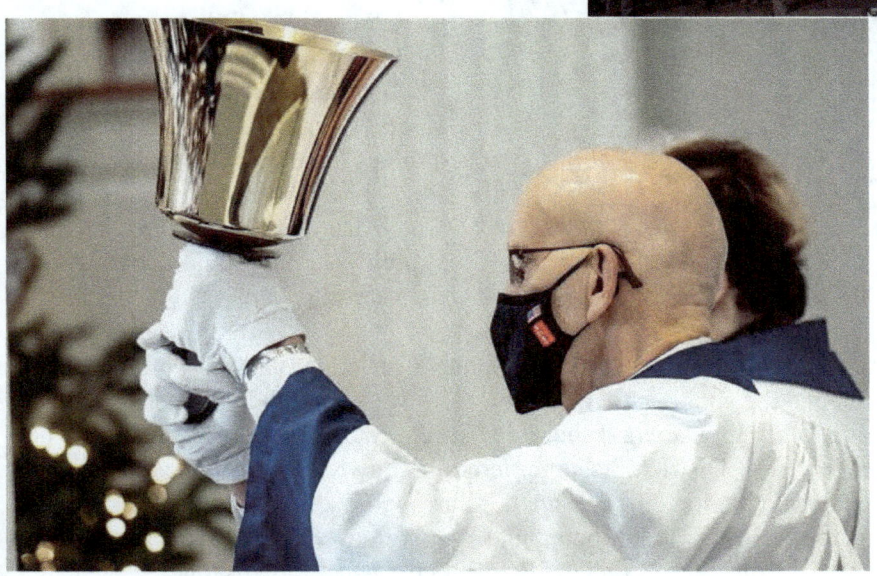

Congregants continued to wear masks in worship well into 2021.

With a key gift from church members Henry and Carolyn Garrard, the church raised $2 million to purchase a new Quimby pipe organ, which was

Henry and Carolyn Garrard
and family in 1990

installed while the congregation was out of the sanctuary for the pandemic. The magnificent four-manual 68-rank pipe organ required expansion of the pipe chambers to include visible pipes on either side of the sanctuary and includes an antiphonal section in the balcony at the rear of the sanctuary. Henry Garrard, a prominent Athens attorney, is known in the congregation for his outstanding barbecue, which has been the center of many churchwide meals and cookouts over the years.

Annual Conference adopted a new districting plan for North Georgia, reducing the number of districts from twelve to eight. Athens First was moved from the Athens-Elberton District headquartered in Athens, to a new Central East District, headquartered in Lawrenceville. The new district included churches in Gwinnett, Barrow, Walton, Clarke and Oconee Counties.Also in 2020, the annual moving day for Methodist pastors was changed from the second week of June to the end of June.

THE YOUNG PARENTS' EXPERIENCE AT AFUMC

GINNY AND JOHN GRAHAM

We both grew up in the United Methodist Church. After we were married, we spent time visiting and experiencing different churches in Athens. We chose Athens First United Methodist because of the strong bond of friendship that we experienced with many of the people that attended. We were welcomed very quickly into a large, loving young adult Sunday school class. We met weekly and with each week we grew closer to the members of that class. Learning and sharing our day-to-day joys, struggles and life experiences helped us to grow in our faith and our church community. We were pregnant at the time when we joined the class and they immediately welcomed us and threw us a baby shower that was not only extremely gracious but made us feel so included in the group we had just joined.

We now have three children and raising them here has been one of the most enriching experiences of our lives. Throughout each phase of their young lives, they have had wonderful parents, teachers, staff and volunteers who have all given their time to enrich our kids and share the great teachings of and the lessons of the Bible. Whether it was nursery workers rocking our infants on Sunday or preschool teachers helping our young ones to learn and develop, the outpouring of love and kindness is overwhelming. As our children have gotten older, celebrating special holidays  with our kids at the church has become part of our family's traditions. One personally impactful experience was our kids learning the Lord's Prayer in Sunday School and hearing them say it in unison with the congregation. Our children feel accepted and secure at the church and no matter what the activity, they are always excited and eager to learn what is being taught to them in an interesting and memorable way.

2021

Joseph Russell, Organist, 2021- 2022

Joe Russell

With the installation of the magnificent new Quimby organ during the Covid-19 pandemic of 2020, search for an organist to meet the challenge of the grand instrument brought the hiring of Joe Russell, previously organist at Christ the Redeemer Catholic Church in Houston. Russell held a Master's in organ performance from Rice University, graduated the Curtis Institute of Music, and was 2013 winner of the Chicago AGO Quimby organ competition.

The Senior Fun Group, known today at Sweet Life, enjoys a program of Christmas music.

Methodist fellowship traditionally involves copious amounts of home- cooked food. At Athens First, we often enjoy covered dish dinners with the fabulous barbecue of Henry Garrard.

৭**2022** ৩

Janis Maxwell, Interim Director of Music 2022

After music director Stephen Mitchell left to assume a position as a program coordinator with the Classic Center, and organist Joe Russell accepted a position as associate organist and associate choir director at St. Thomas Episcopal Church in Houston, Janis Maxwell served in the interim, as the church also was in the midst of a pastoral change and wanted the new pastor to have a role in the selection of the music ministry leadership. Several persons served capably as interim organists during this period.

Jeremy Michael Lawson, Senior Minister, 2022-present

Born in 1980, Jeremy Lawson is a Connecticut native who came south to attend Montreat College, near Asheville, on a basketball scholarship. While in North Carolina, he met his future wife, Sharon Stoneman, whom he married in 2003. Sharon and Jeremy have three children. Their daughter, Anna, was born in 2006 and their twin sons, James and Luke, were born in 2008. Jeremy received his Bachelor of Science in 2002

Rev. Jeremy Lawson

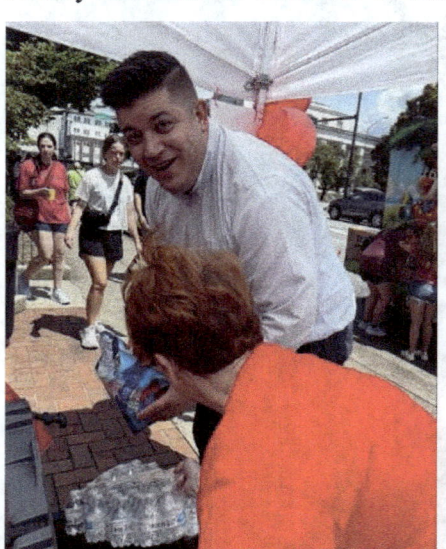

from Southern Connecticut State University and the Master of Divinity from Candler School of Theology in 2006. The North Georgia Conference admitted him as a probationary member in 2007 and an elder in full connection in 2010. His appointments have been: 2007 Briarcliff; 2009 Level Creek; 2014 Clayton; 2018 Hamilton Mill; 2022 Athens First.

Nancy Ann Johnson, Associate Pastor, 2022-present

Nancy Johnson was appointed associate pastor at Athens First in 2022, arriving the same week as Jeremy Lawson became senior minister. Born in 1967, she married Todd Pierson in 1995. Todd is son of longtime North Georgia clergy Marion Pierson and nephew of the late Athens First member and trustee Lee Pierson. Nancy was admitted as a probationary member in 2003 and ordained elder in 2006. Her appointments to date are: 2001 Underwood; 2003 Cascade; 2005 Peachtree Road; 2008 The River UMC; 2010 New Church Development; 2011 Christ UMC, Roswell; 2019 Lewis Memorial UMC; 2021 Marvin UMC, Martinez; 2022 Athens First associate.

Rev. Nancy Johnson

Ryan Ferguson, Director of Music and Worship August 2022 – present Raina Wood, Organist and Music Assistant January 2023 - present

Rev. Jeremy Lawson arrived in Athens in July 2022 facing vacancies in both the positions of Director of Music and Organist. The vacancies had occurred earlier that calendar year and were held open so that the newly appointed pastor could be involved in the selection process. In both cases, national searches brought in many fine candidates, from which two were selected who elevated the already well-respected music program to an even higher level.

Ryan Ferguson came to Athens First from his position as Director of Music and Worship at Calvary UMC in Annapolis, Maryland and at Saint James UMC in Marriottsville, Maryland.

Ryan Ferguson

Sanctuary Choir members at their 2023 fall workshop at the UGA Hugh Hodgson School of Music.

Ryan quickly proved to be a passionate and versatile conductor who enjoys collaboration and education. He oversees a vibrant worship arts ministry with vocal and instrumental choirs for adults, youth and children, as well as a collegiate choral intern program and community concert series. A native of Fort Gaines in southwest Georgia, Ryan graduated magna cum laude with an Honors Bachelor of Music in Music Education degree from Shorter College where he studied piano with Mary Ann Knight. He holds the Master of Music in Conducting from the Peabody Conservatory of the Johns Hopkins University as a student of Harlan D. Parker and Markand Thakar. He is a member of the American Guild of Organists, the American Choral Directors Association and the Chorister's Guild. Growing up playing piano and organ, rotating as needed among churches of several faiths in his small South Georgia hometown, Ryan exhibited the talent that carried him to a career as pianist and guest conductor for community and professional orchestral, choral and wind ensembles in the Baltimore-Washington

area. He was Assistant Conductor of the Baltimore Philharmonia, Cover Conductor of the Greenspring Valley Symphony, Assistant Conductor of the Peabody Modern Orchestra, Wind Ensemble and Youth Orchestra. Guest conducting engagements included the Smith College Symphony, Queens College Symphony, Norwalk Chamber Players, Symphony Tacoma and the Baltimore Chamber Orchestra.

Raina Wood is a native of Asheville, North Carolina and holds a Master of Sacred Music in Organ Performance from Emory University and a double Bachelor of Music in Organ and Piano Performance from Furman University, studying with Derek Parsons, Charles Tompkins and Timothy Albrecht. She is a member of the American Guild of Organists and has been featured on National Public Radio 's Pipe Dreams. Prior to her tenure at Athens First, Raina served as Organist at Meridian Street UMC in Indianapolis and Organist and Music Associate at Church Street UMC in Knoxville. She is admittedly

Raina Wood

reticent in personality until she takes her position at the console of the church's magnificent Quimby organ installed in 2020. Her ability to utilize all the capabilities of the instrument to enhance worship and bring glory to God through music never cease to amaze. We have become that rare church where a crowd gathers for the postlude and stays until the last note to applaud her outstanding work.

୨**2023** ୧

Under a policy known as disaffiliation adopted by a special General Conference in 2019, some 7,000 congregations nationally and 261 in North Georgia left the United Methodist denomination primarily over the issue of homosexuality before the disaffiliation window closed at the end of 2023. This represented 25 percent of churches nationally and 41 percent of churches in North Georgia. Athens First stood fast with the North Georgia Conference of the UMC.

Natalee Y. Dukes-Hamby, Associate Pastor, 2023-present

Rev. Natalee Dukes Hamby

Natalee Dukes-Hamby, who had served as an associate pastor at Hamilton Mill UMC with Jeremy Lawson, was appointed associate pastor at Athens First in 2023. Her duties are all ministries involving persons ages birth to 22. Born in 1992, she married William Montana Hamby in 2014. She entered probationary membership in 2017 and was ordained elder in 2020. Meeting the special challenges of appointing a clergy couple, Natalee's husband, Montana Hamby, was appointed pastor at Princeton UMC at the "other end" of Lumpkin

Street in Athens in 2023 and is an active clergy spouse in the life of Athens First when his own clergy duties at Princeton UMC allow.

BY THE NUMBERS

AS OF DECEMBER 2023

The annual statistical report by Athens First UMC to the North Georgia Conference at the close of reporting year 2022 showed 4,226 total members on roll. During the ensuing year, four were received on profession of faith, 32 by transfer from another UMC, 23 by transfer from another non-UMC church. In the same year, 22 transferred out to another UMC, 44 transferred out to a non-UMC church, 26 were removed by death, leaving enrollment at the close of the 2023 church year at 4,193. The church was 99.66% White, with four Asian members, six Black members and four Hispanic members. By gender, the membership was 53.7% female and 46.3% male. Average attendance at all weekly worship services was 593 plus an average of 484 worshipping online. 27 infants were baptized during the year and three adults received baptism. There were 713 persons in the church who have been baptized but have not yet become a professing member. The church carries 441 constituents on roll. In Sunday School and other Christian formation groups there were 307 children ages 0-11, 126 youth ages 12-18, 35 young adults ages 19-30 and 724 adults ages 31+. Confirmation preparation

for the coming year enrolled 38 youth. Average weekly Sunday School attendance was 284 in 24 different classes offered. There were 366 participants in the year's Vacation Bible School. There were 63 ongoing small groups, support groups and other classes offered other than Sunday School. 1,604 persons from the congregation were engaged in mission to the community serving 6,605 community members. The church property was valued at $32 million. The church paid 100% of its conference apportionment for the year, which was $264,821. $34,452 was given to General Advance specials and another $10,580 to Annual Conference Special Sunday offerings. $68,230 was given to non-UMC charitable causes. Total personnel costs including salaries, pensions, benefits, travel and housing were $1,807,000. Church operating expenses were $772,733 and program expenses were $232,465. The church was debt-free, with capital expenditures during the year of $150,439. Total expenditures for the year for all purposes were $3,339,592. Gifts received during the year were $2,484,524 from pledging members, $766,015 from non-pledging but identified givers and $32,171 in unidentified gifts. Interest and dividends yielded $11,220, another $4,285 in building use fees, $16,775 in capital donations and $19,208 from memorials, endowments and bequests.

❾2024❾

The 2024 North Georgia Annual Conference met in Athens for the 22nd consecutive year and for the 33rd time in the history of our church.

2024 Annual Conference delegate Cassie Folsom with her parents Henry and Mary Folsom in 1987

The Athens First delegates were Cassie Folsom, Kim Griffith and Tom Jackson. Annual Conference determined to reduce further the number of districts in North Georgia from eight to five, having gone from twelve to eight districts only four years prior. The further reduction was dictated by the loss of 41 percent of the conference's churches during disaffiliation. Athens First was moved from the Central East District, which included five counties stretching from Gwinnett to Clarke, to a new South East District, which includes a total of 67 churches in 22 counties stretching from Barrow to Richmond. The District headquarters returned to Athens from Lawrenceville. Tom Jackson was named lay co-leader of the new district.

Descendants of Rev. Lovick Pierce, the first appointed pastor of Athens Methodist Church, are recognized in morning worship on October 13, 2024, as we kicked off celebration of the bicentennial of the church's location on its current site. The Pierce-Troutman-Wilson family has had eight generations in a direct line from Rev. Pierce as members at this church.

Easter Sunrise Service 2024

At the final Church Council meeting of 2024, Trustees chair Ben Griffith announced a resolution had been reached with the Athens-Clarke Unified Government after the church filed suit over the city's five-year refusal to approve a demolition permit for the Saye Building. As this book went to press, the city still had taken no final vote, as the church drew plans to remove the building and replace it, at least temporarily, with parking. Long-term use of the property is yet to be determined.

The AFUMC Sanctuary Choir closed out 2024 with an historic Christmas visit to New York City, including performing a concert of Christmas anthems in the iconic St. Patrick's Cathedral on December 3, 2024.

FORWARD through THE AGES

BICENTENNIAL
ATHENS FIRST UNITED METHODIST CHURCH

Forward into
the Third Century

2025 & Beyond

୨2025ୡ

On January 9, 2025, Bishop Robin Dease announced the "One Georgia UMC" initiative to study potential unification of the North Georgia and South Georgia Annual Conferences. The original Georgia Conference first separated into North and South Georgia in 1866, but remained under one Bishop until 1992. After only 32 years with separate Bishops, Dease was appointed over both Conferences effective September 1, 2024. A study group of six people from each Conference met three times with the Bishop in fall 2024 before commencing the larger study, to be facilitated through some 20 working groups on the various issues that would be involved in unification. A full report of the Unification Task Force was scheduled to go before the annual meetings of the two Conferences in June and July 2025, with potential final action in June 2026. If affirmed, it was anticipated full unification could take place as early as January 2027, with a first Annual Conference for the new entity held in June 2027. The Conference announced the plan was a projection "dependent on the findings, prayerful discernment, and actions of the South and North Georgia Annual Conferences and the Southeastern Jurisdictional Conference."

Athens First United Methodist Church celebrated the bicentennial of its location on its present site, remembering its past with its eyes set firmly on the future as we move "Forward Through the Ages."

If our bicentennial observance has left members of Athens First United Methodist Church with no other impression, let it be an appreciation that we are drinking water from wells we did not dig and resting in the shade of trees we did not plant. Others before us have worked for two centuries to provide what we have here today. We stand on their shoulders. It is now our time to dig wells and plant trees so that others will have water to drink and shade in which to lie. Those who will stand on our shoulders are counting on us to make firm the foundation of the Athens First United Methodist Church of the coming century and beyond. Let us be about the task of building a strong church that can well carry out the mission of making disciples of Jesus Christ for the transformation of the world.

THE MISSING CHURCH RECORDS

As this bicentennial history of Athens First United Methodist Church was being researched and compiled, the church received a phone call from Mr. David Pass, an antiques aficionado from Rocky Face in northwest Georgia. While perusing a Dalton antiques mall for treasures, he came across seven journal books of historical minutes which were part of an estate. They turned out to be historic minutes from Athens Methodist Church, and Mr. Pass, a UMC member himself, knew our church should have them back. A note in the front of one of the journals reads, "Athens, Ga., August 30, 1930. This record found in trash box upstairs on the N.E. corner Clayton and Thomas Sts. (signed) H.V. Hood." That book is: "Record

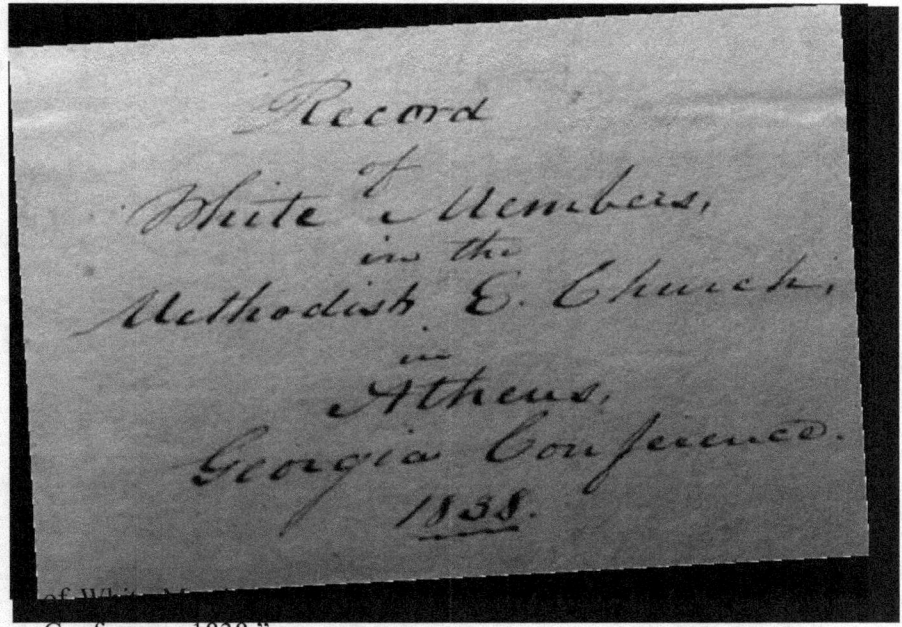

Conference. 1838."

This book found in the trash by Mr. Hood was returned to the church in 1930 and placed in the safe at Dozier Lumber Company, the offices of trustee A. W. Dozier, along with other records of the church. Upon the death of Mr. Dozier in 1948, none of the records could be found. Unbeknownst to anyone, they apparently had become mixed in with other records of the Dozier company when it was sold to the Tanner Lumber Company of Athens. They eventually landed in an estate sale of a member of the Tanner family, were purchased by the antique mall owner, and thus were recovered by Mr. Pass. The other records found are:

Quarterly Conference Record, Athens Station, Beginning with 1866. Ending with 1877.

Proceedings of the Stewards, The Methodist Church Athens, Georgia, Commencing Dec. 1870.

Quarterly Conference Record Book, 1st Church Athens, Geo. 1878-1879-1880-1881.

Quarterly Conference Record Book, 1st Church Athens, Geo. 1882-1883-1884-1885.

Quarterly Conference Record Book, 1st Church Athens Ga. 1886-1887-1888-1889.

Quarterly Conference Record Book, 1st Church Athens Ga. 1890-1893.

Quarterly Conference Record, M.E. Church, South, 1st Church Athens District 1894.

Quarterly Conference Record, M.E. Church, South, First Church Athens District 1895-1898. (The book contains separate handwritten pages which are minutes of the 38th session of the North Georgia Annual Conference of the M.E. Church, South, meeting November 1897 in the sanctuary of Athens First Church).

Quarterly Conference Record, First Church Athens, Methodist Episcopal Church, South, 1911 to 1914.

Minutes, Board of Stewards, 1st M.E. Church, Athens, Ga. 1913-1916.

While the church had records of the Board of Trustees back to 1901, all other records from 1838 to 1916 were missing for more than 70 years. This treasure trove of records fills gaps that otherwise were dark holes in our history. It helped us create a more complete record of church trustee membership and succession and provided valuable insight into decisive periods over the past two centuries. It is unfortunate that these important books were lost, with one of them winding up in a trash bin on the upper floor of a downtown Athens building. It is astonishing that it was rescued from that trash bin and returned to the church, only to be lost again, along with numerous other books of church records. Ninety years after being found in the trash, the historic and oldest book wound up in an estate sale along with the other records. Our boundless gratitude is extended to Mr. Pass for returning them without question to the church of their origin.

The efforts of previous church historians Robert C. Wilson (1930) and John P. Bondurant (1988) were hampered by the absence of these records. That the contact to return these books to our church was made in June 2024 as this bicentennial history was in preparation is no less than Providential. The information presented in this history is richer and more complete because these sources were available to this author, as they fill large gaps that had existed in our knowledge of our own past for almost a century.

As a result of the unfortunate loss and very fortuitous rediscovery of these historic records, the church in 2025 has taken steps to place the historic records in the Special Collections Library at the University of Georgia, where they will be preserved in climate-controlled archives and can be digitized for general research access.

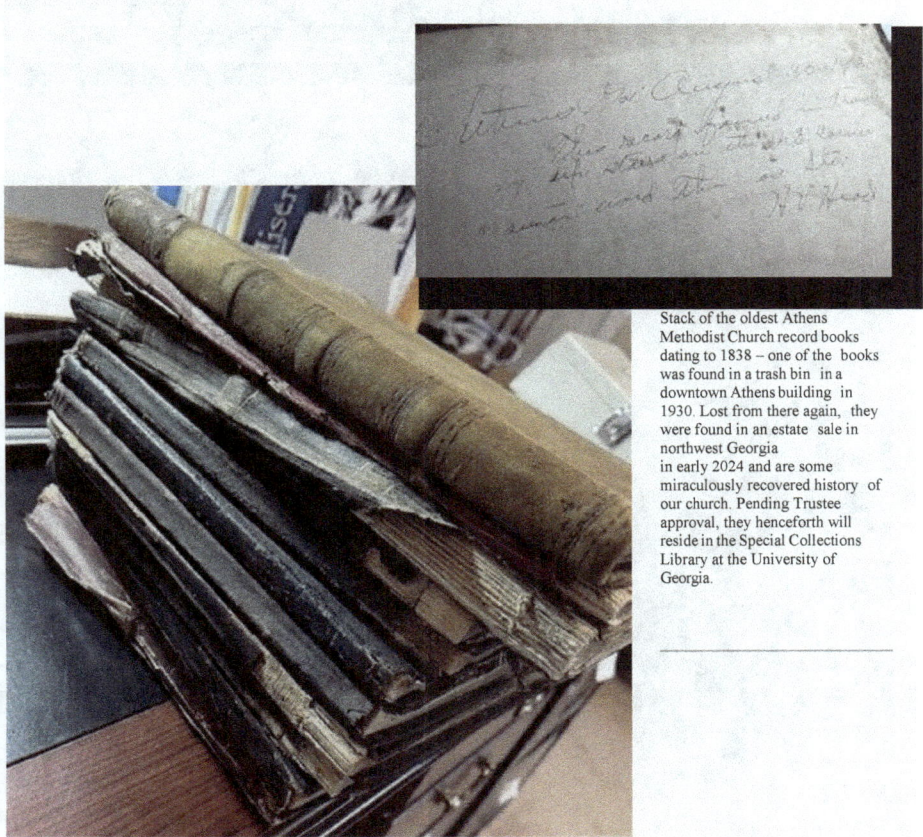

Stack of the oldest Athens Methodist Church record books dating to 1838 – one of the books was found in a trash bin in a downtown Athens building in 1930. Lost from there again, they were found in an estate sale in northwest Georgia in early 2024 and are some miraculously recovered history of our church. Pending Trustee approval, they henceforth will reside in the Special Collections Library at the University of Georgia.

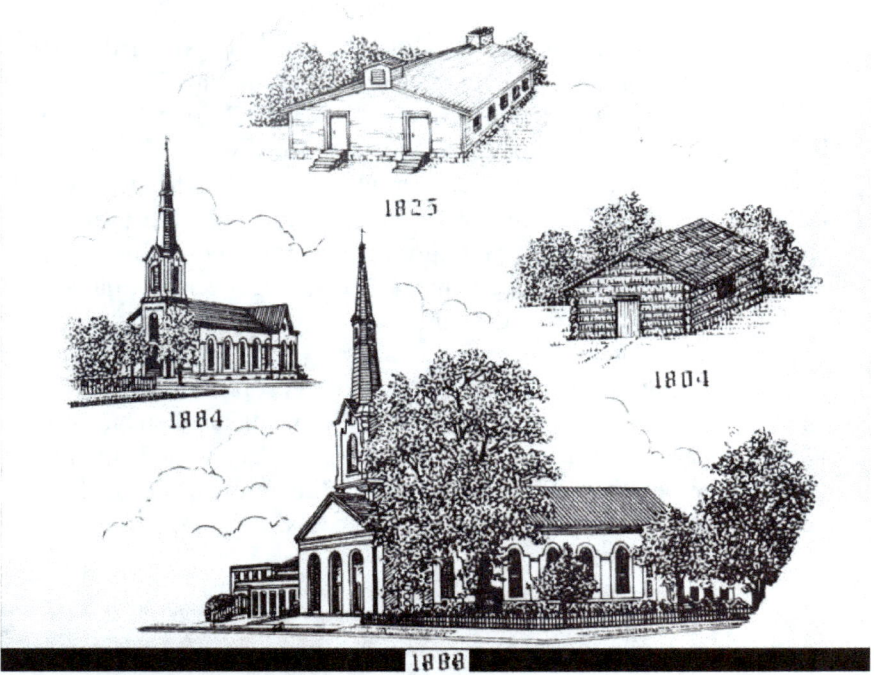

Athens First United Methodist Church on September 30, 2024

298

APPENDIX

METHODISM IN ATHENS -
A HISTORICAL SKETCH

BY ROBERT C. WILSON, CHURCH HISTORIAN, 1953

"The full history of a church cannot be expressed in words but is written in the minds and hearts of the ministers who have served it and of the members whose lives have been spent in its service or glorified by its influence. Since an institution such as a church is born of the dim and distant past, and while it is a throbbing agency of the present and will live on in eternity, all of us, pastors and members alike must

recognize that we are but incidents in its life. Under our Methodist system, whereby a pastor is assigned to a charge for one year at a time, he becomes more of a temporary incident than is true of the average layman since all or a large part of his life is spent in that church. We laymen look to the pastor for religious instruction and leadership, but so far as the continuing life of the church is concerned, we laymen because of our more permanent status must assume the responsibility of carrying the work of the church forward and, by our lives, exemplify to the world what the church teaches and stands for. All of us, pastors and members alike, might profit by Cicero's statement: 'If we fail to make use of the knowledge and the labors of past ages, we will forever remain in the infancy of knowledge.' We of the present generation, profiting by the knowledge and labors of our Methodist forebears in Athens First Church have the responsibility of passing on to succeeding generations those principles which will enable the church to expand its service in the cause of Christ."

ATHENS BANNER-HERALD

SERVING ATHENS AND NORTHEAST GEORGIA OVER A CENTURY

Vol. CXXI, No. 85.   Associated Press Service   ATHENS, GA., SUNDAY, APRIL 19, 1953.   Read Daily by 35,000 People In Athens Trade Area

YOU NEED CHRIST NOW!

METHODIST *Evangelistic* **MISSION** SOUTHEAST

No Increase Of Interest In Religion Is Daily Evidenced

Call To Evangelistic Committee

J. C. CALLAWAY

Message From Bishop Arthur J. Moore

Call To Prayer Is Issued By Eleven Bishops

Radio Programs Reach Nation By 190 Stations

A Bicentennial Within a Bimillennial

By Tom Jackson

A Lay Sermon Delivered Sunday, March 9, 2025
First United Methodist Church
Athens, Georgia

It's finally here! We've been anticipating and planning the bicentennial of this great church now for more than a year. And today we start our three weeks of concentrated celebration, within our year-long observance. I hope you're as excited as I am. I know my wife is excited…I'll finally have my nose out of the research materials and the writing after all these many months.

And I can tell that YOU'RE excited by all the questions I've been getting.
Like – when is the book going to be ready?
Like – are you going to do an in-depth talk on the history?

But the question I've gotten most is – now tell me again about the BUILDINGS? Now when was it that they flipped the sanctuary around? Well, that part actually happened twice, but OK, here's the Cliff Notes version of the buildings.

Hope Hull came to Athens in 1801 and started the Methodist Society. In 1803 he and the Methodists built a log meeting house on South Lumpkin between Pinecrest and Milledge. That was followed by a larger log meeting house built in 1810 where the UGA track is today on South Lumpkin. Hope Hull's house was about 150 yards east of there, I'm guessing somewhere up the hill above where Foley Field is now.

Then in 1825, the Methodists finally obtained THIS lot on which we stand today, and built a wood-frame sanctuary 40x40 feet.

About 1835, they expanded it on the west end by 20 feet, so now we're 40x60 feet. I realize that space would fit into this room comfortably – in fact, it probably was about right here where the middle of this room is today.

In 1852, that wooden church was removed and rolled on logs down Hancock to Foundry Street, where it served the Black congregation for some years. And here in its place, was built a new Brick church, one of the first brick churches in Georgia, with a magnificent steeple, still the same steeple we have today, but only about half the size of this sanctuary.

The Brick church didn't last but 30 years. In 1884, they removed the entire building, except for the steeple, and built a new sanctuary here. And if you can use your imagination, you can see its walls here. The outer walls lined up with these columns. And the front wall was right here across this line where the pulpit and lectern are today, with the altar and pulpit right out front here.

Then in less than another 30 years, they were out of space again – the church particularly needed Sunday School rooms. So in a 1910 renovation, the sanctuary was flipped around so that the altar was on that end, the organ and choir were up where our balcony is today, and on this end they added a rounded section right here, not as large as this chancel is today, that was divided off into Sunday School rooms, and there were large doors they could slide open right here and it all became part of the sanctuary for a worship service, facing that way.

Then in 1952, the Chapel and the front third of the Sunday School building were added.

And ten years later, in 1962, it was the largest project yet. They took almost all of the sanctuary down again, except for the steeple. They propped up the roof, moved the side walls out 15 feet each – and these columns were put in place where the old outside walls used to be, and on this end, they removed everything and started over, all the way back to the red clay earth. Everything from right here where I stand back to the stained-glass windows is new construction from 1963, both upstairs here in the sanctuary, and down below in the basement, where what was then

the Fellowship Hall was expanded and a new kitchen installed.

That same 1963 project added the back two-thirds of the Sunday School building, the portico across the front of all three buildings, and the connecting hallway here between the sanctuary and the Sunday School building.

And finally, from 2000 to 2002 came construction of the Family Life Center which includes Hancock Hall, the gym, a Youth Center, and new church offices.

So there, in a nutshell, is the building summary. Like I said, if you want to see and hear more about that, come at 4 o'clock today, AND order a copy of the book.

But you know, in the end, it's not about the buildings. The buildings are just a means to an end. The history of a church is about people, not structures. It is, first of all, personal. It's our individual stories in this space....

For your family and ours, this church means baptisms, and confirmations, and funerals, and meaningful worship experiences, and a place we come for solace in a time of upset or heartbreak. It's a place that is holy ground and has been so for thousands of Athens Methodists over two-plus centuries.

The bicentennial brings to mind Janus, the Greek God for whom the month January is named. Janus had two faces – one looking forward and one looking back.

We look back so that we may learn lessons. We look forward so that we may implement the better and best ways we have learned from those lessons.

As we consider some of the stories today of those who have gone before us – as Ryan Ferguson said to me – it's sort of like a roll call of the saints – just not on All Saints' Day.

Let's start that roll call with the person most responsible for starting our church, Rev. Hope Hull. He was quite the firebrand. You could call Rev. Hope Hull an inciter, an instigator. He certainly was an exhorter, or one who encourages people to engagement and action. Hull is considered by many to be the founder of Methodism in Georgia.

Crowds gathered to hear him, and other crowds gathered to protest him, leading to confrontation. It's because he preached things that were not in line with the established church order of the day. In Savannah in 1793, a crowd gathered outside a church as Hull preached, shouting and throwing STONES, breaking windows, seeking to break up the gathering of the Methodists they saw as non-conformists … as troublemakers. You could say it was a ROCKY start – see what I did there?

Through Hope Hull this church is only one degree of separation from John Wesley himself. Because one of Wesley's first persons called to join him in ministry was Francis Asbury, who came to British North America in 1771, preaching up and down from New York to the Maryland eastern shore. That's where he was encountered by young

Hope Hull, barely 20 years old and already a veteran of the Revolutionary War. Hull became Asbury's disciple, and then a close colleague -- they were traveling companions for several years. In 1784, Asbury ordained Hull as a Methodist clergyman and set him off on his own path.

Hull rode thousands of miles on horseback, planting churches all along his way… in Virginia and the Carolinas, at Amelia Island and Savannah. But then, he married and settled down in Washington, Ga., where he was teacher in a preparatory school he helped build, literally, as a carpenter. His reputation was such that in 1801 he was lured out here to the frontier in Athens as one of the first faculty members of the new Franklin College.

Here in Athens, using the method of church-planting that John Wesley taught, Hull held meetings in local homes, and started a Methodist Society. And I've described for you how that led to the establishment of this congregation on this site 200 years ago this year.

But it wasn't easy. Hull died in 1818, so for seven years Methodism in Athens was held together by the other circuit riders of the Apalachee Circuit – Lovick Pierce, Benjamin Watts, Eppes Tucker, and Joseph Tarpley. And by Hope Hull's son, Asbury Hull, (catch the name – named after Bishop Asbury). Asbury Hull was the linchpin who held the Methodist Society together and was a leading member of this congregation until well after the

Civil War.

Another determined member of the Methodist Society during those critical interim years was Thomas Hancock, who had a home across the street here on Lumpkin at Hancock and relinquished THIS lot, which he was in the process of purchasing from the UGA Trustees, and arranged for them instead to give it to the Methodist Society. And another influential person was the local judge, Augustin Clayton – who oversaw the construction of that first sanctuary on this site. Those names – Hull, and Hancock, and Clayton – sounds like a map of downtown Athens, does it not? They left a lasting witness of dedication to this church.

There's William Few, who was on that first Board of Trustees of the University, who was the first White person to own this land on which we now stand, who was instrumental in picking the site of the University – without which we would not be here. Perhaps you remember my story from last fall of how he became Georgia's first United States Senator, but grew disenchanted with having to defend southern slavery in Congress, so moved to New York City, where he became mayor.

And when his brother ran into a bitter divorce, William Few took in his young teenaged nephew, Ignatius A. Few, who grew up in New York, at first an avowed infidel. But later, Ignatius became a successful Augusta lawyer, and then heard a call to the ministry. Ignatius Few's first appointment was as pastor here at Athens Methodist Church. And after that? He became the founding president of Emory College, which today is Emory University.

Another of those early saints was Thomas Stanley. He was a Methodist minister who was head of the Athens Female Academy located down here on Broad between Lumpkin and College. When the church needed a pastor and before the Conference could appoint one, Stanley took on the job. He was the first pastor in the first building on this site…in the year 1825.

The next year, 1826, the Conference first appointed a pastor, Lovick Pierce, who had been one of our circuit riders. Lovick Pierce would spend the rest of his life associated with Athens Methodist Church in one way or another. He was pastor here three different times. But he also served all over Georgia, and now is known as the father of Methodism in Columbus and West Georgia.

Lovick Pierce had a son, George Foster Pierce, who was a teenager when his father first moved the family to Athens. At age 16, he was perhaps the first great success story of this church's youth program. Young Pierce was converted in a revival here. He then attended Franklin College, and came under the influence of our next pastor, John Owen Andrew, who counseled him through a call into the ministry. As such, he became friends with Pastor Andrew's son, James Osgood Andrew.

Like Pastor Pierce's son, Pastor Andrew's son also experienced a call into the ministry, and by 1832, young James Osgood Andrew was elected Bishop. It was Bishop Andrew whose purchase of a mulatto girl as a slave, purportedly to rescue her from abuse by her previous owner, and his third wife's owning two other slaves when he married her, led to the 1845 split between the Northern and Southern churches.

Meanwhile, George Foster Pierce became pastor of churches at Augusta, Savannah and Charleston, and by age 33, he was the chief spokesman for the Southern viewpoint at the 1844 General Conference in New York City, where he found himself defending the slave ownership of his almost lifelong friend from this Athens church, Bishop Andrew. And just two years later, George Foster Pierce became pastor here at Athens, then President of Emory College in 1849, and following the lead of his friend, Bishop Andrew, the younger Pierce was elected Bishop in 1854, serving until his death in 1884.

In the years leading up to the Civil War, Blacks and Whites worshipped together in our church in great numbers. At one point, the membership of this church was about 60 percent White and 40 percent Black. Of course, the Black members were slaves of the White members. One wonders how the pastors of that time did not perceive the irony of teaching the love of Jesus Christ to such an assembly of masters and slaves, separated in their seating arrangements by both race and gender. But they did have one of the basic principles correct – that one God loves us all, every one. God's love is without condition or distinction based on who we are or what we do.

There was a great revival here in 1858. In that revival was a slave boy, Lucius Holsey. Lucius was converted and called to the ministry. When the slaves were freed at the conclusion of the Civil War, Blacks largely left to form their own churches – the AME and CME churches. Lovick Pierce of our congregation helped found a church called Pierce's Chapel AME over in the next block here on Hull Street that is still here and active today as Athens First AME. Our church had its last seven Black members join in 1866. It would be more than 100 years before another Black member would join Athens First Methodist.

Lucius Holsey became a founder of the CME denomination. Bishop Pierce officiated at Holsey's wedding, and gave him land on which to build a church. And Holsey was elevated by Bishop Pierce to be one of two Bishops over the CME.

Holsey was instrumental in the founding of Paine College, and was a key figure in working with Atlanta's White leadership to quell the 1906 Atlanta race riots. He worked diligently to stop lynchings that swept Georgia in the early 20th century. It's the poignant story of a young slave who became bishop, converted in a revival at Athens Methodist Church.

Another side to that coin is the story of Clement Anselm Evans, a

22-year-old lawyer from far Southwest Georgia, who found himself swept up into the Civil War, where he quickly rose to Brigadier General and led his own Evans' Brigade at Gettysburg and numerous other battles ending at Appomattox, where he led the last charge before the surrender. He was wounded five times in battle. It was after the Battle at Fredericksburg, that General Evans stood looking over the devastation and carnage of the battlefield, and made a vow to God that if he would just get him out of this and home safely, he would devote the rest of his life to the church. He did just that, being admitted on trial as Methodist clergy in November 1865, and went on to serve many of Georgia's leading churches. General Evans was appointed to Athens Methodist Church in 1869 when he still was only 36 years of age, but he arrived with a lifetime of experience. Even though he became a noted minister, he always was considered a military hero of the South. When Evans died in 1911, his body lay in repose at the State Capitol, and the legislature name Evans County for him. But amid all that, his wish was to be remembered most for his time in the pulpit of this church and others across Georgia.

There's Isaac Stiles Hopkins, a Methodist preacher who taught technology at Emory College in Oxford in the 1870s, became President of Emory, then went back into the ministry, becoming pastor at Atlanta First Methodist, only to be chosen as founding president of the Georgia Institute of Technology –yes – that school over on North Avenue in Atlanta. Then back into the ministry and appointed where? Yes, Athens First Methodist – the former president not only of Emory but of Georgia Tech was the pastor here at Athens. Today we hardly can comprehend.

We've had a number of UGA presidents as lay members here, among them Walter B. Hill, and David Barrow, who chaired our board of stewards and was a trustee for years, and for whom Barrow County is named. And O.C. Aderhold, and Henry King Stanford, and our current university president, Jere Morehead, who was the chair of the church staff-parish committee when Bill Britt became our pastor.

And many UGA Vice Presidents and deans, not the least of which was the legendary Dean of Men William Tate, who taught Sunday School here for 40 years. And another legendary Dean of Students, Louise McBee, who championed the rights of women students, and after retirement became a revered member of the Georgia General Assembly representing Athens. She left an extraordinary bequest to the church that endowed a scholarship program for students who otherwise would not be able to attend college. There's a quote from Dr. McBee that we all should take to heart – she said, "We are born obligated to pour back into the stream that nourished us."

Perhaps you're familiar with the name Young Harris. But I wonder how many of you know that Judge Young Harris was superintendent of our Sunday School for 40 years, chair of the Board of Stewards, and a man of considerable means who was able to do a lot of good, which he did very quietly. Few of his contemporaries in this church were aware of the full extent of his charitable giving. He built the Athens YMCA when it was located down here on Lumpkin at Broad. He purchased a home for the Emory President at Oxford, Ga., which ironically is the home my grandmother grew up in. He built a large hall and a dormitory at McTyeire Institute in Brasstown Valley, in honor of which the names of the college and of the town both were changed to Young Harris. And if you peruse the minutes of the various meetings of trustees and stewards of this church over many years, you will read them written in the exquisite longhand of Judge Young Harris – I have never seen a more elegant handwriting…and he kept those minutes for decades.

When other pastors and laity may have shied away, our pastors helped lead the charge during the Civil Rights movement. Lester Rumble, who served in the 1930s, was a leader in the Conference who chaired a committee to formulate the response of the North Georgia Methodist Conference to the 1954 U.S. Supreme Court Brown v. Board of Education decision. Rumble called for showing greater consideration toward Blacks by placing them on local boards of education and finding other ways for Blacks and Whites to work together in community. Believe it or not, that was a controversial statement in 1954.

Dow Kirkpatrick, who was pastor here 1951-57, and Bevel Jones, who came here in 1976, both were among a group of Atlanta pastors, including Doctors Martin Luther King Senior and Junior, Joseph Lowery, Ralph Abernathy and others, who met regularly at Paschal's Restaurant to help steer Atlanta and the state relatively peacefully through a period when other Southern cities were having riots in the streets. Just by meeting at Paschal's Restaurant, which seated Black and White patrons together, they were in glaring violation of the state's segregation laws. They were among the original authors of the Atlanta Ministers' Manifesto, a 1957 statement calling for racial reconciliation and backing integration of the Georgia public schools. It was not an easy stance to take in Georgia in the 1950s, Kirkpatrick in particular received harassment and threats for his stances not only on race, but on the Vietnam War, and on gay rights.

Bev Jones went on to be elected Bishop, serving 12 years in North Carolina and then as Bishop-in-Residence at Candler School of Theology until his death in 2018. Bev spoke at Dow Kirkpatrick's funeral at St. Mark's UMC in Atlanta, where he said Dow's emphasis was integrity, consistency between belief and action. If you believed it, you had to live it." He described how Dow followed the firm belief that Jesus identified with the poor and oppressed.

When Bev Jones died in 2018, Emory historian Gary Hauk described Bev as "Georgian by birth, Christian by faith, Methodist by conviction, proud Emory alumnus, seeker of justice, advocate for peace and unity among peoples, engaging teacher, eloquent preacher, and pastor to the despairing and dispossessed as well as to the powerful and the privileged."

But I'll tell you one thing about Bev that he tried hard to keep under wraps while he was our pastor – Bev was a closet Tech fan. He could sit in the UGA president's box and wear red & black with the best of them, but it was a learned skill that went away as soon as he moved back to Atlanta.

Rev. Frank Prince served here as pastor in the early 1970s. A member from those days told me a sermon by Frank Prince would make you want to rush into the streets carrying a protest sign.

Two others out of our church became bishops. Joseph Staunton Key was senior minister of Athens First Methodist in 1854-55. He was elected bishop in 1886. And there was William Cannon, a UGA student from Dalton, who joined our church as a constituent in the 1930s and would go on to become dean of the Candler School of Theology before serving as Bishop from 1968 until his death in 1997. He delivered the invocation and the benediction at the Inauguration of Jimmy Carter as President of the United States in 1977, and was an offical Protestant observer at the Vatican, becoming a personal friend of Pope John Paul II.

There are so many other people and stories that time just doesn't allow this morning, you'll just have to read the book for stories about ceremonies held in the church to send troops off to the Civil War, or to mourn those killed in action in World Wars I and II. We remember that first Sunday after September 11, 2001, when people packed this church as I've never seen it packed before – looking for solace, and guidance, and really at a loss as to what had happened to our country.

We think of the devoted laypersons over all these years who came in early to build the fire to warm the sanctuary in time for worship, who served as volunteer church technicians and mechanics.

The people who took up the collections and helped keep the finances going in some tough times, at times quietly giving extra out of their own pockets just to cover a shortfall.

Those who built the buildings, secured the land that put us first on this lot, and then expanded the church property all the way to Hull Street to the west and over to Dougherty Street to the north.

And then there was Covid. The church was closed from March to August 2020, with pastor Chuck Hodges standing here alone with Mark Maxwell on the camera and Janis

Maxwell on the piano, sending out a worship service to members watching online in our homes. We were still a congregation, yet isolated, literally, in our separate homes.

I think of those who were not members but who participated here – like former U.S. Secretary of State Dean Rusk, who was a member across the street at the Presbyterian Church, speaking here about his role in the Cuban Missile Crisis and the Vietnam War. Who can forget him saying, "We're eyeball to eyeball, and I think the other fellow just blinked."

Or South African Archbishop Desmond Tutu standing in this very pulpit in the 1990s, preaching about the evils of apartheid.

Or the singer Kenny Rogers, who occasionally attended worship here while he lived in Athens – there's just something about seeing Kenny Rogers sitting down here in front as we would sing a hymn like Amazing Grace – you just wanted to slip a little closer to hear.

It's a story of how WE HAVE faced the times, endured, advanced, prospered, comforted one another. All the weddings, the funerals, the baptisms, the confirmations, new members welcomed, even a few expelled in times past .

The consistent motivator in all of this is the love for Christ by the people of Athens First Methodist; their, and our, dedication to his great commission, admittedly all done within the context of the times in which they were and we are living. The many lives that have been changed, the many many people who have stood at this altar, whether it was on this end of the building or on that end, to dedicate their lives to Christ and his church.

All because Hope Hull was willing to be a rabblerouser. Because people heard his message and have kept the flame alive all these years, not a few of them doing some rabblerousing themselves.

We're celebrating the anniversary of Hull's arrival in town 224 years ago and the bicentennial of the founding of this church on this site 200 years ago.

But we're also observing another important anniversary. That of another rabblerouser who was willing to turn over tables in the temple and upset the status quo 2,000 years ago. Jesus, who was born between 6 BC and 4 BC by our current calendar, and whose ministry began when he was 30, therefore performed his first miracle at the wedding at Cana 2,000 years ago this year. It's the bimillennial of the beginning of the ministry of Jesus Christ. The next three years mark exactly 2,000 years from the stories in the Gospels telling us of his great works. About 2028 will come the 2,000th anniversary of the Crucifixion and Resurrection.

It's the history written by this congregation over they years as they followed the living history of the scriptures. Their dedication has brought us now to the doorstep of our third century as a Methodist congregation in this place.

And on this, our 200th anniversary as a congregation, it's the 2,000th anniversary of what is written here in the Gospels of the New Testament – the story of a Christ who came, taught, died, to save us. And commanded us to go therefore and do likewise…making Disciples for transformation of world.

How can we not – How can we not carry it forward -- given the examples of those on whose shoulders we stand, who now are in the Great Cloud of Witnesses -- who set the example following that Great Commission of Jesus Christ, and who are watching as we cross this threshhold into our third century. Let us continue to strive to make Athens First United Methodist Church a beacon shining out the bright light of that Good News, as this great church moves Forward Through the Ages.

O God, Our Help in Ages Past
Our hope for years to come.
Be Thou Our Guide While Life shall Last
And our eternal home.

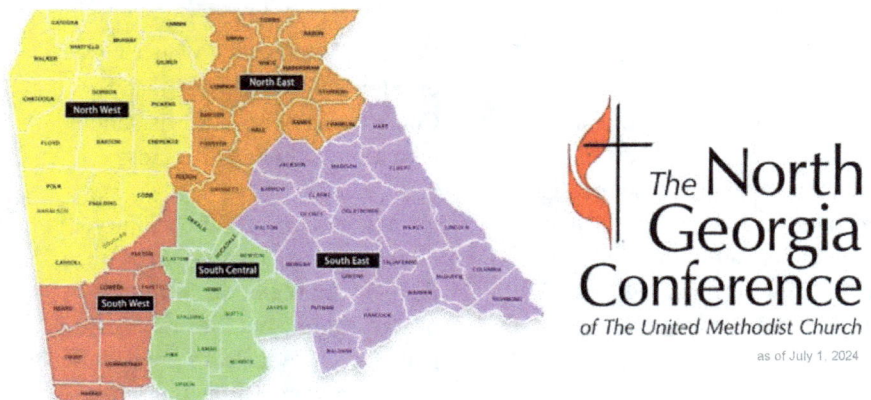

The North Georgia Conference of The United Methodist Church

as of July 1, 2024

Organizational Membership of the Athens Methodist Church

- 1801 - 1825 The Methodist Society at Athens,
  Apalachee Circuit, Oconee District,
  South Carolina Conference,
  Methodist-Episcopal Church

- 1826 - 1830 Apalachee Circuit, Oconee District,
  South Carolina Conference, Methodist-Episcopal Church

- 1830 - 1845 Athens District, Georgia Conference,
  Methodist-Episcopal Church

- 1845 - 1866 Athens District, Georgia Conference,
  the Methodist-Episcopal Church, South

- 1866 - 1939 Athens District, North Georgia Conference,
  the Methodist-Episcopal Church, South

- 1939 - 1968 Athens-Elberton District,
  North Georgia Conference, the Methodist Church

- 1968 - 2020 Athens-Elberton District,
  North Georgia Conference, the United Methodist Church

- 2020 – 2024 Central East District,
  North Georgia Conference, the United Methodist Church

- 2024 - South East District,
  North Georgia Conference, the United Methodist Church

Bishops from Athens First United Methodist Church

Three Bishops arose from our church membership:

- George W. Foster Pierce, Bishop, M.E. Church, South 1854-1884, grew up in the church when his father was pastor, and attended the church when a UGA student.

- Lucius Holsey, Bishop, CME Church, 1873-1920, grew up in the church as a slave member.

- William Ragsdale Cannon, Bishop, The United Methodist Church, 1968-1997, a constituent member at Athens First Methodist while a UGA student, graduating in 1937.

Three Athens First pastors have become Bishops:

- George W. Foster Pierce, Bishop, M.E. Church, South 1854-1884, pastor of Athens Methodist Church 1846-47

- Joseph Staunton Key, Bishop, M.E. Church, South, 1886-1920, pastor of Athens Methodist Church 1861-62 and associate pastor 1854-55

- L. Bevel Jones III, Bishop, The United Methdodist Church, 1984-2018, pastor of Athens First United Methodist Church 1976-82

Two Bishops were sons of Athens First pastors:

- James Osgood Andrew, Bishop, the M.E. Church and the M.E. Church, South, 1832-1871, son of our pastor John Owen Andrew who served 1829-30

- George W. Foster Pierce, Bishop, M.E. Church, South, 1854-1884, son of our pastor Lovick Pierce who served 1826-27, 1830-32, and 1834

Presiding Elders/District Superintendents

Oconee District 1801-1830

Records not clear prior to 1834

1809-1811	Lovick Pierce
1817-1820	Joseph Tarpley

Athens District 1830 – 1939

1834 – 1836	William Arnold
1837 – 1840	William S. Parks
1841	William Arnold
1842 – 1845	John W. Glenn
1846 – 1847	Samuel Anthony
1848	H. P. Pitchford
1849	Russell Reneau
1850 – 1853	William J. Parks
1854 – 1857	John W. Talley
1858	Alfred T. Mann
1859 – 1861	J. O. A. Clark
1862 – 1865	Robert W. Bigham
1866 – 1868	Walter R. Branham
1869 – 1871	Thomas F. Pierce
1872 – 1873	Eustace W. Speer
1874 – 1877	Thomas F. Pierce
1878 – 1881	Robert W. Bigham
1882 - 1883	George W. Yarbrough
1884	Jesse Boring
1885	John D. Hammond
1886 - 1889	S. P. Richardson
1890 – 1893	H. H. Parks
1894	Luke G. Johnson
1895 - 1897	W. P. Lovejoy
1898 - 1900	J. B. Robins
1901 - 1904	W. P. Lovejoy
1916 - 1919	S. P. Wiggins
1920 - 1923	G. R. Venable
1924 - 1927	W. S. Robinson
1928 - 1932	J. L. Allgood
1933 - 1934	Jesse W. Veatch
1935 - 1938	Charles C. Jarrell

Athens-Elberton District 1939 - 2020

1939 – 1941	Charles L. Middlebrooks, Sr.
1942 – 1945	J. Hamby Barton
1946 - 1950	Horace S. Smith
1950 - 1954	J. C. Callaway
1954 – 1955	Paul A. Turner
1955 - 1957	Harvey C. Holland
1957 - 1962	Paul A. Turner
1962 (Jun.-Aug.)	Harry Lee Smith
1962 - 1968	W. H. Ruff
1968 - 1974	Lamar Cherry
1974 - 1980	Eugene T. Drinkard
1980 - 1986	Charles L. Middlebrooks, Jr.
1986 - 1991	M. Eugene Dunn
1991 - 1999	Carolyn Morris
1999 – 2002	J. Harold Smith
2002 - 2007	John Simmons
2007 - 2009	Robin Lee Lindsey
2009 - 2017	Gary L. Whetstone
2017 - 2020	Brian Eugene Clark

Central East District 2020 - 2024

2020 - 2024	Rodrigo Cruz

314

APPENDIX

1905 - 1908   J. S. Bryan
1909 - 1911   W. L. Pierce
1912 - 1915   B. P. Allen

South East District 2024 -

2024 -   Beth Sanders

Chronological List of Pastors
Athens First United Methodist Church

Elder-in-Charge/Senior Minister

1801 – 1818   Hope Hull, pastor of
the Methodist Society

In addition to Hope Hull, circuit riders
of the Apalachee Circuit who preached
to the Methodist Society at Athens
were: Benjamin Watts, Eppes Tucker,
Lovick Pierce, Joseph Tarpley, James
Russell, and Judge Hilliard.

1818 – 1825   Asbury Hull, head of
the Methodist Society
1825   Thomas W. Stanley,
pastor, Athens
Methodist Church
1826 – 1827   Lovick Pierce, first
pastor appointed by
the Conference
1828   Ignatius A. Few
1829 – 1830   John Owen Andrew
1830 – 1832   Lovick Pierce
1833   Benjamin B. Pope
1834   Lovick Pierce
1835   William R. H. Moseley
1836 – 1837   Jeremiah Norman, Jr.
1838 – 1839   Whitefoord Smith
1840   James E. Evans
1841   Daniel Curry
1842   Walter R. Branham, Sr.
and Daniel Curry,
co-pastors
1843   Alfred Turner Mann
1844 – 1845   William Justice Parks
1846 – 1847   George W. Foster Pierce

1848   Samuel W. Anthony
1849   Jesse Boring
1850 – 1851   Eustace W. Speer
1852 – 1853   Alfred Turner Mann
1854 – 1855   Joseph Staunton Key
1856   Alexander McFarlane Wynn
1857 – 1858   Harwell Hodges Parks
1859   Eustace W. Speer
1860   James Wooten Hinton
1861 – 1862   Joseph Staunton Key
1863   William J. Scott
1864   Patrick Arminius Wright
1865 – 1868   Harwell Hodges Parks
1869 – 1870   Clement Anselm Evans
1871   Eustace W. Speer
1872 – 1874   Josiah Lewis, Jr.
1875 – 1878   Weyman H. Potter
1879 – 1880   George Wesley Yarbrough
1881   Willard W. Wadsworth
1882 – 1884   John Dennis Hammond
1885 – 1886   Anderson Joseph Jarrell
1887 – 1890   William D. Anderson
1891 – 1892   Thomas Rogers Kendall, Sr.
1893 – 1894   William P. Lovejoy
1895   George Wesley Yarbrough
1896 – 1897   William Robert Foote, Jr.
1898 – 1900   John Wesley Heidt
1901 – 1902   Joel T. Daves, Jr.
1903 – 1906   Isaac Stiles Hopkins
1907 – 1908   Luke G. Johnson
1909 – 1912   Marcellus Littleton
Troutman, Jr.
1912   James C. Morris, interim
1913 – 1916   Charles Crawford Jarrell
1916   James C. Morris, interim
1917 – 1918   Samuel Robinson Belk

316

From 1919-1923, the Athens First appointment included a proposed Milledge Avenue mission

1919 – 1920	Elam Franklin Dempsey
1921 – 1922	Walter Anthony
1923 – 1926	S. E. Wasson
1927 – 1928	William Peter King
1929 – 1935	Lester Rumble
1936 – 1939	George McDonald Acree
1940 – 1946	Harvey Columbus Holland
1947 – 1951	James William Oscar McKibben
1951 – 1957	Dow N. Kirkpatrick
1957 – 1964	Charles Boleyn
1964 – 1970	Frank Prince
1970 – 1976	T. Cecil Myers
1976 – 1982	Lewis Bevel "Bev" Jones III
1982 – 1984	William R. "Bill" Floyd
1984 – 1987	William Albert "Bill" McKoy
1987 (Aug-Dec)	Bishop (ret.) Joel C. McDavid, interim
1988 – 1992	Larry A. Bauman
1992 – 1997	Garnett S. Wilder
1997 – 2008	William Oslin "Bill" Britt IV
2008 – 2022	Charles Edward "Chuck" Hodges
2022 –	Jeremy Michael Lawson

Pastors of the Athens Colored Mission

1847	John M. Bonnell	1858 - 1859	William Asbury Parks
1848	W. M. Crumley	1860	Henry Crawford
1849	Joseph Staunton Key	1861	Cicero A. Mitchell
1850 – 1851	James L. Pierce	1862	William S. Turner
1853 - 1854	John H. Greghan	1863	George Wesley Yarbrough
1855 – 1856	A. H. Palmer		
1857	John H. Harris	1864 – 1865	William P. Pattillo

Associate Pastors[1]

1868 – 1869	I. M. Kinney, Factory Mission	1872	Charles J. Oliver, Oconee Street Station
1870	Peter A. Heard, Oconee Street Mission	1873 – 1874	Miles W. Arnold, Oconee Street
1871	Ellison D. Stone, Oconee Street Mission	1873	Elison D. Stone, Factory Mission
1871	Charles J. Oliver, Factory Mission	1874	J. E. Sitton, Factory Mission
1872 - 1881	Peter A. Heard, retiree serving as associate	1875 – 1876	A. W. Williams, Oconee Street

1876	G. L. McCles, Factory Mission	1963 – 1966	Roy F. Major
1877	A. C. Thomas, Oconee Street	1966 – 1968	William R. Garrard
		1968 – 1969	Oscar D. Crosby, Jr.
1877 – 1878	W. T. Beall, Factory Mission	1969 – 1972	Ernestine Adams (Director, Christian Education)
1878 - 1879	W. R. Branham, Jr., Oconee Street	1970 – 1971	Malcolm Paterson III
		1972 – 1976	Clarence L. Harris
		1972 – 1983	Charles Johnson

From 1880, Oconee Street and the Factory Mission (later Princeton) ceased being missions of Athens First and received their own direct pastoral appointments.

		1976 – 1991	Wesley Daniel Stephens (continued as a retiree through 1998)
1882	Cicero A. Mitchell	1982 – 1986	Phillip Barrineau, Minister of Education and Youth
1901 – 1902	R. T. DuBose		
1928 – 1931	Clifford Byrd Harbour, student pastor	1984 – 1985	Ronald Emaile Preuss
		1985 – 1991	Diane Neely Shedd
1928 – 1931	W. B. Dillard	1986 – 1987	Charlie Shedd
1953 – 1954	Omar Fink, Jr.	1986 – 1995	Micheal Lee Selleck
1955 – 1958	W. M. Barnett	1991 – 1993	Grady Wigley (continued as a retiree through 2008, Minister of Pastoral Care)
1955 – 1958	Paul H. Hanna		
1956 – 1958	Victor Hugo "Hugh" McKee		
1958 – 1960	Emory R. Brackman	1991 – 1993	Carol Russell Scroggs
1958 – 1961	Charles Frazier (and Minister of Education 1960 – 1961)	1993 – 1996	Elizabeth Camak "Beth" LaRocca-Pitts
		1993 – 1998	Ricky Kevin "Rick" Price
1958 – 1966	William Russell Edwards (and Director, Wesley Foundation)	1996 – 1998	George Earl "Chip" Wilson, Jr.
		1995 – 2006	Margaret Davis Freeman
1960 – 1962	Sidney S. Tate	1998 – 2003	Carolyn Capers Moore
1961 – 1962	R. Gene Wiggins (Director, Christian Education)	1999 – 2004	Susan Carse-McLocklin
		2003 – 2007	David Francis Moore
1962 – 1963	Eugene T. Bell	2004 – 2022	Martha Lee Aenchbacher
1962 – 1967	Virginia Crowell (Director, Christian Education)	2006 - 2007	Nohemi Vivas de Ramirez, Hispanic Ministries
1963 – 1964	Kempton Haynes, Jr.		

Associate Pasters, cont.

2006 – 2009	William Carter Zant	2013 – 2024	Elizabeth Marie
2007 – 2011	Amihan "Amy" Valdez-		"Betsy" Butler
	Barker	2017 – 2021	Robert Wayne "Bob"
2008 – 2010	Haydee Vidot Ortiz,		Winstead
	Mision Latina	2017 – 2019	Susan Martin Taylor
2009 – 2013	John Anthony Page	2019 – 2021	Joshua David "Josh"
2010 – 2014	Eric Victor Fessler		Miles
2013 – 2017	Elizabeth Lockerbie	2022 –	Nancy Ann Johnson
	"Beth" Dickinson	2023 –	Natalee Y. Dukes-Hamby

Directors of Music and Organists[1]

1870 - 1871	Miss Susie Still, choir director
1870 – 1871	Miss Clara Sparrow and Miss Sawyer, co-organists (volunteer)
1871 – ?	Mrs. William King, organist
1871 – ?	Misses Belle Hardeman and Sallie Stanley, substitute organists
? – 1887	Mrs. T. C. Hampton, organist
1888 – 1890	Mrs. Emma Mell, choir director
1887 – 1888	Mrs. H. N. Wilcox, organist
1888	Miss Furlow Anderson, organist
1888 – 1891[2]	Mrs. Mary Nicholson, organist
? - 1914	Mrs. Richardson, choir director
1952 – 1973	Reginald Smith, director of music and organist
1973 – 1977	Herbert P. Hoffman, director of music
1973 – 1975	Andrew Andela, organist
1975 – 1976	Grover McNeill, organist
1976 – 1977	Michael Shawgo, organist
1977	Pierce Arant, interim director of music
1977	Jane Palmer, interim organist
1977 – 1982	John Hebblethwaite, director of music and organist
1982	Gwyn Spell, interim director of music
1982	Debbie Henson and Woody Entrekin, interim organists
1982 – 1986	Michael Moffitt, director of music
1982 – 1986	Martha Braswell, organist
1986 – 1999	Martha Braswell, director of music and organist
1994	David Smith, Chancel Choir director
1999 – 2001	Janis Maxwell, Beverly Brown and Carol Reeves, Interim co-
directors 1999 – 2001	Janis Maxwell and Beverly Brown, interim co-organists

2001 – 2022	Stephen Mitchell, director of music
2001 – 2005	Janis Maxwell, Mary Ann Fitzgerald and Beverly Brown, co-organists and accompanists
2005 – 2007	Mary Ann Fitzgerald, organist
2007 – 2021	Janis Maxwell, organist
2021 – 2022	Joe Russell, organist
2022 (Feb. - Sept.)	Janis Maxwell, interim director of music
2022 (Oct .- Dec.)	Interim organists
Oct. 2022 –	Ryan Ferguson, director of music and worship
Jan. 2023 –	Raina Wood, organist and music assistant

Trustees of the Methodist Church at Athens

1828 - 1840	James Meriwether	1901 - 1908	James S. King
1828 - 1840	William Lumpkin	1908 - 1944	Thomas Fletcher Johnson Comer
1828 - 1830	Cicero Holt		
1828 - 1866	Asbury Hull	1908 - 1947	David F. Miller
1828 – 1845[3]	Right Rogers	1908 - 1948	Augustus W. Dozier
1842 – 1845[3]	Daniel Grant	1912 - 1943	Edward Deloney Sledge, Sr.
1842 – 1866[3]	Francis Gideon		
1842 - 1888	James R. Carlton	1920 - 1959	Madison Gartrell Nicholson, Sr.
1845 - 1881	Henry Hull		
1845 - 1866	Ross Crane, Sr.	1923 - 1937	George Deadwyler
1866[3] - 1866	A. S. Hill	1923 - 1966	Robert C. Wilson
1866 - 1890	Marcellus Stanley	1926 - 1949	Robert L. Patterson
1866 - 1890	John W. Nicholson	1930 - 1932	Walter B. Hodgson
1866 - 1873	Reuben Nickerson	1933 - 1934	Thomas Fitzgerald Green
1873 - 1930	John (or James) A. Hunnicutt		
		1935 - 1958	Percy L. Huggins
1873[4] – 1879	William King	1937 - 1953	Henry Haynes West
1879 - 1899	Manasseh B. McGinty	1943 - 1985	John P. Bondurant
		1945 - 1974	Carter W. Daniel
1886 - 1887	S. P. Thurmond	1947 - 1971	Edward Scott Sell, Sr.
1887 - 1901	Rufus K. Reaves	1948 - 1978	Howard B. Higginbotham
1888 - 1891	Peter A. Summey	1949 - 1956	Harold Hopkins Hinton
1890 - 1920	Edward R. Hodgson	1954 - 1963	Joseph Kenneth Patrick
1892[3] - 1911[3]	F. W. Lucas	1956 – 1988	James Inman Akins
1872[4] - 1912	Rufus LaFayette Moss	1958 - 1986	J. Smiley Wolfe
1899[4] - 1901	Thomas H. Dozier	1959 - 1981	Arthur F. Darden
1901 - 1926	Emmet J. Bondurant	1963 - 1966	Nathaniel G. Slaughter

Trustees of the Methodist Church at Athens, cont.

1966 - 1988	M. Troutman Wilson	1994 - 2007	Richard Morgan
1966 - 1986	Jenkins Comer Whitehead	1999 - 2010	Dan Blitch
		2000 - 2012	Patrick Haggard
1971 - 1988	Eugene A. Epting	2000 - 2001	Ken Daniel
1974 - 1990	William Eugene Hudson	2001 - 2013	Margie Shedd
1978 - 1988	Carlton M. James	2002 - 2014	Mason McWhorter
1982 - 1990	Lee Pierson	2004 – 2016	Tom Hollingsworth
1985 - 1992	H. Edsel Benson	2004 – 2016	Holley Schramski
1986 - 1998	Louis Turner Griffith	2006 - 2022	Henry Garrard
1986 - 2007	Allen Russell Green	2008 – 2017	Larry Webb
1988 - 1991	J. Reid Christenberry	2009 - 2020	David Shipley
1988 - 2001	Gerald Driver	2011 - 2016	Diane Wall
1988 - 2007	Roger Roemmich	2015 - 2026	Mack Guest
1988 - 2001	Elbert N. "Bert" Whitmire III	2015 - 2026	Lisa Hudson
		2015 - 2026	Duke Lindsay
1988 - 2001	Betty Whitten	2017 - 2022	Charley Whittemore
1990 - 1996	Bob Brown	2019 - 2024	Ben Griffith
1991 - 2003	C. Patrick Allen	2019 - 2024	Spence Johnson
1991 - 2003	Bert Maxwell	2021 - 2026	Grant Tribble
1993 - 2005	Lewis Gainey	2022 - 2027	Carrie Scruggs
1993 - 2005	Louise McBee	2024 - 2029	John Graham

Compiled by Tom Jackson
2024

---

[1] This list is likely to be incomplete and may not cover all possible items or details.

[2] After: Listed date

[3] Before: Listed date

[4] About: Listed date

BIBLIOGRAPHY

Athens First Baptist Church website, https://firstbaptistathens.org

Atlanta Constitution, "General Evans at Oxford," November 4, 1907, p. 8.

Atlanta Constitution, "Ministers are Still at Work, North Georgia Conference Has a Busy Day in Athens," November 28, 1897, p. 2; "All Accused Were Vindicated," November 30, 1897, p. 4.

Bondurant, John P. *The First United Methodist Church, Athens, Georgia: Some History and Recollections, and its Trustees*. (self-published), 1988.

Brooks, Robert Preston. "A Brief History of First Methodist Church, Athens, Georgia." (unpublished manuscript), 1924.

Centennial Alumni Catalog, The University of Georgia, published 1901.

Coleman, Kenneth and Charles Stephen Gurr, eds., *Dictionary of Georgia Biography*, Athens: UGA Press, 1983.

Dempsey, Elam Franklin. *Life of Bishop Dickey.* Nashville: Publishing House of the Methodist Episcopal Church, South, 1937.

Eskew, Glenn. "Lucius Holsey." *New Georgia Encyclopedia.* https://www. georgiaencyclopedia.org/articles/arts-culture/lucius-holsey-1842-1920/

Find-a-Grave online, multiple listings and photos of gravesites.

Georgia Archives "Virtual Vault." https://vault.georgiaarchives.org/digital/collection/adhoc/id/1051

Hauk, Gary. *A Legacy of Heart and Mind: Emory Since 1836.* Atlanta: Bookhouse Group, Inc., 1999.

Hayes, Zach C. "Bishop George Foster Pierce." *The Georgia Review*, Vol VII, No. 2, Summer 1953.

Hill, Walter B., papers, University Archives, Hargrett Rare Book and Manuscript Library, The University of Georgia Libraries.

Holcomb, Walt. *Sam Jones: Celebrating the Centennial Year of the Birth of Sam Jones*. Nashville: Parthenon Press, 1947.

Hull, Augustus Longstreet. *Annals of Athens, Georgia, 1801-1901.* Henry Hull, editor. *Athens Banner*, 1906.

Hull, Henry. *Sketches From the Early History of Athens, Georgia. 1801-1825.* Hull, A. L., ed. Athens, Ga.: H. L. Cranford, job printer and book-binder, 1884.

Jackson, Thomas H., Jr., *King James: James Edward Dickey (1864-1928), Emory College President and Methodist Bishop*, doctoral dissertation, University of Georgia, 2008. http://getd.libs.uga.edu/pdfs/jackson_ thomas_h_200812_phd.pdf

Journal of the Alabama-West Florida Conference, Southeastern Jurisdiction, The United Methodist Church, 1972.

Journals of the North Georgia Annual Conference of the Methodist Episcopal Church, South, 1878-1939.

Journals of the North Georgia Annual Conference of the Methodist Church, 1940-1967.

Journals of the North Georgia Annual Conference of the United Methodist Church, 1968-2023.

Lane, Richard B., Ronald L. Bogue, Thomas Bowen, Sam Thomas, editors. *The First Presbyterian Church of Athens, Georgia; A Bicentennial History 1820- 2020*, Marceline, Mo.: Walsworth Publishing Co., 2021.

Lawrence, Harold. *Methodist Preachers in Georgia 1783-1900*. Lawrenceville, Ga.: Boyd Publishing Co., 1984.

McClintock and Strong Biblical Cyclopedia, online retrieved October 2, 2024, https://www.biblicalcyclopedia.com/C/curry-daniel-dd-lld.html

Minutes, Board of Stewards, 1st M.E. Church, Athens, Ga. 1913-1916.

Morris, Sylvanus, L.L.D. "Strolls About Athens During the Early Seventies." 56 pp. pamphlet self-published with the permission of *The Athens Banner*, 1912.

Myers, Robert Manson. *The Children of Pride: A True Story of Georgia and the Civil War*. New Haven: Yale University Press, 1972.

NCPedia. https://www.ncpedia.org/biography/norman-jeremiah. *Dictionary of North Carolina Biography*, Powell, William S., ed., University of North Carolina Press, 1979, 1996.

New York Times, "Gen. Clement A. Evans Dead," July 3, 1911.

Northen, William J., ed., *Men of Mark in Georgia*. Atlanta: A.B. Caldwell, 1910.

Northern Illinois Conference Minutes, 2004.

Paschal, Paul Holmes, *A Tribute to Young L. G. Harris*. Franklin Springs, Ga.: Advocate Press, 1977.

Pierce, Alfred M. *A History of Methodism in Georgia February 5, 1736 – June 24, 1955*. North Georgia Conference Historical Society, 1955.

Proceedings of the Stewards, The Methodist Church Athens, Georgia, Commencing Dec. 1870.

Quarterly Conference Record, Athens Station, Beginning with 1866. Ending with 1877.

Quarterly Conference Record Book, 1st Church Athens, Geo. 1878-1879-1880-1881.

Quarterly Conference Record Book, 1st Church Athens, Geo. 1882-1883-1884-1885.

Quarterly Conference Record Book, 1st Church Athens Ga. 1886-1887-1888-1889.

Quarterly Conference Record Book, 1st Church Athens Ga. 1890-1893.

Quarterly Conference Record, M.E. Church, South, 1st Church Athens District 1894.

Quarterly Conference Record, M.E. Church, South, 1st Church Athens District 1895-1898.

Quarterly Conference Record, 1st Church Athens, Methodist Episcopal Church, South, 1911 to 1914.

Record of White Members in the Methodist E. Church in Athens, Georgia Conference. 1838.

Reul, Myrtle R., editor. *Beacon on the Hill: Ashford Memorial Methodist Church*. Athens, Ga.: ABC Printing, 2003.

Sheets, Herchel H. *Methodism in North Georgia: A History of the North Georgia Conference*. Milledgeville, Ga.: Boyd Publishing Company, 2005.

Smith, George G., Jr. *History of Methodism in Georgia and Florida from 1785 to 1865*. Macon: Jno. W. Burke & Co., 1877.

APPENDIX

Smith, George G., Jr. *History of Georgia Methodism from 1786-1866.* Atlanta: A.B. Caldwell, 1913.

Tate, Benjamin. "David C. Barrow Jr." in *New Georgia Encyclopedia.* https://www.georgiaencyclopedia.org/articles/education/david-c-barrow-jr-1852-1929/.

Trustees of the Methodist Church at Athens in Clarke County, *Minutes Books*, 1901-1970, two bound volumes.

West Virginia Conference Minutes, 2018.

Wilson, Robert C. "Methodism in Athens, A Historical Sketch, 1801-1953." (manuscript held by the Church and included in the 1953 church directory).

Wilson, Robert C., file of original papers held by the Church.

Index

Individual churches not listed may be found under the city/town/county where located.
Counties listed are in Georgia unless otherwise indicated.
Churches listed are Methodist/UMC/ME South unless otherwise indicated.

327

INDEX

Birmingham College/Birmingham
  Southern University 72, 125, 257
Bishop, Ga. 21, 242
Bishops (and see individual names) 5, 7, 8,
  17, 21, 25, 29, 30, 33, 35, 36, 37, 38, 43,
  44, 47, 48, 51, 52, 55, 57, 58, 68, 69, 70,
  77, 81, 83, 88, 104, 109, 114, 122, 129,
  151, 157, 168, 179, 191, 196, 213, 214,
  225, 233, 242, 248, 249, 253, 263, 298,
  315, 318, 323, 324
Black (see also African-American, Colored)
  8, 16, 28, 34, 38, 39, 51, 55, 58, 156,
  186, 188, 193, 287, 302, 306, 308
Blackstone College 141
Blairsville, Ga. 22
Blalock, Elizabeth (Anthony) 40
Blitch, Dan 255, 322
Bloomfield Street 101
Blue Ridge Church 147, 164, 222, 242
Blue Ridge, Ga. 29
Board of Education 73, 84, 90, 94, 111, 120,
  130, 142, 144, 152, 163
Boggs William E. (Chancellor) 104
Bold Springs Campground 49
Boleyn, Charles Wheatley (Rev.) 165, 170,
  171, 172, 173, 179, 187, 275, 318
Boling, Jay 112
Bolkcom, Penny (Hodges) 264
boll weevil 155
bonds, bond issue 114, 133, 153
Bondurant, Birdie Moss (Clower) 107
Bondurant, Emmet J. 97, 106, 114, 117,
  120, 125, 138, 149, 238, 239
Bondurant Hardware Co. 106 Bondurant,
John P. II I, 6, 14, 36, 76, 106,
  118, 132, 147, 149, 152, 162, 179, 191,
  238, 301, 321, 323
Bonnell, Cornelia Frances 38
Bonnell, John M. (Rev.) 38, 39, 40, 318
Bonner, Edna L. (Scott) 56
Booth, John Wilkes 31
Boring, Harriet 42
Boring, Jesse (Rev.) 42, 48, 53, 66, 73, 79,
  84, 316, 317
Boston, Mass. 271
Boulevard 113, 213
Bowden (Ga.) Methodist Church 238
Bowen, Judson A. 195
Bowman, Thomas (Bishop) 31

Boy Scouts 175
Boys' High School, Atlanta 171
Brackman, Emory R. (Rev.) 173, 319
Branham, Junius 32
Branham, Walter R., Jr. (Rev.) 32, 78, 111,
  319
Branham, Walter R., Sr. (Rev.) 30, 31, 32,
  53, 78, 111, 316, 317
Brasstown Valley (Young Harris), Ga. 308
Braswell, Martha 190, 211, 222, 223, 228,
  254, 258, 320
Braucher, Charles 188
Braucher, Sara 188
Breckenridge, John C. 65
Brenau College 195
Briarcliff Church, Atlanta 217, 283
"Brick Church," the 45, 46, 50, 67, 73, 87,
  302
Bridge Community Church, The 114
Briercrest Bible Institute 197
British Columbia, Canada 197
Britt, Sara 248
Britt, Will 248
Britt, William Oslin "Bill" IV (Rev. Dr.)
  118, 188, 318, 245, 248, 251, 252, 255,
  277, 259, 307
Broad Street, Athens 7, 155, 305, 308
Broad Street Church, Columbus 58
Broad Street Mission, Augusta 65
Broadway Church, Augusta 122, 129
Brockman, Mrs. C. Joseph 209
Brookhaven Church 193
Brooks, Robert Preston (Dean) 138, 323
Brown, Beverly 230, 254, 320, 321
Brown, Bob 322
Brown, Joseph E. (Gov.) 69
Brown v. Board of Education 162, 308
Brown, William 27
Brunswick, Ga. 195
Bryan, J.S. (Rev.) 316
Buchanan, Ga. 196, 235, 237, 238
Buford First 194, 245
Buie, Archie 194
Bulloch County 168
Bull Run, Battle of 90
Burch, Charlie 118
Burke County 5
Burlington, Iowa 204
Bush, George H. W. (President) 224, 261

INDEX

INDEX

E

INDEX

INDEX

337

INDEX

H. W. Gray Company 159
Hymn Society of America, the 211

I

Illinois 172, 215, 218, 325
Illinois Wesleyan University 215
India 149, 242
Indianapolis, Ind. 285
Inman Park Church, Atlanta 95, 245
Interlochen Arts Academy 280
International Nursing Services Association 225
Iowa 204, 230
Ipsen Church Interiors 184
Iron Foundry, Athens 62
Isle of Hope Church, Savannah 28, 49, 79

J

Jackson, Angelique "Angel" 355
Jackson, Brett 355
Jackson County 3, 4, 5, 42, 147, 152
Jackson Forest Academy (N.C,) 127
Jackson, Ga. 32, 103
Jackson, Sharon (Sherry) I, IV, 210, 233, 234, 323, 355
Jackson's Hotel 22
Jackson, Stanley D. (Stan) 233, 355
Jackson Street 42, 61, 70, 130, 150
Jackson, T. Harold "Hal" III 233, 355
Jackson, Thomas H. "Tom" Jr. (Dr.) IV, 66, 210, 233, 235, 236, 238, 244, 253, 255, 256, 288, 302, 322, 323, 324, 355
Jackson, Thomas Jonathan "Stonewall" (Gen.) 64
Jacksonvile, Fla. 272
James, Carlton M. Jr. 231, 271, 322
James, Claire 232
Janus (Greek god) 303
Japan 139, 141, 189
Jarrell, Anderson Joseph (Rev.) 56, 87, 88, 120, 317
Jarrell, Charles Crawford (Rev.) 120, 122, 124, 125, 128, 132, 138, 143, 144, 147, 316, 317
Jasper, Ga. 76, 122, 245
Jefferson College 38
Jefferson, Ga. 3, 8, 89, 237
Jefferson, Thomas (President) 15

Jeffersonville, Ga. 57
Jesus, Christ, Christian VI, 39, 118, 139, 158, 156, 213, 225, 239, 242, 244, 264, 280, 283, 287, 306, 310, 311
Johns Creek, Ga. 227
Johns Hopkins University 284
Johnson, Charles (Rev.) 197, 219, 319
Johnson City, Tenn. 216
Johnson, Luke G. (Rev.) 110, 316, 317
Johnson, Lyndon B. (President) 191
Johnson, Nancy Ann (Pierson) (Rev.) 283, 320
Johnson Organ 69, 107
Johnson, Spence 322
Johnston, Richard Malcom 52
Jonesboro, Ga. 80, 188, 243, 276
Jones Chapel Church, Augusta 88, 102
Jones, C. O. (Rev.) 56, 128
Jones County 87
Jones, David Bevel (Rev.) 214
Jones, Deana 226
Jones, Henry H. (Rev.) 151, 323, 355
Jones, Joseph B. 27
Jones, Lewis Bevel "Bev" III (Bishop) 157, 176, 187, 211, 213, 214, 219, 222, 223, 225, 248, 308, 309, 315, 318
Jones Memorial Church, Morrow/Lake City 226, 237
Jones, Sam 104, 324
Jones, Steven 226
Jones, Thomas 225, 226
Jones, W. L. 61
Joy Choir 190
Juilliard School of Music 159

K

Kendall, Thomas Rogers, Sr. and Jr. (Rev.) 94, 95, 96, 317
Kentucky 39, 156, 166, 172, 201
Kentucky Wesleyan College 172
Key, Caleb Witt (Rev.) 47
Key, Joseph Staunton (Bishop) 43, 46, 55, 60, 213, 309, 315, 317, 318
Kidd-Key College, Sherman, Tex. 47
Kidd, Lucy C. 47
Killingsworth, Conn. 140
kindergarten 192
King, Barrington 70
King Center, Martin Luther Jr. 53

339

INDEX

INDEX

INDEX

INDEX

S

INDEX

T

INDEX

350

INDEX

INDEX

INDEX

9ABOUT THE AUTHOR 9

Thomas H. Jackson, Jr.

Tom Jackson was born into the Methodist church, grandson of Rev. Henry H. Jones and great-grandson of Methodist Bishop and Emory President James E. Dickey, who was subject of Tom's doctoral dissertation. He was president of the MYF in high school and Wesley Fellowship in college. He directed the Chancel Choir at Allen Memorial UMC while a student at Emory's Oxford College. Transferring to UGA in 1971, Tom joined Athens First UMC and over these many years has served as chair of the Administrative Board, a member of the building committee for the Family Life Center, and on the finance, staff-parish, worship and executive committees. He twice chaired the annual stewardship campaign, taught Sunday School more than 20 years, and sings in the Sanctuary Choir. A lay delegate to Annual Conference from the church or District for most years, he is a District trustee and lay leader. At the Conference, he served on the Bishop's Leadership Forum, the Council on Finance and Administration, the Annual Conference host committee, and study committees regarding staffing, organization and communication. He delivered the Laity Address at 2019 Annual Conference and was named Conference Communicator of the Year in 1999. He was elected to Jurisdictional Conference five times and General Conference four. He served on the Georgia Methodist Commission on Higher Education, the UGA Wesley Foundation board, the Foundation for Wesley Woods, and is a trustee of Wesley Woods Senior Living, Inc.

Tom headed public relations for the University of Georgia 1988-2015, the last eight years as Vice President for Public Affairs. From 2015-2017, he was in the University System chancellor's office on special assignment as Executive Director of the Georgia World War I Centennial Commission. He previously was Athens Bureau Chief for WXIA-TV in Atlanta and worked ten years in radio news, management, and as an on-air personality in LaGrange and Athens. He was a state news correspondent for the *Atlanta Constitution* 1974-1980.

He holds an A.A. degree from Oxford College of Emory University (1971) and three UGA degrees: A.B. (1973), M.P.A. (2004), and Ph.D. (2008). He was named a Distinguished Alumnus of Oxford College in 1989. Tom recently marked 50 years and counting as "Voice of the Redcoats," stadium public address announcer for the UGA Redcoat Marching Band.

He and his wife Sharon (Sherry) married in the AFUMC sanctuary in 1975, as did their sons Hal (Brett, 2001) and Stan (Angel, 2006). There are five wonderful grandchildren.

www.ingramcontent.com/pod-product-compliance
Lightning Source LLC
Chambersburg PA
CBHW071703120626
46550CB00001B/93